# The Poetics of Shadows: The Double in Literature and Philosophy

Edited by Andrew Hock Soon Ng

Andrew Hock Soon Ng (ed.)

# THE POETICS OF SHADOWS:
# THE DOUBLE IN LITERATURE AND PHILOSOPHY

*ibidem*-Verlag
Stuttgart

**Bibliografische Information der Deutschen Nationalbibliothek**
Die Deutsche Nationalbibliothek verzeichnet diese Publikation in der
Deutschen Nationalbibliografie; detaillierte bibliografische Daten sind im
Internet über http://dnb.d-nb.de abrufbar.

**Bibliographic information published by the Deutsche Nationalbibliothek**
Die Deutsche Nationalbibliothek lists this publication in the Deutsche Nationalbibliografie;
detailed bibliographic data are available in the Internet at http://dnb.d-nb.de.

Cover illustration: "Ying Yang" by Petr Kratochvil.

A CIP catalogue record for this book is available from:
Die Deutsche Bibliothek
http://dnb.ddb.de

∞

Gedruckt auf alterungsbeständigem, säurefreien Papier
Printed on acid-free paper

ISBN-10: 3-89821-735-3

ISBN-13: 978-3-89821-735-4

© *ibidem*-Verlag
Stuttgart 2008

Alle Rechte vorbehalten

Printed in Germany

# Contents

## Acknowledgement

I would like to thank Melissa Wong Yuet Fun for her conscientious indexing work on this project.

# Introduction: Reading the Double

Andrew Hock Soon Ng

The essays in this volume attest to the incredible dexterity of the trope of the double in illuminating ambiguities embedded in literary and philosophical writings. While the literary double often centers on questions about the self, the double in philosophical writings manifests at the level of rhetoric, confirming Protagoras's dictum that "on every question there are two opposing answers, *including this one*" (in Gordon: 1). Regrettably, scholarly forays into the philosophical double are few,[1] and psychoanalytical criticism continues to direct studies of the literary double. This is perhaps unsurprising, given the fact that the double is almost always studied in relation to a branch of literature known as the Gothic, of which psychoanalytical criticism predominates. Another reason for this lacunae is perhaps the fact that the notion of writing as *trace*, which suggests that writing is always *at least* double in "meaning" (and I use this word loosely), has only more or less recently motivated a recapitulation (in the musical sense) of the study of philosophy and literature prompting scholarship to pay heed to the "language" of philosophy and literature, and how it generates meaning, rather than just what it means *per se*. In this introduction, I will briefly touch on the double in contemporary theory, and discuss how the "double" is to be read with regards to this volume, before introducing the essays.

## Two Theories of the Double: Theology and Psychoanalysis

The trope of the double is most familiarly recognized in literary works especially those which arose from the Romantic era. Although literary doubles have a much longer and older history,[2] it was during this period that its popularity in literature, especially prose fiction, became most prominent. As Eugene Crook asserts, this was because the double reflected "the basic tenet" of this period, that was:

---

[1] The most extensive study of the philosophical double that I know of is Paul Gordon's *The Critical Double: Figurative Meaning in Aesthetic Discourse* (1995).
[2] According to Eugene Crook, the earliest known double story is the Egyptian tale, "Two Brothers". Crook also sees examples of this trope in the Babylonian *Gilgamesh*, in biblical stories (Cain/Abel, Jacob/Esau), Plautus's *The Menaechmi*, Spenser's *The Faerie Queen*, and of course, the plays of Shakespeare (Crook: 9).

1

the concern with the creative, passionate, and transcendental self. The Double figure is an appropriate agent for these ideas in prose fiction, with a propensity for abrupt comings and goings, for stealing reflections and appropriating shadows, and for acting out the central character's secret fears and desires. (Crook: 10)

In the branch of Romantic writing known as the Gothic, the double has been heavily exploited for it multifarious possibilities in foregrounding the subject wrecked by opposing but equally compelling forces. From Frankenstein and his monster, to Jekyll and Hyde, and to Dorian Gray and his portrait, these characters have exemplified Romanticism's and post-Romanticism's perpetual concern with the (il)legitimacy of the secret self, which, despite being often repressed by the *status quo*, is where the creative and transcendental force resides. But this force, as many Gothic narratives seem to suggest, is also aligned with evil, and hence is destructive. This insinuates the extent of fear and trembling which accompany the Romantic hero/ine's quest, akin to the Faustian myth, for aesthetical overreaching. For in desiring transcendence, in pursuing passion that transgresses the boundaries of propriety, it becomes unclear where virtue ends and villainy begins.

Some Gothic theorists, like John Herdman, discuss the double's alignment with evil from (among others) a theological perspective (Herdman: 1–10). According to Herdman, the double demonstrates the conflicting wills inherent in humans, in which the natural is morally opposed to the spiritual. The self is torn between flesh and spirit, good and evil, God and the Devil, and Gothic narratives such as Hogg's *The Private Memoirs and Confessions of a Justified Sinner* (1824) and Godwin's *Caleb Williams* (1794) immediately lend themselves to such an interpretation. As Karl Miller further asserts:

Demonic possession and the transmigration of souls are dualistic categories which indicate that the subject has been due both to the dark ages and to the enlightenment of the past. The resemblance of sound and sense between "double" and "devil" has weathered the passage of the centuries, and is a specimen of the superstitions which have lent their forebodings to the common knowledge of the subject which is still about [...]. The self is violated, invaded, destroyed, on such occasions: but it may also be saved. The loss of the self is supernaturally defied and averted. But there are many premonitions of its loss, as of its dispatch beyond nature to a regime of punishment. (Miller: 30 – 31)

As a theological signifier, the double signals the battle between good and evil for the human soul. The double is an external, diabolical agent bent on destroying the hapless self by instigating the latter's proclivity towards sin. This self will either resist, and thus be saved, or give in, and be eternally damned. The story of Faust is the supreme example, but Hogg's narrative, and the tales of Hoffman, Brockden-Brown and Hawthorne can also be read from this theological angle.

Other theorists tend to read the trope's ambiguity as an instance of "madness" which ultimately engulfs the self. Such a reading follows from an idyllic view reminiscent of Rousseau that humankind is essentially good, and that depravity is a psychological condition effected by external factors such as, say, metropolitan life.[3] Hogg's narrator's deviance, for example, has been recast as delusion due to excessive exposure to religion.[4] Such a reading, despite its psychological flavor, continues to hark back to a theological understanding of the human self as persistently wrestling with external forces which threaten to corrupt it. But with the advent of psychoanalysis, psychological interpretations of the double became increasingly staple. The decline of religion in eighteenth-century Europe and the rise of scientific enquiry, coupled with the sophistication and refinement of the theoretical framework of psychoanalysis, were largely responsible for an increasingly psychoanalytical reading of the literary double.[5] Eugene Crook, for example, declares in his 1981 study that "[c]ontemporary scholars of the Doppelgänger are virtually unanimous in stating their position that our understanding of the Double (in fiction or otherwise) is directly related to Freud's breakthrough in understanding the human personality" (Crook: 11) – and he provides an extensive list of scholarship to prove this as well. Despite the availability of substantial studies of the double from a variety of theoretical perspectives (such as anthropology and deconstruction),[6] that reading of the literary double, especially in the Gothic, tend to recourse to psychoanalysis remains evident in contemporary literary analyses.[7] In psychoanalytical criticism, the double is no longer a nemesis without, but has become an enemy within, a shadowy other residing within the psyche, threatening to disrupt the stability and coherence of the self. Edgar Allan Poe's "William Wilson" (1840) is arguably the first narrative of the double based on a psychological model, but the paramount tale of the psychological double is certainly Stevenson's *The Strange Case of the Dr Jekyll and Mr Hyde* (1886) (the title itself suggests a "medical" condition).

---

[3] Linda Dryden, for example, posits that "[u]nstable identity [is] closely linked in [Gothic] fiction with the labyrinthine metropolis and its teeming population. Issues of duality – split personalities, physical transformations, mistaken identities, doppelgangers – were found to be manifested in social, geographical and architectural schisms of the modern city" (Dryden: 19).

[4] See Elizabeth McAndrew (209–213).

[5] The classic psychoanalytical studies of the double are Freud's essay, "The 'Uncanny'" (1919) and Otto Ranks's *The Double: A Psychoanalytical Study* (1971).

[6] Respectively René Girard's *Violence and the Sacred* (1977), and Derrida's *Dissemination* (1981).

[7] For example, see Andrew J. Webber, *The Doppelgänger: Double Visions in German Literature* (1996), John Pizer, *Ego-Alter Ego* (1998), Valdine Clemens, *The Return of the Repressed* (1999) and Andrew Smith, *Gothic Radicalism* (2000)

This twin aspects of scholarship on the double – that it is often studied as a Gothic trope, and that it deploys psychoanalysis to unpack the double's layered nuances – have, unfortunately, reduced the interpretive possibilities of the trope. This is in no way a criticism of psychoanalytical interpretations which have admittedly provided a fundamental basis for understanding this rather slippery trope, and whose framework will continue to prove useful for yielding careful insights into the mechanisms of, for example, the uncanny, the unconscious, the schizophrenic – all of which are somewhat related to the doppelgänger. But to privilege psychoanalysis over other possible theoretical and philosophical directions is to construct a kind of meta-theory for the investigation of the double, which would severely limit its signification, however far-reaching a psychoanalytical interpretation may be. Furthermore, interrogations of the double deploying a psychoanalytical perspective tend to concentrate primarily on "characters" or "personas" of a literary work. This is the conventional approach in scholarship from Freud to contemporary Gothic criticisms. An area which has remained largely unexplored with regards to textual scission is the performance of doubling inherent in the act of writing itself, or what Paul Gordon terms the "critical double", which understands the double "as a model of the way all rhetorical and poetical works construct and destruct – de-construct – their own meaning" (Gordon: 12). Gordon's observation is especially pertinent to (post)modern writings which increasingly question the nature and limits of the creative process, and of the text itself. If Barthes, in his important essay "The Death of the Author" (1977), has announced that the text now takes on an existence independent of the author, and allows for a confluence of multifarious meanings imposed by the reader(s), then literature is, in a sense, not only double, but multiple. Hence, it is not just characters who ought to be investigated when discussing the double, but the act of writing (together with its ideological thrust) as well (in both senses of writing as performance and performing writing), of which characterization is but one integral part. In this sense then, psychoanalysis is insufficient, and perhaps even ineffective, in grappling with doubling at the level of "meaning", that is, "the way all literary and rhetorical texts utilize structures of meaning to deny the very structures of meaning on which they are based" (Gordon: 12).

It is the contention of this collection of essays that the trope of the double can yield further and deeper significances with regards to meaning, rhetoric, and identity (of the characters, the authors) when scrutinized from various philosophical perspectives. While some essays directly address doubling as fundamental to the process of writing and meaning-making, others discuss the ontological, epistemological and axiological dimensions of the double by subscribing selected literary texts to philosophical unpacking. Again, this is not to downplay the importance of psychoanalytical readings, but to enable other thought and belief-systems to tell us something (else) about the double, and in turn, allow the double to tell us something (more) about literature and philosophy, about meaning, and about ourselves. But before I introduce the essays in this volume, some further observations of this trope is useful.

## The Double in/as Derrida's Hymen, and Gadamer's Bildung

Although most frequently rendered "the double", this trope is known by many other aliases – the second self, the shadow self, alter-ego, and doppelganger. This last term, a German word literally meaning "double-goer", was introduced into the literary tradition by Jean Paul Richter "who in 1796 defined the word in a one sentence footnote: 'So heissen Leute, die sich selbst sehen' ('So people who see themselves are called')" (Crook: 5). Such a phenomenon is portentous, and individuals who glimpse themselves externalized onto an identical, physical other are usually doomed. The reason for this, as Crook surmises, can be found in mytho-religious explanation. To see oneself suggests the soul's departure from the body, thus signaling the impending death of the latter (within which the soul is housed): "The concept of the Double, then, results when this inner being has in fact made its escape and exists without" (7). Early Gothic writers are, of course, quick to appropriate this idea, evidenced in the many damned tragic-heroes who people the genre. On the other hand, the term "alter-ego" is immediately derived from psychoanalysis. Here, within the self-as-ego, is secretly lodged an alter-ego who, under certain circumstances, surfaces to disrupt the ego's hitherto seamless existential trajectory. This alter-ego is often the site of forgotten, forbidden desires which have been carefully locked away in the unconscious until a fateful event triggers its return. It is upon such a framework that Freud built his theory of the uncanny – a theory which has become foundational in psychoanalytical readings of the double (Gordon: 12).

But the double, as Albert Guerard contends, is an "embarrassingly vague" concept (in Crook: 5), and despite theoretical advances in delineating its significance and function, necessarily continues to exceed them. This does not mean that interpreting the double is always a futile attempt, but that the double cannot be defined within any theoretical position. One useful way for us, then, to reconsider this trope is *via* Derrida's discussion of mimesis in writing (language). Derrida argues that the operation of mimicry (the "adequation between a presence and a representation" [Derrida: 218]) does not lead to any "truth", but is an imitator with no imitated, a "signifier having in the last instance no signified, this sign having in the last instance no referent" (218). Writing (language), rather than referring to a transcendental signified, is nothing more, in the end, "than the space of writing" itself: "in this 'event' – hymen, crime, suicide, spasm (of laugher or pleasure) – in which nothing happens, in which the simulacrum is a transgression and the transgression a simulacrum, everything describes the very structure of the text and effectuates its possibility" (218). If I understand Derrida correctly, he is proposing that any meaning that can be at all possible in writing (be it literature or philosophy) is within writing itself, and not something external to it. As such, meaning is always only a "possibility", that which is effectuated by the event of writing, but never definite or absolute. It is perhaps not surprising that Derrida titles his essay "The Double Session", immediately signaling the literary trope, and at the same time, upholding the trope's irreducibility to meaning. In fact, more than just a particular feature recurrent in Gothic literature, doubleness is a fundamental aspect in all writings, whose effectuation already functions as a palimpsest of what cannot be written, must be repressed, or denied. Directly related to his view on mimesis, Derrida introduces another concept, the "hymen", which is curiously similar to the way in which the double has been theorized:

> "Hymen" (a word, indeed the only word, that reminds us that what is in question is a "supreme spasm") is first of all a sign of fusion, the consummation of a marriage, the identification of two beings, the confusion between the two. *Between* the two, there is no longer difference but identity. Within this fusion, there is no longer any distance between desire (the awaiting of a full presence designed to fulfill it, to carry it out) and no longer any difference between desire and satisfaction. It is not only the difference between difference and nondifference. Nonpresence, the gaping void of desire, and presence, the fullness of enjoyment, amount to the same. By the same token [*du meme coup*], there is no longer any textual difference between the image and the thing, the empty signifier and the full signified, the imitator and the imitated, etc. But it does not follow, by virtue of this hymen of confusion, that there is now only one term, a single one of the differends. It does not follow that what remains is the fullness of the signified, the imitated, or the thing itself, simply present in person. It is the difference between the two terms that is no longer functional. The confusion or consummation of this hymen eliminates the spatial heterogeneity of the two poles in the "supreme spasm", the moment of dying laughing. (220)

Derrida's "hymen" therefore, signals the double on both rhetorical and thematic levels. In the case of the literary double, its presence at once suggests a rupture, or split, in the self, as well as points to, when considered alongside the self, a fusion, or consummation with the self. Or to state it in a different way: the double, because it announces the incompleteness of the self, is therefore ultimately *not* the "other" of the self (although this is how the double is normally viewed) but is integral to *self* – "no longer difference but identity". As such, desire is not located in an alter-ego, but

6

within the very ego itself, which now functions as both the locus of desire and satisfaction, presence and nonpresence. On a rhetorical level, the doubleness/hymen inherent in language is precisely its ability to both mimic the object signified, as well as refuse, or deny, this identification. As Derrida says ("But it does not follow [...]"), language may point to a signified ("consummation"), but it also collapses altogether this structural binarism, rendering the two terms "signifier" and "signified" incompatible or completely meaningless in light of language's underlying mechanism to deconstruct itself. As such, whether the double is personified by a character in a narrative, or whether it is the hymen operating rhetorically, its essential characteristic is "inscribed at the very tip of [...] indecision" (230).

In the New Testament, the disciple of Christ who doubts is named Thomas. This is perhaps not a coincidence, as the name Thomas, in Greek ("Didymus"), suggests duality (see Claire Potter's essay in this volume). Thematically, this implies that doubt renders the character suspicious of himself, that he "may be his own worst enemy, and may not belong to himself" (Miller: 47). Literature abounds with examples of self-doubt, leading to the creation of the double upon which the self's unacknowledged, dangerous secrets are projected. Rhetorically, and especially important in the study of philosophy and philology, duality implies that to read the/as double is always to remain doubtful of what writing signifies. Interestingly, stories of the double are often configured as a Bildung (a quest) of self-discovery. If this relationship is adopted to the study of literature and philosophy, then recasting the act of reading the double as a form of a journey would directly confirm Derrida's prescription of the hymen as guiding interpretation. According to Gadamer, "Bildung [...] describes more the result of the process of becoming than the process itself. The transition is especially clear here because the result of Bildung is not achieved in the manner of a technical construction, but grows out of an inner process of formation and cultivation, and therefore constantly remains in a state of continual Bildung" (Gadamer: 10).[8] Appropriating this to the current study, I want to propose that the act of interpreting the double should be construed as a continuous journey in which the acquisition of various theories ("acquiring Bildung always involves the development of theoretical interests" [12]) – of which psychoanalysis is only one – helps to unpack the potentially endless significations of the trope. Understanding the function and the meaning of the double will be enriched when placed "under [theoretical] glass", which would

---

[8] See Paul Gordon's study for an analysis of Gadamer's theory in light of the "critical double" (in Introduction)

also mean that this tropic structure "cannot be described, only interpreted" (Derrida: 242).

## The Poetics of Shadows

The aim of the essays in this collection is to put the literary double under the glass of a variety of philosophical enterprises in order to investigate what it tells us about the nature of writing and being. Broadly divided into four parts (each comprising two essays), the essays attest not only to the richness of the double's significance but, as in Derrida's "hymen", the wonderful ambiguity inherent in this trope and its defiance against becoming subscribed to any one theory or interpretation. The two essays in part one concentrate on writings which blur the distinction between literature and philosophy; through investigating this ambiguity, what is unveiled is the doubling nature of writing itself as containing its own unmeaning even as it stretches towards creating a recognizable "world of the text" (to borrow a phrase by Ricouer). The first piece, Daniel Watt's "Edmond Jabès: Double Exile and the Uncanny Fragment", demonstrates that the act of writing in modernist literature is already "ghosted" by the presence of its non-writing. Focusing on Edmund Jabés works and reading them against Derrida and Blanchot, Watt's central thesis is that the act of literature itself is always haunted by its own impossibility of telling, which results in writing becoming fragmentary. Drawing on Blanchot's argument with regards to writing and disaster, Watt sees Jabès's writings as "studded with blank spaces". This fragmentation of the text is then conceptualized as a doppelgänger presence that disturbs narrative linearity, stability and coherence.

The second is Claire Potter's essay on Blanchot's experimental fiction, *Thomas L'Obscur,* in which she concentrates on the "name" as signifier of doubleness. Blanchot's *Thomas L'Obscur* tells the story of a man who, as his name foretells, is existentially caught within the matrix of his own self (that is, obscurity/obliteration/nothingness). Of particular interest to this work is how the grammatology of Blanchot's novella functions within a literary space that encapsulates the reflexivity inherent to the multifarious character(istic) of Thomas. Indeed, in the French, *Thomas L'Obscur* makes overt use of the reflexive form of the verb which immediately inserts an injunction between the subject and the object of action. Equally, the use of oxymoron, rhetorical question, tautology and repetition paint the text of *Thomas L'Obscur* in recurrent diptych inasmuch as the tragedy of the text is precisely that there is no mysterious double in whom Thomas hides; rather he is, by virtue of an existence riveted to itself, always already *at least* double.

Part two considers the manner in which several European narratives grapple with various philosophical conundrums by exploiting the doppelgänger as a guiding principle. The first essay in this section is Søren Landkildehus's "Taxonomy of the Double: Struggles of Cognition in the works of Vita Sackville-West and Walter de la Mare". This essay develops a theory of the double as a signifier of cognition, but rather than drawing on psychology to explain the trope, Landkildehus privileges philosophies of the mind from Kant to Kierkegaard to interrogate narratives by Dickens and especially, Sackville-West and de la Mare. Landkildehus suggests that several models of "cognitive" doubling can be affected through different combinations of three key concepts – (as)symmetry, inwardness and (dis)semblance – the most radical of which, according to him, results in what Sackville-West would term a "fundamental" change of mind. To an extent, de la Mare's *The Return* succeeds, as Landkildehus's essay demonstrates, in exemplifying this

The second essay in this section interrogates the relationship between the double and "Jewishness" in Paul Celan's narrative poem, *Conversation in the Mountains*. Expanding on Emmanuel Levinas's observation that the ambiguity of the poem is its difficulty in verifying if there are "two Jews [...] or one Jew tragically divided against himself, J.D. Mininger demonstrates that the seeker and the sought in Celan's poem are ultimately a single entity. In the poem, a Jewish man wanders through the mountains in order to understand himself, his world, and how language positions him in it, and in the process encounters his other in the guise of a bigger, older cousin. The thematic double, in Mininger's view, is mirrored in the *form* of the poem as well. Indeed, if subjectivity is interpellated by the symbolic structure of language, then through its many uses of  repetitions, alliteration, assonance, rhyme, and so on, Celan's poem is able to show how intricately the subject is related to language, and that the doubling of the latter would result in the fragmentation of the former as well.

The two brief essays in part three draw on Eastern religio-philosophical traditions to understand the function of the shadow self. Investigating the double through Eastern belief-systems, these essays target important issues of consciousness and identity formation that are wedded to politics, art, iconography, and religion. They demonstrate the effect on subjective formation when such apparatuses of power clash on the site of the self. As in the essays in part one, Jonathan Ganeri's essay rehearses the troubled space of writing as always already doubled, but makes this point by considering the nature of the embedded, or "nested", story (that is, a story within a story). Analyzing the narratives of lesser known Indian writer, Mauni, Ganeri (who develops his theory from Borges) states that this form of story-telling creates an "insider relationship" between the nested tale and the main narrative frame, especially between the narrators in each frame. The self of the main frame is not the mirror-image of the "nested" double, nor are they straightforwardly identical. Instead such a mode of storytelling creates a bridge between narratives, permitting the narrator to explore the reaches and limits of subjectivity while reserving the flexibility that comes with writing in the third (as opposed to the first) person. Thus, the narrator can speak of two separate others, and is able to analyse the intimacy and asymmetry in their relationship with each other. For Ganeri, such a narrative structure has important ethical implications as well. Reading Mauni's narratives against Hinduism, Ganeri argues that Mauni's doubled narrative structure mirrors the distinctive discomfort which the "present self" (the main self/text) is made to feel because of unacknowledged "past selves" (the embedded self/text) that continue to haunt it – a concept aligned to the Hindu view of history which (unlike its Western counterpart, which posits history as progressive and linear) is circular and recurring.

Mustafa Kirca's and Firat Karadas's intriguing essay, "The Problem of Miniaturist Art as Reflection of Reality in Orhan Pamuk's *My Name is Red",* provides a unique perspective on doubling as a "problem" in Muslim art. In Pamuk's narrative, the distinction between art as a representation of objective reality (as in Western art), and art as a reflection of God's greatness is foregrounded to demonstrate the extent to which a Muslim painter must resist replicating (or doubling) objective reality in his work but instead, focus on eliciting the message "behind" this reality in order to proximate God's hidden reality. Art as God's double and as human's double become a matter of contention when the Sultan, fascinated by Frankish art, commissions a miniaturist artist to emplace his (the Sultan's) portrait at the centre of an artwork. This is not only in violation of Islamic artistic principles which prohibit the drawing of portraits, but a blasphemous act as well in its request for centrality, for only God can occupy this position. Through a series of dialogues between figures depicted in artworks, the narrative pits Western and Muslim art theories against each other, to culminate in a sympathetic pronouncement that echoes its opening epigraph, "To God belongs the East and the West".

The last section in this collection will consider the double in the postmodern context. Two American novels, Don Delillo's *White Noise*, and Chuck Palahniuk's

*Fight Club*, are discussed. In his essay, "Confessing the Post-Romantic Subject: *Fight Club* as "Rematch" of Rousseau and Hobbes", Brian Burns argues that despite *Fight Club*'s postmodern concerns about the crisis of masculinity and the overwhelming of the subject by the consumer culture, at the core of the narrative are two familiar perspectives on human culture and temperament that have played central roles in both philosophy and anthropology since the Enlightenment. Palahniuk's narrator and his doppelgänger personify and confusingly scramble both the mild-mannered and pugilistic human temperaments (respectively) that Thomas Hobbes and Jean-Jacques Rousseau have located in human prehistory. This essay considers the similarities between Palahniuk's, Rousseau's, and Hobbes's configurations of masculinity, and reads *Fight Club*, at the same time, as depicting a symptom of the increased postmodern confusion regarding what is essentially human. Indeed, as Burns argues, the confessional rhetoric of the confused first-person narrator of the novel reengages the work of Jean-Jacques Rousseau in its efforts to frame a cultural critique within a narrative of selfhood invested with the idea that there is still something *authentic* to be found in human prehistory

Finally, Natalia Lizama's essay, "A Body of Information: Posthumanism, the Digital Doppelgänger and Don DeLillo's *White Noise*", completes this volume by considering the double from a bio-technological perspective. Lizama contends that despite an obvious correlation between doubling and bio-technology, critical studies of such an interfacing are scarce, often focusing – predominantly and somewhat simplistically – on the figure of the clone or cyborg (this is particularly in relation to science-fiction texts). To correct this oversight, this essay will put forward the notion of a medico-informatic double, a double that is not made of flesh, *but rather of data*. This medico-informatic double will be discussed in relation to Don Delillo's *White Noise*. In this context, Lizama's essay radically departs from familiar depictions of the doppelgänger motif. Rather, the medico-informatic double, made up of digital information and images, functions as an immaterial and informatic entity that is unique to late twentieth-century notion of subjectivity.

There is a noticeable absence of literature by women writers studied in this collection (Sackville-West is the sole representative). Although stories by women with the double as a theme and/or a trope are not uncommon (the novels of the Brontë sisters, and the narratives of D. K. Broster, and more recently, Angela Carter and Emma Tennant, will testify to this), they remain few and far between, possibly due to the fact that, as Andrew Webber observes, whenever female doubling is effectuated, "it would have little to do with altered or divided states of female subjectivity. Instead, the female Doppelgängers are typically in the service of male fantasies of the other, corresponding to the time-honoured polarization of madonna and whore, the sexless and the over-sexed" (Webber: 20). For this reason then, women writers would tend to subscribe their representation to this polarization when deploying the double (as in Charlotte Brontë's *Jane Eyre* and Tennant's *Two Women of London*), or reject the trope altogether. The more subversive utilization of the trope, such as those exemplified by Carter, has yet received much attention from scholarship. It is my conviction that if the hymen-al quality of the double is to be interpreted for its variegated possibilities, this will certainly contribute toward the Bildung of exploring the literary double, one that is more sensitive to gender and sexual (rather than just psychological or philosophical) dimensions.

## Works cited

Barthes, Roland. "The Death of the Author" in *Image, Music, Text*. Trans. Stephen Heath. London: Fontana, 1977.

Clemens, Valdine. *The Return of the Repressed: Gothic Horror from* The Castle of Otranto *to* Alien. New York: State Univ. of New York Press, 1999.

Crook, Eugene J. *Fearful Symmetry: Doubles and Doubling in Literature and Film.* Tallahassee: Univ. Presses of Florida, 1981.

Derrida, Jacques. "The Double Session" in *Dissemination* (1981). Trans. and with an introduction by Barbara Johnson. London/New York: Continuum, 2004.

Dryden, Linda. *The Modern Gothic and Literary Double*. Basingstoke: Palgrave, 2003.

Freud, Sigmund. "The Uncanny" (1919). Ed. and Trans. under the supervision of James Strachey. *The Standard Edition of the Complete Psychological Works of Sigmund Freud.* Vol. XVII. London: Hogarth Press, 1957: 217–252.

Herdman, John. *The Double in Nineteenth-Century Fiction.* Basingstoke: Macmillan, 1990.

Gadamer, Hans-Georg. *Truth and Method* (1975). Trans. Joel Weinsheimer and Donald G. Marshall. London/New York: Continuum, 2004.

Girard, René. *Violence and the Sacred.* Trans. Patrick Gregory. Baltimore/London: The Johns Hopkins Univ. Press, 1977.

Gordon, Paul. *The Critical Double: Figurative Meaning in Aesthetic Discourse.* Tuscaloosa/London: The Univ. of Alabama Press, 1995.

McAndrew, Elizabeth. *The Gothic Tradition in Fiction.* Columbia: Columbia Univ. Press, 1979.

Miller, Karl. *Doubles: Studies in Literary History.* Oxford: OUP, 1987.

Pizer, John. *Ego-Alter Ego: Double and/as Other in the Age of German Poetic Realism.* Chapel Hill/London: The Univ. of North Carolina Press, 1998.

Rank, Otto. *The Double: A Psychoanalytic Study.* Trans. Harry Tucker Jr. Chapel Hill/London: The Univ. of North Carolina Press, 1971.

Smith, Andrew. *Gothic Radicalism: Literature, Philosophy and Psychoanalysis in the Nineteenth Century.* Basingstoke: Macmillan, 2000.

Webber, Andrew J. *The Doppelgänger: Double Vision in German Literature.* Oxford: Clarendon Press, 1996.

**Part One**

# Edmond Jabès: Double Exile and the Uncanny Fragment

Daniel P. Watt

Much of the criticism addressing Edmond Jabès has dealt with his "main" and monumental work, *The Book of Questions*, whose six volumes begin with a relatively straightforward narrative, the story of Sarah and Yukel, which then gradually fractures and dissolves. As Paul Auster describes in his introduction to "An Interview with Edmond Jabes":

> isolated statements and paragraphs are separated by white spaces, then broken by parenthetical remarks, by italicized passages and italics within parentheses, so that the reader's eye can never grow accustomed to a single, unbroken visual field. One reads the book by fits and starts — just as it was written (Auster: 6).

Throughout this interview it becomes clear that the presentation of the text, its fragmented structure and halting dislocated narrative are the most vital aspect of Jabès's concept and practice of writing, whether it be the italicized passages which he describes as being "from another book", or the longer passages which "belong to the book itself, to the book that is being written, and they are there to continue the story, or to continue the questioning". Also the use of aphorism is important as it "comes from a need to surround the words with whiteness" (17). Later Jabès is very clear concerning the disruption within his texts: "All my books are about cutting, about disjunction. From one end to the other the book is fragmented, cut up constantly [...] and in the last book [of *The Book of Questions – El*] I wanted to show how this plays on the level of the word itself". Jabès then describes the centre of this text where a chart appears containing the word *nul* (nothing) and *l'un* (one) which are turned around to mirror, or uncannily double, each other at the top and bottom of the page: "The whole work, in effect, takes place in this 'one' and is finally canceled to become this 'nothing'. This reveals the essence of the fragmentation, and in some way this chart is an image of all my books" (23). Jabès's concern with the visual architecture of the book, the artistic development of the text, emphasizes his interest in both the experience of the text at a micro, aphoristic, level, and at the level of the total work; the book: "Totality is an idea [...] and it can be shown only through fragments [...]. For example, we are in this room and cannot see the whole house. But we know that

17

we are in the house. The same thing happens in the book. We know that we are in something immense, but at each moment we only see what is in front of us" (20). This repeats a similar assertion made by Jabès in *Ça suit son cours* (1975), which later appears collected in *The Book of Margins*:

> Only in fragments can we read the immeasurable totality. Hence it is with reference to a fabricated totality that we tackle a fragment, which always represents the accepted, traditional part of the totality, yet at the same time renews its challenge of the beginning and, taking its place, becomes the beginning of all possible beginnings that can be brought to light. (Jabès 1993: 42)

Jabès uses the fragment as both an individual component but also the collective, or total, ensemble of fragments, rather than the purely ruined fragment of antiquity. For Jabès the fragment is a central process through which the text operates, in fact it is the structure through which any textual component, whether it be the aphorism, sentence, paragraph, or chapter would relate to the broader structure that is called the book – this structure existing provisionally as a "fabricated" system even before we encounter the fragment within. It is only because the fragment is the sign of this decomposed unit that the book can cohere. Without the spacing inherent in the fragment there could be no book. The significance given to the fragment leads to a very powerful regenerative urgency at each moment within the book: "The book carries all books within itself, and each fragment is the beginning of the book, the book that is created within the book and which at the same time is taken apart" (Auster: 22). This continuous process is not a decision on the part of the writer – today I shall write fragments – but the very manner in which a text goes beyond each separate, fragmented moment and appears as a series of possible books. It is that structure of dissolution and possibility that gives the fragment its forceful opportunity and seems to be the only way in which his text could be written as Jabès clarifies in his interview with Auster: "The book that would have a chance to survive, I think, is the book that destroys itself, that destroys itself in favor of another book that will prolong it. This is the point, if you will, of my deconstruction of the book"(22). Again a similar statement appeared in *The Book of Margins*, which reiterates the dependency of the text on the manifestation of the fragment as a visual unit of writing, Jabès claims that the work of the eye is also a part of the relation between the totality of the fragmentary work and the dissolution, or withdrawal, of that totality in each fragment: "The eye is guide and beacon for this fertile 'deconstruction' which works in two directions: from totality toward the ultimate fragment, and from the tiniest fragment, through its own rescinding, its own gradual fading into the void of preponderant fragmentation, toward restoration of this very totality"(Jabès 1993: 42). In Jabès one finds a continual assessment of the figure of writing as it appears, it is a bridge between the fragment and the visual arts, without in any way being able to unite them. It seems both compelling and dishonest for a reader of Jabès to deploy his work in a strategic and theoretical manner. As Warren F. Motte Jr. declares in *Questioning Edmond Jabès*: "The Jabesian text is 'irrecuperable': it is different from other texts, it is marginal. Its key integer is the 'fragment': fragmentary writing proclaims its difference by its very form; its shape on the page advertises its marginal character" (Motte: 15). However, as shall become apparent, a certain amount of infidelity is required, for the work of the fragment also begins with a deceit that cannot be unmasked by a purely critical positioning. It is such a demand, an obligation of the critic or commentator encountering the work, that Motte examines so carefully in his book. Motte's examination of Jabès's work explores how to react to the work, and from what position it is to be received. It is a sustained analysis of much of the commentary and criticism that had appeared by 1990, including Derrida and Blanchot, to whom this essay turns later. Motte's argument seems to ask for a different engagement with the fragmented works of Jabès. Motte traces Jabès reaction to Adorno's statement that there can be no more poetry after the Holocaust, and discovers a writing that demands to be written because of the Holocaust. The interstice of the fragmentary becomes an obligation in such a damaged world.

The collection of essays in which the interview with Auster appears, *The Sin of the Book*, is the most comprehensive selection of Jabès criticism to date. Derrida also brought Jabès's work to a wider readership by including two essays on him in *Writing and Difference*: "Edmond Jabès and the Question of the Book" (1964) and "Ellipsis" (1967). It is to the dialogue between Jabès and Derrida, with consideration of the idea of 'nomadism' as presented by Richard Stamelman and Gilles Deleuze, that this essay now turns before considering some of Jabès' texts that have received little critical discussion. Later the essay shall turn to Freud's concept of the Uncanny and the figure of the double, which appears throughout Jabès' work, to demonstrate the conflict between the fragment and the book, between writing and reading, and the difficulty of simply separating the task of criticism from that of writing.

Derrida's short essay "Ellipsis" is concerned with the nature of wandering and return, repetition, writing and death. At the heart of Derrida's discussion is a question concerning whether the loss of centre in the doubling of the sign is to be mourned or affirmed:

As soon as a sign emerges, it begins by repeating itself. Without this, it would not be a sign, would not be what it is, that is to say, the non-self-identity which regularly refers to the same. That is to say, to another sign, which itself will be born of having been divided. The grapheme, repeating itself in this fashion, thus has neither natural site nor natural center. But did it ever lose them? Is its excentricity a decentering? Can one not affirm the nonreferral to the center, rather than bemoan the absence of the center? Why would one mourn for the center? Is not the center, the absence of play and difference, another name for death? The death which reassures and appeases, but also with this hole, creates anguish and puts at stake? (Derrida: 297)

This issue of the double sign, already formulated in his earlier essay on Jabès "Edmond Jabès and the Question of the Book" will form the basis of the link between the fragment and the "Uncanny double", as discussed by Freud. The fragment affirms the 'nonreferral to the center' and plays out its loss in a continued deferral between its instance as individual fragment and its indication towards a collection of fragments. It will be in a mirroring of the total work and its fragmented double that many of Jabès's commentators will also find their own work doubled. These two essays by Derrida are infused with a poetic reflection upon Jabès's writings, and especially when repeating Jabès's primary concerns: the possibility of the book, the ongoing process of writing and the relation between the reader and the work, critical distance is under continual erasure as writing asserts its power to evade attempts at exegesis.

Later in the same year, May 1964, Blanchot too addressed Jabès's work in his essay "Interruptions" that appeared in *La Nouvelle Revue Française*. In this essay, which appears in two separate sections, "Interruptions as if on a Riemann Surface" from *The Infinite Conversation* (1993) and "The Book of Questions" from *Friendship* (1997), Blanchot located the quality of Jabès's work in exceeding the possibility of establishing a coherent and linear reading of the text. In *Friendship*, "The Book of Questions" appears as a sub-section within a larger essay, "Traces", and there Blanchot offers his most succinct and clear explanation of the functioning of the enigmatic and disruptive "neuter", which effects the decentring power of which Derrida discusses:

The neuter is a threat and a scandal for thought. The neuter, were we to think it, would free thought of the fascination with unity (whether the latter be logical, dialectical, intuitive, mystical), turning us over to an exigency that is altogether other, capable of failing and of escaping all unification. The neuter is not singular, nor does it tend towards the Singular; it turns us not toward what assembles but equally towards what disperses, not toward what joins but perhaps what disjoins, not toward work but toward idleness, turning us toward that which always diverts and diverts itself, in such a way that the central point toward which we would seem to be drawn when writing would only be the absence of a center, the lack of origin. To write under the pressure of the neuter: to write as if in the direction of the unknown. This does not mean to speak the unspeakable, to recount the unrecountable, to remember the immemorable, but to prepare language for a radical and discreet mutation, as can be foreseen if we recall the following statement that I will be content to repeat: the unknown as neuter, whether it is, whether it is not, could not find its determination there, but only insofar as the relation to the unknown is a relation that light will not open, that the absence of light will not close – a neuter relation; which means that to think in the neuter is to think, that is to write while turning away from all that is visible and all that is invisible. (Blanchot 1997: 221–22)

These comments also recall the important remarks that Blanchot offers before *The Space of Literature* (1982), where the centre of the book acts to attract the reader whilst also turning such theoretical assimilation of the work aside. The neuter attracts so as to disperse, it turns outwards towards the double work of writing, which is also to dissolve (as Jabès describes in *The Book of Margins*) the total work of the book. Jabès's use of fragmentation is part of the repetitive structures of doubling and otherness, centre and decentred, and as Derrida points out, this work is born of division. Jabès's fragmenting work begins by being double. As we can see from Jabès's own response to Derrida's early essays it is a far from straightforward celebration of the polysemous and disseminated aspects of fragmentation. [1] The fragment becomes the mode more suited to Jabès because it does not contain the closure of the aphorism, although the aphorism is itself never completely whole. The aphorism becomes a device through which to argue against narrative and novelistic structure, whereas the fragment disarms as it proceeds carrying ruination and dislocation wherever it occurs. This is not to say that there exists some pure division between the work of the fragment and that of the aphorism, as though the latter belonged to some tradition of reason and understanding to which the former was opposed. Instead the aphorism makes clear its opposition to unified presentations of writing whilst the fragment continually conceals its individual message, deferring its own work towards that of the ensemble of fragments, which itself refers back to the

---

[1] This is particularly apparent in Jabès's response to Derrida, published in *The Book of Margins* entitled "Letter to Jacques Derrida on the Question of the Book". It appears inside a work called "The Moment After" which begins with reflections on the work of the eye in reading and writing. Jabès's response to Derrida is very idiosyncratic, being neither poetry or criticism, but having the tone of someone addressing an errant teenager, with a respectful distance, but also an attempt to make a forceful point. Jabès speaks to Derrida directly in this letter explaining his own reading of terms such as *Différance*, Hymen and Tympanum with the continual attempt to demonstrate that "the question of writing truly arises on abyssal ground – the question of being likewise, the two being riveted to one another" (Jabès 1993: 45). Jabès shows that the work of writing is "explosive" and that "at the same time [it is] a space for leaving traces" (47) but these traces are black fire on white fire – the pages of a book. Jabès warning is that such a fire must be allowed to burn in its own way. He is cautious, as Derrida is, of not allowing 'deconstruction' to become a term that explains the movement of writing but rather that it put such a movement into effect.

individual fragmentary component, becoming a constant interplay of relations. Eric Gould makes this point when considering the potential of the aphorism:

> The aphorism reveals a self-containedness that seems only available in excessive speech, an overstatement that wants to be transparent, a fundamentalist faith that yearns for less restraining boundaries of wisdom. It demands a body in which to live – the reader – and there, ironically, it must set history in motion again in order to be new, restoring the play of the imagination. (Gould: 164–65)

Of particular interest here is Gould's use of the term "transparent", for whilst the aphorism may want to be transparent it does not necessarily achieve it precisely because of the "other", this reader. This will become Jabès's concern, as the text seems unable to release itself from the tyranny of the paradox of writing: "Every text, every discourse, witnesses the final triumph of the other. He will always lord it over us, and we probably write to escape his irksome sway. From this perspective, we might consider writing as an act of liberation, but it liberates the writer only to subject him more" (Jabès 1993: 189). However Jabès can find no clear separation between the self and that 'irksome' other. Instead what becomes of supreme value is the *encounter*, another word for writing, the remains of which is always the fragment.

In perhaps Derrida's most important point in "Edmond Jabès and the Question of the Book" he makes clear that the fragment is not opposed to meaning, pure and simple, but is instead the mark of the gap between signification and meaning:

> The other originally collaborates with meaning. There is an essential *lapse* between significations which is not the simple and positive fraudulence of a word, nor even the nocturnal memory of all language. To allege that one reduces this lapse through narration, philosophical discourse, or the order of reasons or deduction, is to misconstrue language, to misconstrue that language is the *rupture* with totality itself. The fragment is neither a determined style nor a failure, but the form of that which is written. (Derrida: 71)

Everything written can be read as a fragment, or certainly the manifestation of the fragmentary distance from meaning and closure, the delay at the centre of all forms of the word, whether it be "narration" or "philosophical discourse". This extension of the realm of the fragment is, of course, vital to the futurity of the fragmentary "project", the fragment being always a work of the future, or one held open to be begun again and again. What Derrida clarifies here is that the fragment operates behind, or within, all writing, but that the aphorism would be considered one of a multiplicity of genres within which the fragmentary occurred. As Blanchot also describes, the interruptive event of the fragmentary is also the event of all writing, as it is spaced by punctuation marks and gaps. Derrida continues: "But, primarily, the caesura makes meaning emerge. It does not do so alone, of course; but without interruption between letters, words, sentences, books no signification could be awakened"(71).

Throughout criticisms of Jabès, the confused definitions of aphorism and fragment enact a doubling process in which each occupies the place of the other, at times the aphorism standing for dissociated witty statement, complete within itself but reflective of a total structure. At the next turn though the fragment represents this potential aspect of literature. What this confusion demonstrates is not an incompetence or inability to define either of these terms on the part of each critic, but rather it shows the entirely ungraspable nature of the *fragment*, which in Jabès's work frequently presents itself as the aphorism. It becomes an experience of the fragment, as each of its definitions gradually slide away into other forms, themselves fragmented. In Jabès's work fragmentation becomes a repetitive structure that threatens to assimilate the fragment into a teleology, the total work, the fragment book, a collection. Richard Stamelman's excellent study, *Lost Beyond Telling* (1990), continually grapples with the issue of the aphorism and the fragment and it will be useful here to trace through some of his definitions. Concerning aphorism and fragment, he states that "the aphorism (like the quotation and the question) is a fragment: it is a miniature text whose beginning and end are telescoped so that they happen almost within the same moment" (Stamelman: 243). This experience of fragmentation can be found in other similar genres, which arise from fragmentation: quotation, aphorism, question. This experience of fragmentation becomes one of exile when Stamelman writes: "Jabès's rhetorical figuration of exile thus depends on the genres of quotations, aphorism and question, which are literary forms that not only represent mimetically the errancy of Jewish existence but also give an experience of errancy itself by being inserted as nomadic participants in a series of decentered, wandering books" (246).

Stamelman wishes to assert the consistency of Jabès's project in terms of the history of the Jewish identity as repeated in those figures of exile: quotation, aphorism and question. A chain of dependence is engendered in Stamelman's argument which is structured by his earlier statement:

> The aphorism literally cannot contain itself. It is a fragment, complete in itself, and yet exploding into further fragments. So reduced is its meaning, at least in Jabès's hands, that the aphorism comes to signify a plurality of possible, sometimes contradictory meanings. There is no finality, therefore, to the interpretation of the aphorism in Jabès's writing; it stimulates endless thought. The reader moves into it as toward a centre of meaning, only then to be thrust centrifugally away in a plurality of indeterminate meanings. In form, the aphorism is implosive; in meaning explosive. It concentrates writing but only in order to scatter meaning. It is a

force of dispersion, contributing to the nomadism of words and the diaspora of signification in Jabès's works (245).

Stamelman's analysis of the aphorism, as it fragments, depends upon a particular reading of Deleuze's essay "Nomad Thought" in *The New Nietzsche*, where he states that Deleuze clarifies "the link between the aphorism and the textual fragment" (245 n24). Stamelman's insightful and poetic description of the process of decentring that takes place in Jabès's work is very compelling but once again asserts the fragmentary aspect of the aphorism. This is the problem at the heart of criticism concerning the fragment: it is already engaging with a writing that is in continual movement, offering, as Stamelman observes, contradictory meanings. The doubling that occurs between the aphorism and the fragment is one such contradiction, and perhaps this danger is also what gives the aphoristic and the fragmentary their power to innovate and oppose rigorously structured systems of philosophy and literature. For Stamelman this shows the need to see in Jabès the "nomadism of words" and "diaspora of signification". However I believe that it is clearly demonstrated throughout Jabès's work that such nomadism and diasporic identities are also part of the urge to assign meaning, and that Stamelman, whilst attempting to describe the peculiar and ambiguous nature of a writing that erases as it inscribes, has ultimately repeated the error of signification through the ascription of the nomad identity to Jabès' work.

What Derrida finds so unusual, and so important, about Jabès is how the book itself, and in relation to the book, the fragment, already contain the issues so forcefully developed throughout Jabès's oeuvre:

> The radical illegibility of which we are speaking is not irrationality, is not despair provoking non-sense, is not everything within the domains of the incomprehensible and the illogical that is anguishing. Such an interpretation – or determination – of the illegible already belongs to the book, is enveloped within the possibility of the volume. (Derrida: 77)

This possibility of writing is discussed by Jabès in his most frequently cited quotation: "I brought you my words. I talked to you about the difficulty of being Jewish, which is the same as the difficulty of writing. For Judaism and writing are but the same waiting, the same hope, the same wearing out" (Jabès 1991: 122). This waiting is also to be emphasized because it demonstrates the difficulty of the purely "nomadic" writing that Stamelman wishes to underline, via a reading of Deleuze. Whilst Jabès repeatedly asserts the importance of the wait, gap or void through which the writer works, the "nomadic" thesis – as proposed by Deleuze – is driven by a critique of the philosophical petrifaction of the signifier. Deleuze's arguments offer Nietzsche as an anti-philosopher, via the aphorism, who mobilizes a "nomadic war machine" to oppose the "utterances of a rational, administrative machinery, whose philosophers would be bureaucrats of pure reason" (Deleuze: 148–49). What writers such as Stamelman and Deleuze do not address, the issue so continually raised through Derrida's essay and Jabès's own writing, is the inscription of the double desire for such nomadism and the homeliness of the total work. This is Jabès' relation to the spiritual, a writing exchange system that mirrors prayer, another doubling of the work of writing. Eric Gould is very clear here: "Writing, as Jabès puts it, is giving words 'back to God' through the seemingly endless transformations of the sign: the innumerable supplanting the unique" (Gould: 169). Gould substitutes the aphorism for the fragment though:

> Yet, "original sin", as Jabès points out, "was only an insane quest for divine harmony", and the aphorism pursues that end. For the sacred is impossibly appropriative. It demands the removal of itself from its hypothetical origin in order to make itself known, which means that God is, if nothing else, a concept of infinite play in the gap. (169–70)

What Jabès succeeds in setting in motion is the play between the moment of creativity and the act of writing. The fragment is the work through which such a gap might be affirmed, the aphorism attempts to bridge the gap.

Jabès demonstrates the dangerous double at the heart of the fragment, which strives for both the infinite space of textual play but also elaborates quite specific limits to its own form, limits which are continually transgressed. Even Blanchot, the clearest recent proponent of fragmentation, does not create fragmented *fictions* of the same intensity as Jabès. This has everything to do with humour, poetic laughter and irony, as I will discuss further on. However, Blanchot does provide continual *definitions* of the fragmentary impulse. An early definition that appears in *The Infinite Conversation* will be useful when considering Jabès's *Desire for a Beginning/Dread of One Single End* (2001). Blanchot directs the fragment towards a questioning of the artist and of the society that is to receive the work:

> The fragmentary work – the fragmentary exigency of the work – therefore has a very different meaning depending on whether it appears as a renouncing of the act of composing, that is, an aggressive imitation of a pre-musical language (which expressionism attempted to arrive at with sophistication) or, on the contrary, as the seeking of a new form of writing that would render the finished work problematic. Problematic not because it refuses accomplishment, but because it explores with an inexorable rigor – beyond the conception of the work as something unified and closed upon itself, as organizing and dominating the values transmitted by a tradition already established and attained – the infinite space of the work, though with a new postulate: namely, that the relations of this space will not necessarily satisfy the concepts of unity, totality, or continuity. The problem of the work of the fragment poses a problem of extreme maturity: first of the artist, and also of society. (Blanchot 1993: 348)

Here the fragment becomes a challenge to society, to ways of living, in that it will not obey the designated confines of a desire for unity: it announces a new writing that questions itself even as it seems to conclude, engendering a radically uncertain future ungovernable by previous modes of knowledge. Such a radical description of what the fragment offers shows just how much the concept has been transformed, from German Romanticism into our contemporary environment. It still retains a concern for the total work, not as absolute but as symptomatic of problems within the work. The fragment becomes the textual enterprise which accompanies the artist and society as they question themselves. The fragment enables literature to encounter itself in the process of writing and it is this possibility that liberates the fragment from simply becoming an event in literary history.

*Desire for a Beginning/Dread of One Single End* is a short book, and one of Jabès's last, with a more than usually aphoristic style. It appears later than most of the important essays collected in *The Sin of the Book* and also after Motte's work. In the space of its fifty-one pages the nature of the book, writing and authorial identity, being Jewish, and the fragmentary text, are all explored. Again we have a face-to-face encounter, both within the book itself and also its own separate parts, page-to-page and section-to-section, which is likened to both Judaism and the work of a book: "The Jew faces the Jew, as a page of the Book, a page of the book" (Jabès 2001: 22), and then later, to explore the strangeness and irregularity of the encounter between these parts: "In my bathroom mirror I saw a face appear that could have been mine, but whose features I seemed to discover for the first time" (32). The mirror here reveals the face of the writer encountering another self, almost identical but slightly different. This passage follows up a detail which Jabès mentions earlier concerning his own date of birth: "My father – I have written this before – at the registrar's office declared me born two days before my actual birth. Ever since, I have lived beside another self, my senior by forty-eight hours" (19).

This delayed entering into the world, or ghosting of his own existence, leads Jabès to postulate the existence of a doppelgänger which is his elder, thus also conjuring the possibility of a worldliness of his spectral kin that Jabès himself does not possess. Interestingly here this story is itself a repeat from another time that the tale was written. It develops into a palimpsest of memorial writing at the same time that he writes his own existence as double. The mirror scene that occurs later in *Desire for a Beginning/Dread of One Single End* then tells, again, of that double Jabès who both

26

gazes into and looks back through these mirror pages. The event of the double writer is the conflict of a fragmentary work which seeks to assert itself as a book, whilst in the continual problematic position of dissolving such a possibility with each fragmentary passage. To say this another way then, Jabès's texts will be fragmentary as they assert the event of the book and in doing so they will deny such a book the possibility of existing other than as a collection of fragments: as a non-book, or a double text which ghosts the existence of *the* book that has been asserted throughout the text. Such an aporia is very much the environment of the fragmentary text, whose aphoristic structure both asserts and denies the correlations developed by a linear reading of them. Indeed the doubling that Jabès puts into play here depends entirely upon recognition of the other face being different, it is based entirely on a knowledge of what belongs and what is alien. So too will the fragmentary text always be seen in relation to the narratively coherent text to which it is both parasite and necessary supplement. Yet such assurances of the situation of fragmentary writing (in pure opposition to the linear text) are, as I have shown, difficult to sustain. The fragment is an insidious work of writing, one that occurs where it seems least likely to be; entire novels can become fragments.

Freud's essay "The 'Uncanny'" has importance here, for Jabès' account of his mirror encounter "mirrors" that which occurs in Freud's essay. In a footnote Freud describes Ernst Mach's surprise when he did not recognize himself, thinking the "stranger" to be rather "shabby-looking" when it was in fact himself. Freud reports a similar experience, when thinking that someone had taken a wrong turn into his train compartment:

> [...] an elderly gentlemen in a dressing-gown and a travelling cap came in. I assumed that in leaving the washing-cabinet, which lay between the two compartments, he had taken the wrong direction and come into my compartment by mistake. Jumping up with the intention of putting him right, I at once realized to my dismay that the intruder was nothing but my own reflection in the looking-glass on the open door. I can still recollect that I thoroughly disliked his appearance. Instead, therefore, of being *frightened* by our 'doubles', both Mach and I simply failed to recognize them as such. (Freud: 371 n.1)

Freud speaks here of the *intruder*, and the essay makes much of the importance of the sense of being "at home" contained in the words *heimlich* and *unheimlich*. The intrusion of the double is an important phenomenon because it also betrays the doubling that occurs in literature when it is faced with the intrusion of fragmentary writing. The ancient *fragment* is a confirmation of the whole from which it is a part, it confirms literature's self-identity and promises a restoration of the shattered work.

Where the German Romantic fragment differs is in conception. It is generated in dissolution, and reflects and speculates on both the complete work and the ideal work in each of its disparate fragments. The fragment repeats a discourse with doubling that becomes important in much of twentieth century thought. So whilst Jabès continues his discussion of the double: "Face of another and yet so familiar. Sorting through my memories I recognized him as the man I'm mistaken for. I am the only one to know he has always been a stranger to me" (Jabès 2001: 33): we read on with the uncanny feeling that it has all been said before, attending at the event of our own inadequate memory, or side by side with another self at once unwelcomed and also familiar.

Jabès's writings repeatedly questions the nature of the book and its relation to the work of writing (questions which Blanchot finds so central), asking what meaning is retained in a fragmentary work "studded with blank spaces". The fragment can be understood as a doppelgänger to modern literature, an uncanny sibling, at once the same (aiming at coherence, clarity and understanding) but radically different; disturbing narrative and disordering linear reading. The demand of the fragment becomes impossible to respond to, requiring an ear attuned to the polyphonic variety of possible readings. Motte identifies the issues of impossibility that Jabès addresses throughout his texts. This makes the fragment a work of resistance and affirmation. Jabès uses impossibility:

> not merely to valorize his writerly activity and to suggest analogies between writing and reading (according privilege in this fashion to the reader's role) but also to protect his text from any threat of recuperation: 'To put oneself back into question, for a writer, is to abstract one's book from any eventual attempt at appropriation by the reader, depriving the latter of the possibility of undertaking a global reading of the work' (*Du désert au livre* 13). Impossibility arises in part at least from fragmentation and multiplication, processes which are inimical to any *possibility* of stable meaning. (Motte: 5)

For Jabès, in *The Book of Shares*, the book offers both the stabilization of such disruption:

> The order of a book often means victory over oblivion.
> How could we read a book studded with blank spaces?
> It would quickly seem incomprehensible. We must appeal to recall, give in to memory. (Jabès 1989: 11)

and also works under both the weight of the ending and the intervals leading towards that ending:

> With supporting arguments, every page of writing tries to persuade the following one that it must continue.

> A book is a series of mutual concessions. But to what can we trace the persuasive power
> of the word?
> Perhaps to the intensity of its silence. (35)

Such a silence is vital in Jabès's work and is commented upon frequently by many writers who have been concerned with his work, especially Blanchot. Fragmentation and multiplication operate against the establishment of authorial identity and power, offering a work that situates itself outside the marketplace of literature and into what Blanchot would term the singularity of the work. What strikes the reader as particularly ironic here is that this singularity is only confirmed, if identifiable explicitly, as double. It is already the registering of a double work, a text and a book. The proliferation of similar terminology: book, the book and The Book, text, the Text and intertext, all serve to confuse and alienate the hermeneutic desire, even – and perhaps most especially – the ability to read sequentially. This functioning of failure enables the "series of mutual concessions" and for each page to "persuade the following one to continue". It is such a momentum which is so apparent in the separate structure of fragmentary writing that returns each of Jabès's passages of text in each of his works back to the beginning, to be reread and doubled. Such a movement, especially in Blanchot's intricate fictions, can seem burdensome. But there is enough humour in Jabès to avoid becoming tiresome, his poetic laughter in a sense locates our sense of being lost, or of losing an ability to identify ourselves outside the text. So a passage such as: "'Do not ask me who I am', said a sage. 'I do not even understand the question. Hence I have long stopped asking it'" (63), can restore, momentarily, a reader's ability to relate to the work experientially as well as cognitively. The imaginary Rabbis that are so prolific in *The Book of Questions* also serve this function which is both a real and surreal experience of reading.

The figure of the double becomes one that informs a reading of Jabès as a writer of fragments, because the fragmentary work is the sinister double of the book, suggesting that writing may be more at home in the fragment, which is itself already double: "What remains to be seen, what promises a voice after silence, fascinates us. The field of writing is twofold. The place of the book is a place already lost" (Jabès 1993: 42–43). Derrida had already stated that the idea of the book is:

> profoundly alien to the sense of writing. It is the encyclopedic protection of theology and of logocentrism against the disruption of writing, against its aphoristic energy [...]. If I distinguish the text from the book, I shall say the destruction of the book, as it is now under way in all domains, denudes the surface of the text. That necessary violence responds to a violence that was no less necessary. (Derrida: 18)

Jabès repeats this violence in *Ça suit son cours* where he states: "Reading a text involves several degrees of violence; this is sufficient warning that there is danger in the house" (Jabès 1993: 42). These opposing violent forces (with the provision that they do not establish the conflict of the rational and irrational that Derrida so carefully avoids throughout his essays on Jabès), the encyclopaedic and the aphoristic, find themselves combined within the fragment, and it is such a coupling that makes the fragment work so much more volatile and resistant than either of these forces, or genres, alone. For the reader cannot help but resist the ironic tendency of the aphoristic (the reader desiring some level of closure), but also the appropriative tendency of the encyclopaedic (the reader desiring some level of freedom). To fully address everything that Derrida touches on here would take a thorough historical analysis of the event of the novel and the social and economic rise of the book as commodity, against the aesthetic criteria of the "aphoristic" energy of the writerly act. This is not possible here, but it is important to note that this does not imply a clear division between these two sides – the text as commodity and the text as aphoristic shard – but that their relationship and the evolution of the latter is deeply embedded in the cultural artefact of the novel, and book. Much of Jabès's own discussion of "the book" is concerned with this cultural "quality" and the opportunity that the fragment offers to radicalise the book's relation to culture.

At some level then the aphoristic and fragmentary would appear to provide some counter force against the cultural hegemony of the book: the reduction of the singularity of the text to a cultural field of economy based success and failure. Such a possibility also explains the tendency of writing such as that encountered in Blanchot, Jabès, Borges and many others, including Kafka and poets such as Baudelaire and Mallarmé, for the surreal and symbolic. Many of these writers' texts are violently opposed to the collative energies of the novel and its narration, which leads to a quasi-mystical repetition of the theological into the arcane and mysterious. Certainly this tendency is most noticeable in Jabès; however the transcendental never escapes the level of the text, returning to the writing act the power of genuine creative assertion and energy. Such a double of the theological is the reiterative step of a fragmentary writing infused with talk of God and writing, where the two terms soon fuse and continually take each other's place. It is such a situation, with a focus on the aphorism that Eric Gould debates in "Godtalk" where he states that "however secular Jabès's intentions and however agnostic his Judaism, we find in his work the tendency of post-modernism to actually want to reinvent a sense of the divine and the numinous"

(Gould: 162). Whilst such a desire is present in modernism too it is interesting to find Gould extending it into the work of Jabès, where what he terms as Jabès's "secular intentions" are a doubled desire for the metaphysical domain of an exiled God. The confused exchange process taking place between God and writing throughout Jabès' work leads to what Gould calls an "absolute forgetting" in which each instance of the aphoristic leads to a fresh start, a new immediacy (Gould: 162–63).

In Freud's analysis of E.T.A Hoffman in "The 'Uncanny'" he concentrates on the theme of the double, where an exchange takes place in which "the subject identifies himself with someone else, so that he is in doubt as to which his self is, or substitutes the extraneous self for his own. In other, words, there is a doubling, dividing and interchanging of the self" (Freud: 356). Such a structure also appears in the Jewish concept of *Tsimtsum* which is God's exile from God, within God. Reading and writing then begin to encounter each other in a frightful mirrored moment:

> Could it be that the thinker is a creation of thought?
> Then thinking would mean being shaped by our thought, being the live model to which it sacrifices us: our own frightful double. (Jabès 1989: 64)

This is similar to that encounter described by Derrida in "Violence and Metaphysics" where he asks: "Would Levinas subscribe to this infinitely ambiguous sentence from the *Book of Questions* by Edmond Jabès: 'All faces are His; this is why HE has no face'? The face is neither the face of God nor the figure of man: it is their resemblance. A resemblance which, however, we must think before, or without the assistance of the Same" (Derrida: 109).

Whilst Jabès does not elaborate a clear theoretical position that defines his use of terms such as book, silence, work, and God, it is apparent that his proximity to much of structuralist and post-structuralist theory cannot be denied. Roland Barthes's short essay, "From Work to Text" (1971) describes both the movement from the work (or book, as commodity and closed signified) to the text (playful, plural signifying chain) but also the relation between reader and writer that Jabès returns to repeatedly. For Barthes, this Text is:

> not a co-existence of meanings but a passage, an overcrossing; thus it answers not to an interpretation, even a liberal one, but to an explosion, a dissemination. The plural of the Text depends, that is, not on the ambiguity of its contents but on what might be called the stereographic plurality of its weave of signifiers (etymologically, the Text is a tissue, a woven fabric). (Barthes 1977: 159)

Even a brief wander through Jabès's work provides a reader with the understanding that the emerging sequence of correlations and reflections on the work of writing provide the context for a readerly engagement quite other to that of a conventional text. The relationship between reader and writer is changed throughout the work, not progressively or systematically (and certainly with the fearful ending far from sight), but at the interval of each fragmented passage that redistributes interpretative relations and doubles, or doppelgängers, the urge to interpret into a desire to resist the textual polysemy. Jabès's work is an excellent example of the plural Text that Barthes discusses, but equally Jabès's task of estranging the author is another aspect of Barthes's Text which works against the confirmation of the Work as product of the author: a genuine *Work* that has been *worked* at. Instead the Text offers a network that undermines the organic development of a Work. And Barthes goes even further in stating that:

> no vital respect is due to the Text: it can be broken (which is just what the Middle Ages did with two nevertheless authoritative texts – Holy Scripture and Aristotle); it can be read without the guarantee of its father, the restitution of the inter-text paradoxically abolishing any legacy. It is not that the author may not 'come back' in the Text, in his text, but he then does so as a "guest" (161).

Recalling Blanchot's comments from *The Infinite Conversation* concerning the maturity required of the fragment "artist" and the society into which this work will enter, it is important to emphasize the relinquishing of agency that the fragment demands. Jabès's work here becomes the double of Barthes; they invite each other. For each repeats a desire to have done with the Work, by way of the Text. Writing becomes a production that cannot be predetermined:

> The contradiction is one between writing and the work (as for the Text, that is a magnanimous word: it shows no partiality to this difference). I delight continuously, endlessly, in writing as a perpetual production, in an unconditional dispersion, in an energy of seduction which no legal defence of the subject I fling upon the page can any longer halt.(Barthes 2000: 418–19)

This passage from *Roland Barthes by Roland Barthes* expresses many of the techniques and exigencies of the Jabesian text. However it proceeds: "But in our mercantile society, one must end up with a work, an '*oeuvre*': one must construct, i.e., *complete*, a piece of merchandise. While I write, the writing is thereby at every moment flattened out, banalized, made guilty by the work to which it must eventually contribute" (419). Barthes's work is of much interest in relation to the fragment: *Camera Lucida* (1980) demonstrates the relation of textual fragmentation to photographic image, and a work such as *Michelet* (1954) shows Barthes's interest in fragmentation from early in his writing.

Jabés's relation to the critique of the commodification of the literary work is a complex one, that plays with a deceit: "O sons and grandsons of the sin of writing, lies shall be your breath, and truth your silence" (Jabès 1989: 23). This is similar to Blanchot's "deceit and mystification not only are inevitable but constitute the writer's honesty" (Blanchot 1995: 310) and leaves writing perpetually in the shadow of this deception. The fragment is complicit in "the sin of writing", it works against structures of the book as production, as commodity, for the fragment will always be in abeyance, inconclusive and offering possibilities which will engender error and confusion. The fragment cannot finish, it is always a futural project, one that the writer and reader must await. Jabés's work offers the finality of fragmentation: a double ending that can only end because it provides the opportunity to begin again.

**Works cited**

Adorno, Theodor. Prisms. Trans. Samuel and Shierry Weber. Cambridge, Mass.: MIT Press, 1983.

Auster, Paul. "Book of the Dead: An Interview with Edmond Jabès" in *The Sin of the Book: Edmond Jabès*. Ed. Eric Gould. Lincoln: University of Nebraska Press. 1985. 3–25.

Barthes, Roland. *Image, Music, Text.* Trans. Stephen Heath. London: Fontana. 1977.

Barthes, Roland. *A Roland Barthes Reader.* Ed. Susan Sontag. London: Vintage. 2000.

Blanchot, Maurice. *The Infinite Conversation.* Trans. Susan Hanson. Minneapolis: University of Minnesota Press. 1993.

Blanchot, Maurice.. *The Work of Fire.* Trans. Charlotte Mandell. Stanford: Stanford University Press. 1995.

Blanchot, Maurice. *Friendship.* Trans. Elizabeth Rottenberg. Stanford: Stanford Univ. Press. 1997.

Deleuze, Gilles. "Nomad Thought" in *The New Nietzsche.* Ed. David B. Allison.: Cambridge, Mass.: MIT Press, 1985. 142–49.

Derrida, Jacques. *Of Grammatology.* Trans. Gayatri Chakravorty Spivak. Baltimore: John Hopkins University Press. 1976.

Derrida, Jacques. *Writing and Difference*. trans. Alan Bass. London: Routledge. 1978.

Freud, Sigmund. *Volume 14: Art and Literature*. London: Penguin. 1985.

Gould, Eric. "Godtalk" in *The Sin of the Book: Edmond Jabès*. Ed. Eric Gould, Lincoln: University of Nebraska Press, 1985. 160–70.

Jabès, Edmond. *The Book of Shares*. Trans. Rosmarie Waldrop. Chicago: University of Chicago Press. 1989.

Jabès, Edmond. *The Book of Questions*. Trans. Rosmarie Waldrop. Middleton, CT.: Wesleyan University Press. 1991.

Jabès, Edmond. *The Book of Margins*. Trans. Rosmarie Waldrop. Chicago: University of Chicago Press. 1993.

Jabès, Edmond. *Desire for a Beginning/Dread of One Single End*. Trans. Rosmarie Waldrop. New York: Granary Books. 2001.

Motte, Warren F. *Questioning Edmond Jabès*. Lincoln: University of Nebraska Press. 1990.

Stamelman, Richard. *Lost Beyond Telling*. Ithaca: Cornell University Press. 1990.

# Reading Blanchot's Obscure Double :

## *Le soi comme (dés)astre en orbite avec soi*

Claire Potter

*Would I like to be a comet? Yes. For they have the speed of birds,*
*they flourish in fire and are as children in purity*
*– Hölderlin*

## Introduction

Errancy in criticism, enhanced by erratum inasmuch as the accuracy of interpretation is always predicated on and driven by the essential missing of its mark, develops a particular aesthetic from this default. The authorship of two nineteenth-century figures, S.T. Coleridge and Oscar Wilde, is thus haunted by the spectre of a third — the critic — who, in addendum to their creative work, develops an aesthetic based on misinterpretation, or errancy. Discussing the use of poetics and the role of the critic in society, the critical and philosophical writings of Coleridge and Wilde can be seen to converge on one small but significant point: that there is a language of spirits (*sermo interior*) at work between words which gives life and colour to the literary dreamcloth, but which the critic often misses.[1] Like Salomé's veils, criticism, in the best cases, can reveal itself to be both a red flag of imaginative persuasion and an allegory of the dance-steps of the critic himself. The role of critical theory, then, can be seen to elucidate and articulate paradigms of literary understanding which go hand-in-hand with subjective reading and critique. Furthermore, might we not have recourse to call this discipline *self*-critical theory — not only in Oscar Wilde's sense of the critic being the one painted by his or her critique, but also in the sense that theory is in some ways the thread we pull through the eye of a text in order to widen and illuminate the dimensions of theory itself?

It is from this purlieu that the critical approach, as J. Hillis Miller argues, becomes a form of praxis rather than being "merely theoretical"; it confines itself not to the "ideology that traditional canonical and thematic readings [...] have blindly as-

---

[1] See particularly S. T. Coleridge, *Biographia Literaria* (290), and Wilde's essay "The Critic as Artist" (26–27).

35

serted", but "makes something happen" (48). And yet, as reader and/or critic, how do we understand any literary figuration – such as the trope of the double – in order to articulate how the figure affects and moves us? How, instead of becoming displaced to a critique which, floating above the text in question, does it conceal the countenance, and the hand, of the critic himself?

In this essay I explore how the trope of the double assumes both a metaphorical and ontological function in the writing of French novelist and critic, Maurice Blanchot. Fundamental to this, I argue the double is always *at least two*, and in Blanchot, the figure functions as an axis of repetition and similitude (as opposed to the double being the manifestation of dissimilarity). The focal point of the discussion lies in how character is estranged from as well as riveted to a sense of self; and further, that this ontological duality contravenes the traditional understanding of the double as a sign of two split personalities. Instead, understanding the double to be *at least two* leads us to a conception of character that is based on a necessary antagonism. Such an internally riven character makes sense of the world by perceiving this antagonism allegorically; through the figure of the double, antagonism reflects an unachievable and irreconcilable knowledge of the world and the self within it.

The work of the double in Blanchot is somewhat at odds with the all-too-familiar trope of the doppelganger in nineteenth century Romantic literature. For whereas the latter, for the most part, designates the presence of an extraneous and conflicting *other* set in contrast with the self, in Blanchot there is no other; the self is *already* other. Contrary to many literary representations of the double, the Blanchotian version exists intrinsically, that is, within the self or subject. For this reason, it makes itself felt in his writing negatively. The double in Blanchot marks not the presence of a second entity or an incongruous being hiding in the self, but the infinite repetition of the same.

Ontologically speaking, the figure of the double deepens a character's sense of literary being as a "living" entity within the literary text — a paradoxical bind which at best confers, in the reader, a compassionate assimilation which relies firstly on bringing the characters we read alive, and secondly on the notion that from reading, we ourselves are part of the story. Before examining specific instances of the literary double, via those characters who represent, in the simplest of terms, some sense of duality either in their contextual or ontological roles, we should perhaps first address how the double has traditionally manifested itself in certain key literary texts.

## The Double in Literature

Thirty-four years after the riotous performance of "The Rite of Spring" in Paris in 1913, the Russian composer Igor Stravinsky gave a lecture at Harvard entitled "The Poetics of Music in the form of six lessons". Stravinsky's theory of music was based on the "musical experiencing of time" which he argues gives our nuanced perceptions of reality "a particular tempo" (31). Understanding such perceptions according to how we experience real time, Stravinsky distinguishes two kinds of music whose tempos either "evolve parallel to the process of ontological time [...] or counter to, this process" (32). Ontological time, as opposed to psychological time, proceeds from the principle of *similarity* rather than contrast, and follows the desire for unity between real time and musical time, rather than the compulsive will to expression. He recounts the following experience apropos of the creative process: "Variety surrounds me on every hand. So I need not fear that I shall be lacking in it [...]. Similarity is hidden; it must be sought out [... it] poses more difficult problems, but offers results that are more solid [...]" (34). This declaration is a direct reply to Stravinsky' harshest critics who regarded his work as little more than noise, a modernist cacophony of uncoordinated sound (14). Arguing against both the atonal (variety) and ahistorical (non-similarity) elements in his work, Stravinsky puts forward two interrelated arguments. First, he avers that his music is not atonal, but rather *anti*-tonal, for he is working "within the bounds of the strict order of tonality, even though [he] may quite consciously break up this order for establishing a new one" (41). And second, he stresses that his composition is firmly based in the musical traditions and folklore of his native Russia. Illustrating these two points with the words of Verdi, he voices a paradox: "Let us return to old times, and that will be progress" (46).

Relating these two suppositions to the literary double, we find that while the figure initially implies some kind of antagonism (atonality) in a pre-existing order, it eventually becomes clear that — in classic dialectical fashion — this antagonism negates order without entirely renouncing it. In other words, borrowing from Stravinsky the notion that a suitably visionary new order must develop from what has gone before, we can see the figure of the literary double in more nuanced ways. For alongside the chronic disorder customarily associated with the double, a new order is brought into being, from the break-up but necessary retention of the old.

In nineteenth-century European literary and psychological writing, it was the macabre figure of the doppelgänger that sensationalized difference-as-duality *par excellence*.[2] Perhaps best captured by Goethe's anxious figure of Faust strikingly contrasted with the calm surety of Mephistopheles, the doppelgänger produces an immediate and recognizable effect. Stemming perhaps in part from Plato's allegorical chariot, pulled in opposite directions by recalcitrant horses in the *Phaedrus*, the doppelgänger's presence was narrative suture. In other words, it could provide a convenient textual resolution to incongruities and differences pertaining to the romantic subject caught within hostile societal forces, by externalizing and bracketing such difficulties to a realm "outside" the subject.[3] In addition, the doppelgänger can confer a shared but discrete bond between two disjointed characters – for example, Charles Darnay and Sydney Carton in *A Tale of Two Cities*. And through this bond, certain nineteenth-century writers of the doppelgänger were thus able to acknowledge, as well as make sense of, the seemingly unfathomable. P.B. Shelley makes this point in *Prometheus Unbound* (1820):

> Ere Babylon was dust, / The Magus Zoroaster, my dear child, / Met his own image walking in the garden. / That apparition, sole of men, he saw. / For know there are two worlds of life and death: / One that which thou beholdest; but the other / Is underneath the grave, where do inhabit / The shadows of all forms that think and live / Till death unite them and they part no more [...]. (Act 1, Scene I, 27).

Characters of double cognizance, Stevenson's Dr. Jekyll and Mr. Hyde to name the most illustrious, thus relied on intensive differences (*impulses* or drives, *Triebe*) being attributed to their literary personalities such that the violence of their being indeed one and the same character could ultimately, at the end of the narrative, be brought to rest (*repose*). The wider two portraits were sketched apart and the further asunder their variances were painted, the more cataclysmic and profound was the disclosure of their unity. The Many, again in this case, cede to the One and similarity that was hidden amidst the affluence of variety becomes representative of a greater truth: that within our ourselves, at most times, is the presence of *at least* two forces whose variety and disparity are essential inasmuch as they confer correspondence amidst differ-

---

[2] Concrete examples abound in nineteenth fiction, but perhaps most famously in Goethe's *Faust* (1832), Dicken's *A Tale of Two Cities* (1859), Robert Louis Stevenson's *Strange Case of Dr. Jekyll and Mr. Hyde* (1886), Wilde's *Picture of Dorian Gray* (1890), Dostoyevsky's *The Double* (1846), Joseph Conrad's *Heart of Darkness* (1902), not to mention such twentieth-century inheritors as Nabokov's *Lolita* (1955), and even Bret Easton Ellis' *American Psycho* (1991). I thank Paul Sheehan and Deborah Pike for discussions of the double in these works.

[3] Indeed the German word for the "double", doppelgänger, literally means "doubler-goer" and originally carried a sense of the spectral which we still find in the word "wraith" meaning a ghostly apparition.

ence. As a precursor to Romanticism, this sense of unifying harmony was described in Schiller's theory of aesthetic experience in which a third drive — our "play drive" (*Spieltrieb*) corresponding to poetic imagination — unites opposing impulses by transforming the antagonism between reason and passion into an idealistic interplay.[4]

Such harmony or similarity, understood by Stravinsky to be "born of a striving for unity", is therein often described as teleological, that is, as the bringing together of the familiar with itself into "a succession of *impulses* that converge toward a definite point of *repose*" (Stravinsky: 33, 37–39, my italics). By referring to what has gone before, this *imperfect* hemming together of the similar and disparate elements in literature can lose, in the best of cases, the didactic qualities it might otherwise possess, and instead become, a way of engaging with the impossible, engaging with what Jacques Derrida in *Les Marges de la philosophie* wryly calls *l'esperance heideggerienne* or the "Heideggerian *hope*"[5] – engaging with the poetic cataclysm of, and confrontation with, differences which seem otherwise too ubiquitous.

And yet, the hidden similarity that Stravinsky seeks, exists, I suggest, on a much smaller scale than the example of oppositional modes of character sutured by a democratic awareness that acknowledges the simultaneous presence of good and evil in all of us. Instead, I venture to suggest that Stravinsky is talking about something more akin to the pronounced beat of a heart in love, something Franz Kafka alluded to when he referred to a book being like an ice-axe which cleaves the frozen sea within us[6], or the soul Goethe described as dwelling twofold in the heart of Faust, or even something Heraclitus made reference to when he supposedly remarked that we cannot step twice into the same river (Heraclitus: 90). Stravinsky is discussing the *anima* of a piece of music, its breath or, as he calls it, its *respiration* (Stravinsky: 39). He is discussing motion – the relationship between notes, the flow or rhythm that runs *between* signs and beats, between points of difference – more than he is talking about the gaping and obvious breaches that exist between a played piece of music and its score, between the meaning of a word and its grapheme, between the composer and his or her composition.[7] Rather than analyzing a played piece of music to ascer-

---

[4] See Schiller, *On the Aesthetic Education of Man, in a Series of Letters* (97); the passage in question in Goethe, see *Faust* (lines 1110–117).
[5] In Jacques Derrida, *Margins of Philosophy* (27).
[6] Franz Kafka to Oskar Pollak, 27 January 1904, *Letters to Friends, Family and Editors* (161).
[7] I am indebted to William Martin for making clear to me the etymological origins of the word "rhythm" (from the Greek verb *rhein*, meaning to flow). In this sense, there is an important connection to be made between the moments of overlap and correspondence vis-à-vis similarity and differ-

tain how it matches its score or does not, or using a literary text to explain an author's biography, or even cognitively interpreting a text in order to penetrate what Nietzsche in *The Birth of Tragedy* described as the "deepest abysses of being" (95–96), Stravinsky leads our eye, and moreover our ear, into realms where hidden echoes and subtle degrees of repetition and resemblance are at play in our poetic imagination. He writes: "The unity of the work has a resonance all its own. Its echo, caught by our soul, sounds nearer and nearer. Thus the consummated work spreads abroad to be communicated and finally flows back toward its source" (146). Indeed, what Stravinsky strives with most difficulty to portray is the recurrence, as well as the sharing of, similitude, which does not proceed from the juxtaposition of violent sensations, but from the slow but assured inclination towards repose.

Perhaps even more difficult is the desire to reveal similitude without assuming an origin or a centre-point from and against which to measure not only repetition but also that which turns around itself in rhythmic circles. Here Stravinsky refers us to the word "melody" – the dominant voice of a symphony – which is derived from the Greek *melodia* meaning the intonations of the *melos*, the fragments or parts of a song. As such, the overall voice of a piece of music is made up of smaller voices which confer harmony. Apropos of his own compositions, Stravinsky goes to lengths to explain that it is these fragments which have already belonged, and been familiar (in the *unheimlich* sense of the word), to him. He writes: "renewal *is fruitful only when it goes hand in hand with* tradition" (123). For Stravinsky there is no pure contrast just as there is no pure difference. As Derrida has pointed out, there is no *hors de texte*, and while Locke's *tabula rasa* indisputably exists, it exists only in palimpsest wherein novelty builds itself upon what has gone before.

Thus we arrive at questions linking the workings of similitude, origin and rhythm or flow within a text, which refer us back to our initial questions concerning the employment and representation of the double in literature. The double can function on a broad scale as we have seen: separating and inserting differences between character portraits to have them later rejoined – a working out, we might call it, in terms of a philosophical *qua* literary exploration of questions concerning duality and metaphysics. Or, the figure can work quantitatively, augmenting character traits in

---

ence inasmuch as both exist in a *stream* moving essentially along the same direction: that of repose. Indeed the word "cadence", indicating the flow or rhythm of melody, borrows etymological origins from the Latin verb *cadere* – to fall, presumably from and to a stationary point. The relevance of this movement, indeed inter-play, between opposing states – falling to stationary – to the writing of Blanchot will be developed later in this essay.

order to underscore their textual importance and create the sense of a harmonic theme *between* character and text. And yet, it can also work on a much smaller scale, by exploring ways in which fragments or heterogeneous facets of a *single* character – one's authentic and inauthentic relation to death for example – are held simultaneously apart and together by a sense of (re)doubling that Blanchot in *L'Espace littéraire* calls *désœuvrement* (idleness or inertia). In this instance, language "is not a power; it is not a power to tell" (1982:48), but rather a *dédoublement*,[8] a splitting into (at least) two in which our "two relations with death, one which we like to call authentic and the other inauthentic, only express the *doubleness* within which such an event withdraws as if to preserve the void of its secret" (155).

This itinerancy between selves, and the self's fissuring from within should be seen as one and the same thing: the character not rejoined by an external double but understood to be already doubled in his or her orbital relation to the self turns around the central inability to escape the subject to whom we are ontologically attached. It is the perspective of the double as being *already double* or *at least double* that this work seeks to develop, paying particular attention to the tiny oscillations between difference and similitude so beautifully exemplified by the French author Nathalie Sarraute in her work entitled *Tropismes* (1939). Borrowing from biology referencing the growth of a plant vis-à-vis the external world, the tropism of the plant is essentially its movement towards things such as light and water, in order to foster development. What particularly interests Sarraute is the minute vertical and horizontal movements of plants in relation to the world, which she understands, *mutatis mutandis*, in terms of the tiny movements human consciousness makes and projects into the external world. It was a literature of recording and taking cognizance of these indefinable movements or interior sensations, and transporting them back into the linguistic and literary realm such that their support (or embodiment) – that is, character – was rendered scarcely visible.

My reading of Blanchot's *Thomas l'Obscur* seeks to put into motion such interest in the rapport of sensations between subject and world proposed by Sarraute in which character – reduced to a minimalist support – permits more generalised questions to be foregrounded by a text. Like Giacometti's sculptures, in front of which we cannot help but have the feeling that suspended corporeal weightlessness is predicated explicitly on heaviness and weight, we see movement in stillness because the

---

[8] There is also, in French, the psychological sense of "dual personality" for the word *dédoublement* which I do not intend to develop here..

sculptures are shaped and reduced in such a way that all that is left to them is motion. This emphasis on the perceived motion of a still object, expresses itself in Giacometti, and Blanchot, in tiny increments which confer an underlying order steeped in anything but complacency, perfection and quietness. A Giacometti sculpture, like Blanchot's prose, is anything but quiet.

We find also present in Sartre's *Nausée* an exampled of this disquiet. Sartre brilliantly records certain moments of ontological vertigo such as when Roquentin finds himself "stuck" in the mirror regarding himself. Expressed here is the sense of a brief lag between the self in the mirror and the self looking at it (that is, between being and Being) such that the two faces are not harmonic but loosely adjunct universes – opposed but at the same time riveted together. The mirror in *Nausée* functions as this indefinable, parallel *glissement*, a sliding and slippery existent suspended between the perceiving "I/eye" and the perceived "I/thing" which share the same, but disparate, spatio-temporal frames. *Le soi* – the self – in orbit with self (*soi*) is thus disastrous (*un désastre*) because we never can catch our own shadow, but fortuitous, like a falling star (*un astre*), because it represents the chance that befalls and sustains our desire, permitting thus the possibility that things could be otherwise. The link here with Sarraute is the *double entrendre* inherent to tropism, to the double meaning of *self* – referring concurrently to my "self" and to *some*thing (a noun, a second name) that is outside of and separated from the sense of who "I *am*" in the world. In literature, the self (usually the protagonist) participates disastrously and fortuitously in this orbital recurrence around the self, and it is the purpose of this essay to explore this "self-circling" or inertia Blanchot so well describes in *l'Espace littéraire* as representative of the work of the double: "Whenever thought is caught in a circle, this is because it has touched upon something original, its point of departure beyond which it cannot move except return" (1982:93).

### Work of the Double

Close cousin to tropism is the trope. Stemming from the Greek word *trepo* which signifies "turn", a literary trope is a figure of signification whereby a word or concept, turned in a contrary sense from its usual direction by the alliances and contexts in which it occurs, possesses new signification. As such, metaphor and metonymy are the most common ways in which tropes are expressed. We find example of this in what can be considered as one of the most ancient and nuanced tales of the double the Western canon possesses: Sophocles's tragedy, *Oedipus Rex*. There are, so to speak two *turns*, or moments of *peripeteia*, in *Oedipus Rex*, both taking place offstage. From this displacement or non-inclusion, we can surmise that the scenes are non-representable, or that they signify an excess of what can be represented.

The first of these turns occurs at the beginning of the play when Oedipus is awaiting the news of Creon's return from the Oracle; the second is Jocasta's suicide. Both these events indicate a turn in the text (a swerve in a particular direction if you like) wherein the trope is worked into the story in order to alter meaning on both figurative and literal levels. This interchangeability between the literal and the figurative, of what is posited as reality and what is posited as metaphoric, allows the reader to question how a synthesis between what is at once different and similar and not simply opposite, but rather stitched together in a manner that allocates movement and slippage between meanings and events which echo and repeat themselves.

In *Oedipus Rex*, there is no double *and* there is a double: Oedipus is his own double and he is not. Both contradictory suppositions can be held at the same time, and it is this ambiguity that propels the tragic element in Oedipus's journey, compelling Karl Reinhardt to describe *Oedipus Rex* not as a human tragedy in which the paradoxical is neutralised, but a tragedy of *seeming* which supports the double-bind or flaw inherent to the marred life of the hero (1979: see chapter 4). Indeed, echoed in the word "double" which stems from the two Latin words *du* and *plus* (duo + fold), is this sense of *seeming,* for the etymology of the word itself implies more than two; a fold viz. something twice-folded, gives the sense of having four or more sides. Thus the conjunction of the two words, *duo + fold* into one word — "double" — does not erase the third term — the "and" — which joins the two together, suggesting thus that that which is double is *at least* double. The figure is thus an allegory which occupies the place of the *seeming* – the seam – which in linking opposed/related entities only ever in uneven ways, resists the simplicity of being reduced to either one and/or two.

*Oedipus* is therein not an example of an incongruous paradigm which cathartically resolves the struggle of truth over illusion. Rather it is, as Reinhardt suggests, a "tragedy of human illusion, in which illusion implies reality" (98). In Blanchot, characters are never simply at odds with themselves: they are living in an irreverently empty and in-between place – a space Blanchot, quoting Hölderlin, describes as belonging neither to god nor men ("In such a moment", Hölderlin writes, "man forgets himself and forgets God; he turns his back like a traitor, although in a holy manner" [1982:272]). This is how I think Reinhardt sees the function of "seeming" (*Schein*) that in *Oedipus* infers a double infidelity between self and the Gods. Perhaps all we can do is allude to Aquinas's notion, borrowed from Aristotle, that it is meaningless to ask whether a human being is made up of one or two things; instead we can understand through literature that *to be double* is, in all cases, to be at least two.

## A Stationary Fall

In his article "Un bonheur extraordinaire" Jean Roudaut observes that Blanchot frequently organizes his *récits* in diptych to not only "make heard the repetition, but also to render the disjunction perceptible: in a blank space, he exposes the shift which occurs when we become aware of being, at the same time, living and dead" (2003:50).[9] Of this Blanchotian oxymoron, Roudaut asserts: "A figure of particular style, the oxymoron has the predilection of Maurice Blanchot; it permits him to evoke 'the steps of immobility' or 'a stationary fall', to render reversible an opposition and summons discontinuity, to dismiss the story by marking the passage without fixing it" (51).[10] Against most critics of Blanchot, Roudaut argues that the employment of the incongruous serves to create an *impression* that a conflict is perpetually occurring within the self, which then gives way to figurative language. As Blanchot himself writes in *Celui qui ne m'accompagnait pas*: "[...] I had to go through events so terrible that it would be better to say that they went through me and they are still, ceaselessly, going through me" (265). Here the presence of the passive voice, not so familiar in English, affords a way of understanding and articulating events that were "so terrible"; if the events were described in the perfect (such as, I have experienced these terrible events), then a certain amount of "false finality" to the happenings would be effected. Instead, as Blanchot writes, it is the events themselves which continue to traverse him in a ceaseless and indestructible way, *impressing* upon his body these moments as pure events, resulting in the self becoming its own surplus, where the reliving of events seems to have no end.

As Roudault suggests, more than being mere repetition, doubling in Blanchot is a diptych of similitude which renders disjunction perceptible. To illustrate this point, I relate the story of Martin Guerre, a French peasant of the sixteenth century who became the centre of one of the most famous cases of imposture in French history. Returning home after eight years of absence and recognised and welcomed by his wife and family, Martin Guerre is soon revealed to be Arnaud du Tilh, an

---

[9] Translations of the Roudaut text are my own.
[10] We find this restlessness present also in the poems of William Wordsworth, whom Blanchot greatly admired. See, for example, *The Prelude*, book VI, lines 557–567.

imposter pretending to be the real Martin Guerre. While most representations of the doppelgänger in literature are usually accompanied by a sense of foreboding and macabre (as if their ambiguity menaces human knowledge and is therefore unacceptable), in the case of Martin Guerre, his double succeeds him so well in likeness that he brings to fore not only questions addressing fakery and legitimacy, copy and original, paternity and patency, but raises questions about recognition and how we "see". With these thoughts in mind, let us approach the Orphic character of Thomas in Blanchot's *Thomas l'Obscur* (*récit*) who likewise puts into question the notion of a central motif from which copies and doubles supposedly stem.

Recognised by others (his partner Anne, friends in the hotel) as Thomas but also as having changed – he is asked in a concerned voice if he "swam" today – Thomas's self-coherence or legitimacy is inversely correlated to the demise of his physical body which, paradoxically, becomes stronger and more resilient the more it attaches itself to dying. As the story of *Thomas l'Obscur* develops, Thomas is not, like Arnaud du Tilh, discovered to be a fraud, but rather he becomes fastened more and more to his own existential fraudulence which he cannot draw to a close. And yet, to writes "as the story of *Thomas l'Obscur* develops", is misleading: in *Thomas l'Obscur*, plot, action, denouement, chronology are not superfluous but profoundly vertiginous; there is only the most flimsy indication of time-frame which decentres all sense of linear spatio-temporality in the text. While there have been two versions of *Thomas l'Obscur* published by Blanchot – the *roman* in 1941 and the *récit* in 1950 – it will be the latter *Thomas l'Obscur* (henceforth *TO*) to which this essay refers.[11]

Let us begin our investigation by turning to the title of the work which carries the name of its protagonist: Thomas. Stemming from the Greek word "Didymus" meaning twin, the name Thomas already intimates "twofold", or "double". This is further emphasized by the adjective (*obscure*) and, more interestingly, a definite article (*the*) which underscore the darkness *qua* obscurity inherent to the Orphic Thomas (*orphe* in Greek means darkness). Blanchot's three emblematic words thus confer a title which is at once metaphorical and literal. Like a mirror already unveiled for the

---

[11] All translations of the 1950 version of *Thomas l'Obscur* in this essay are by Robert Lamberton (unless otherwise stated) (*The Station Hill Blanchot Reader*, 1999). For a more thorough account of Blanchot's writing and political activities in the 1930s which led to the writing of *TO* (Blanchot's first novel), see David Urhig's essay "Levinas et Blanchot dans les années 30: le contrepoint critique de la philosophie de Louis Lavelle". Indeed, in 1941, the year that the first version of *TO* was published, Blanchot was already retracting and qualifying certain writings he had made a decade earlier. Ten years later, when the second version of *TO* was published, Blanchot had lived through French occupation and moved to the south of France.

unsuspecting reader, the capitalised "O" in *Obscur*, invites the reader into a circle where boundaries are imaginary and de-constructible, but nevertheless possess the possibility to contain and express circularity negatively. In the case of word "the" in the title, we can take it to mean "Thomas 'who is' Obscure". Here, "the" functions as a conduit or a hinge – a metaphor *in absentia* – points to the contiguity between "Thomas" and "Obscure". It is thus a joint *out of joint* – a third party – which confers the inherent interference and oxymoronic quality in Blanchot to *TO*. The double in *TO* is thus at once singular (in the name) and triple (in the splitting or *dédoublement* of the name).

## Chance/Cadence

The first time we encounter the possibility of the double in *TO* is in the first chapter or first *chant* (as Kevin Hart in *The Dark Gaze* calls the chapters [11]).[12] Having gone for a swim in a sea which gives Thomas only the impression of the sea, and swimming with a body which gives him only the impression of swimming, a storm arrives and the sky is turned "upside-down": "The storm darkened [the sea], scattered it into inaccessible regions; the squalls turned the sky upside down and, at the same time, there was a silence and a calmness which suggested that everything was already destroyed" (*TO*: 10, translation adapted).

Already the order of things has begun to wane, and as readers, we have an impression that it is as though we are being watched by a faraway eye, in whose iris is the scene of Thomas swimming, unable to intervene in any cogent manner a story that is itself becoming undone (or undoing itself). The first word in *TO* is "Thomas", and the last the word, *lui* (him). Between these two keywords – the name and the third person pronoun – are "a thousand of hands which were only his hand" ("mille mains qui n'étaient que sa main" [61]) which, in the logic of the novel, serve to undo any sense of the upright, or the sky being the "right way up" that either Thomas or the narrative might hope to possess or even witness. The name of Thomas — an "I" or a *je* as in *je m'appelle* — becomes, by the end of the work, an *il* (a third person). This

---

[12] The brilliance of understanding the chapters of *TO* in terms of chants cannot be understated. Drawing attention to the poetic rhythm and flow (the text's "musicality") not only gives the reader impression of moving through the months of the year (there are twelve chants, and each is roughly seasonal), but further permits approach to a world where language is temporal and where, as Georges Bataille observes, "words, contestations [...] have something of quicksand about them (1988:14). Indeed, the notion of "chants" furthermore links Blanchot's work with that of Lautréamont's *Chants,* which Kevin Hart suggests, has resonance with *TO* in places. My thanks to Kevin Hart for explaining the motivation to describe the chapters as chants.

*décalage* or gap between the words *Thomas* and *il* is expressed by the third person narrator in the fourth chant after Thomas, having retired to his room to read, is confounded by what he is reading; instead of being the reader, he becomes the "read": "[…] he pitted all his strength in the will to seize it [the text …] even when the words were already taking hold of him and beginning to read him" (68). Moments later, "the word He and the word I began their carnage, while on his shoulders were perched obscure words, disincarnated souls and angels of words which profoundly explored him" (68, translation adapted). Here, an allegorical shift has obviously occurred: instead of wings, words are perched on Thomas's shoulders, which give the impression that his being, like a fallen angel or like Icarus, cannot escape its literary carapace. Although the "I" and the "he" belong to the same person, they are sutured by an interval or, to use musical terms, a pitch relation between two similar tones, which simultaneously cleaves and holds together the ontological melody the character of Thomas is expressing. It is for this reason that a few sentences later, Blanchot tells us that Thomas no longer fights the words he is reading (that are reading him), but offers "his being to the word be" (68).

Held within this fraught and imaginary universe, the negative articulation of "being" (defined not in-itself but by language) is described by Blanchot as a universe which is ocellate – that is, marked by eyes, by the sensibility of body – but it remains a universe which sees nothing. Characters in Blanchot's universe oscillate *en désoeuvrement* between a sensibility they cannot positively describe and matrix of words they cannot directly experience. The carnage between the *I* and the *he* is akin to the carnage between the reader and the read, between the first word (*Thomas* — the I — the *je*) and the last (*lui* — the he — the *il*).[13] Increments of difference exist between these two points, like the invisible threads that emanate from the central character which serve to hold past, present and future in contiguity. Thomas's double in this sense, is the double of what is already double: the name Thomas which already signifies double is in the text held in opposition to its correlative "he", and its subsequent return to the object at the end of the story, *not as a name* but as a third person pronoun, pronounces even further this double separation. We read with a sense that the entire *récit* is thus the impossible striving towards this ambiguous point: the joining of the signifier (the name, the I) to the signified, the object, the *he*.

---

[13] For an extremely nuanced reading of Blanchot's relationship to the "I" apropos of the cogito in Novalis, Descartes and Heidegger, see Kevin Hart, *The Dark Gaze* (chapter 4).

It is this *he* that is the last word of *TO* and that links the first word Thomas with its third person pronoun, thus marking the doubling of the word which contains, and does not contain, the same meaning. The difference and distance that Blanchot foregrounds between the pronouns *he* and *Thomas* are contrasted with the similitude of setting that he gives to the beginning and the end of the *récit*: in both instances, Thomas is at the edge of the sea, waiting his turn to join the others already swimming. This waiting, however, is much more pronounced at the end of the novella: not only is Thomas waiting his turn, he is also witnessing a very particular scene: his fellow beings have become "a troop of constellations [...] men-stars" ("un troupeau des constellations [...] hommes-étoiles" [*TO*: 137]). Echoing the celestial madness that possessed Hölderlin at the end of his life, Blanchot calls these *men-stars* "crude images" (137) who chant the *empty word of Thomas* (135, translation adapted). When his turn comes, Thomas is visited by shame, for like the emperor without clothes, "he" does not possess the means to transcend the emptiness his "name" affords him: "he hastened himself there, but sadly, despairingly, as if the shame had begun for him" (137). But why exactly this shame? We are not told, and for good reason. In leaving this question unanswered we are referred back to the beginning of the novel, implying that meaning is only ever grasped retrospectively: the beginning of the sentence is coherent only by reaching the final full-stop which, like a surrealist arrow, points the reader back along the path whence he or she came.

**Reading Double**

Let us return to the middle parts of the narrative in which the character of Thomas not only enacts various efforts to give meaning to his name, but rigorously struggles with himself so as to prove himself alive. The first instance of this we find in the fourth chant: a short while after reading, *a sort of Thomas left his body*, and the taste of poison or venom becomes present his mouth (69). Thomas's reaction manifests in the desire to become a serpent in order to render the presence of venom relative to his ontological status: unable to *be* a man and have venom in his mouth, he wants "to become" (*devenir*) a serpent to contextualise the venom (*ibid*). This is an interesting reversal to common thinking: rather than reject the presence of venom as an anomaly within the whole, the whole is rejected as the anomaly in relation to the venom which is the "smaller" part, suggesting that it is the smaller parts which triumph and ultimately replace the harmony of the whole. For Thomas, the presence of venom in his mouth (the signified) comes before the idea of incarnating a serpent, suggesting that words or signifiers are themselves empty and seeking objects and concepts to seize upon and indicate. This is exemplified by the impassioned and almost parasitical entry the words make into Thomas as he is reading. Instead of indicating meaning, words in Blanchot search in vain for meaning; more than requiring other signifiers, they search for a concrete body to host them. This world of words, as we are told at the beginning of the *récit*, is upside down and the word "impression", important throughout Blanchot's text, is related to the "tragedy of seeming" that Karl Reinhardt evoked apropos of *Oedipus Rex*: both terms indicate an ongoing sense of deferred knowledge or meaning which is constantly redefining the outward appearance or surface of how things – words, ideas, meanings – appear to be.

Accordingly, in scenes which border upon sexual frenzy, words in *TO* press themselves against us instead of us *impressing* ourselves and our meanings upon them. The scene of Thomas reading and exchanging places with the words he reads causes a double effect in the reader reading Thomas reading which, we imagine, might also have had an effect on the writer of the work – Blanchot himself. We find suggestion of this textual haunting in the last three lines of the fourth chant:

> Each time Thomas was thrust back into the depths of his being by the very words which had haunted him and which he followed like the explication of his nightmare. He found himself always emptier and heavier; he didn't stir other than with an infinite fatigue. His body, after so many battles, became entirely opaque and, to those who regarded him, he gave the peaceful impression of sleep, although he did not cease to be woken (70, translation adapted).

From these lines we have the impression that Blanchot is regarding (and writing about) a sleeping Thomas whom he knows is not sleeping at all, for sleep like death, always falls short of its ultimate possibility. As Blanchot writes in "Literature and the Right to Death":

> [...] original double meaning, which lies deep inside every word like a condemnation that is still unknown and a happiness that is still invisible, is the source of literature, because literature is the form this double meaning has chosen in which to show itself behind the meaning and value of words, and the question it asks is the question asked by literature" (399).

Because the question asked by literature is also the question asked by Blanchot, the theme of being ultimately unsure if a character – indeed a character we are writing about — is sleeping or not recurs in order to maintain the threads of the question throughout his oeuvre; as Blanchot observes in *The One Who Was Standing Apart From Me*: "We stand around him…We don't know if he is sleeping, riveted to his rest, or if he is coming down to us, without knowing it and without seeing us. Our task is to maintain the circle, but why? We don't know" (327). Likewise, the character of Thomas can be seen to embody the writing process itself which is fraught with a dissonance entirely concordant with the manner in which his literary being is sketched: Thomas is always emptier and heavier, sleeping but woken, stirring with infinite fatigue — and this impression Blanchot paints of Thomas's sleep furthermore reminds us of Walter Benjamin's contemplation (apropos of Proust) of how "[...] the day unravels what the night has woven. When we awake each morning, we hold in our hands, usually weakly and loosely, but a few fringes of the tapestry of lived life, as loomed for us by forgetting" (Benjamin: 198). Our watching Thomas sleeping is precisely the mark of our own forgetting: it is a watching whose conclusion (that we are seeing someone sleeping) is determined precisely by its failure (that Thomas does not cease to be woken): life is loomed for Benjamin by the act of forgetting, sleep is conferred upon Thomas by ceaselessly being woken, and fatigue, unravelling any opacity that sleep might possess, is essentially insurmountable.

The words which haunt Thomas (and Blanchot for that matter) clamber to him precisely because he is himself a word – a name *without story* – and nothing more (*TO*: 56, my translation). The only thing he possesses – the presence of venom in his mouth – does not even match his name: he is not a serpent; he carries the name of a man and this is a further cleavage between that which is signified (the venom) and the one who attempts fruitless signification (Thomas). It is for this very reason that while Thomas takes on the impression of sleeping, in the eyes of other viz. the reader, he is merely being awoken again and again by the fundamental rift that has taken place between his "I" and "he", between being and self, between reading and being read. The tautological orbit within the self is therein expressed in these scenes as a fundamental rift not between our variant and contradictory selves which pull us frenetically in opposing directions – like Dionysus and Apollo – but rather, the rift belongs to a situation wherein being is trapped within its-self when faced with a predicament of "self"-expression in language, in writing, in communication.[14] As such, the double in Blan-

---

[14] Indeed this realisation is present in the first version of *TO* where at the beginning of the story, the body, arms and legs of Thomas are described as being pulled in opposite directions by the sea: "Some very violent currents shook the body of Thomas, pulling his arms and legs in different directions, though without giving him the sentiment of being in the midst of the waves and of rolling in elements that he knew" (1941: 24, my translation). In the second version – the *récit* – we find these description of Thomas's body noticeably reduced such that his limbs and body are not only *no longer* pulled in various directions, but there is no need for Blanchot to write of Thomas possessing

chot functions not as the moment of strife, but rather as the turning on the same spot where the impasse inherent to existence is located. The figure functions as a movement which is necessarily a *turning* rather than a *replacement* (as in metaphor) or an *overriding* (as in metonymy). This turning is the site that keeps us outside of reducible meaning, so as to escape becoming *"mastered by the discernment of an either-or* [...] that could authorize a choice and lift from the choice the ambiguity that makes choosing possible" (*EL*: 262). This duplicity inherent to the literary double – to the moments referred to in a text but not made manifest, as in *Oedipus Rex* – instead refers "us back to a still more primal double meaning [... where] meaning does not escape into another meaning, but into the other of all meaning" (263). The double *as evasion* is precisely this: the "I" that recognises itself through dissimulation, through an ontology implying infinite degrees of (re)semblance, through dwelling, movement and zigzagging meaning.

### Resus(citation)

In the fifth chant Thomas leads us on a new adventure: he is in search of a body to occupy, and he momentarily finds one – that of a cat. Hearing the thing that he has embodied "scratch the ground, with its claws probably", Thomas, leaving the imprint of his hands upon the earth, himself scratches out a hole from the earth large enough to fit him (*TO*: 72–73, my translation). The hole becomes a tomb perfect for a vagrant name such as Thomas "whose absence it absorbed" (73). Once the tomb is finished Thomas throws himself into it. In this "grave" – which Blanchot in *L'Espace littéraire* calls "the impersonal place *par excellence*" (*EL*: 259) – he meets another similitude of himself: "This grave which was exactly his size, his shape, his thickness, was like his own cadaver, and every time he tried to bury himself in it, he was like a ridiculous dead person trying to bury his body in his body" (*TO*: 73, translation adapted).[15] But as much as we would like to believe that Thomas has acquired a final resting place, we are brutally reminded, as Blanchot also writes in *L'Espace littéraire*, that the cadaver merely reinforces its semblance to its own Nothingness:

---

either limbs, arms or body: "Currents shook him, though without give him the sentiment of being in the midst of the waves and of rolling in elements that he would have known" (*TO*: 55, translation adapted).

[15] The word "cadaver" shares etymological origins with the word "cadence" (musical or rhythmical fall of the voice) with both nouns stemming from the Latin *cadere*. That Thomas falls into the grave in order to find the cadaver he already is suggests that his interminable swan song, his threnody, is already cadenced – he falls into the cadaver that he already inescapably embodies.

"there was another dead person who was there first, and who, identical with himself, drove the ambiguity of Thomas's life and death to the extreme limit" (*EL*: 258, *TO*: 73). This cadaver is both Thomas and not him; it is his sign, his tomb and as such, is his "double [*sosie*], surrounded by strips of cloth [...] and this double was the only one with whom compromise was not possible, since it was the same as him, realised in the absolute empty (*TO*: 39, translation adapted). The cadaver does/not have a name, the cave is/not an abyss, Thomas does/not have a body: they are one and the same thing.

Deliberating on the Spanish word *sosiego* will illuminate some further insights. Although similar to the French word for double (*sosie*) which Blanchot utilises in *TO*, the Spanish word carries a further meaning apropos of painting. *Sosiego*, (meaning calmness, tranquillity) is a word which also suggests repose.[16] In painting, to capture the natural face of the sitter in their moment of repose is to capture the *sosiego* of the sitter – the appearance of his or her unobserved double which dissimulates the un-comfortable act of being observed and painted. But Blanchot's *sosie* – viz. Thomas' double – is anything but in a state of repose, for in *TO*, there can be no harmonic ac-cord between the impression of repose (*sosiego*) and its absence (after all, death is anything but reposing). In the end, Thomas walks out of his crypt as a "veritable Lazarus whom death had even resuscitated" (42, translation adapted). Having finally encountered his own corpse — his *sosie* without *sosiego* — and therefore being unable to "sink" any further, Thomas leaves the tomb –while the universe falls around him:

> He advanced, passing by the last shadows of the night without losing any of his glory, covered by grass and earth, going under the falling stars at an even pace which, for men not wrapped in a shroud, marks the ascent toward the point the most precious in life (42, translation adapted).

Here we have what I term an anti-onto-theological moment in Blanchot which de-scribes the ascension point in life, the one that men follow when they are not en-shrouded or dead, as one not of personal advancement (progress, forward-moving), but of *stasis*: as long as the universe continues moving and falling around us, we have

---

[16] These thoughts have been inspired by the work of Velasquez, in particular the following com-mentary by Enrique Lafuente Ferrari: "That is why Velasquez's princely portraits seem to us so de-void of the pomposity shown by so many court painters [...]. And in fact, Velasquez's models nei-ther pose nor act, but are merely present. The artist with his rare gift of observation, which was the result of intelligence rather than of his technical skill, knew how to catch the natural face of his sit-ter in that moment of repose, that *sosiego*, to use a Spanish word, when the model relaxes quietly wrapped up in his own dream. (1961: "Introduction", no page number). We recall here Blanchot's *Aminadab*, published straight after *Thomas l'Obscur* in 1942. In this short story, we find the pro-tagonist, Thomas, in an artist's studio standing before his portrait for which he cannot remember posing, and moreover cannot in the image find his face.

the impression of ascendance. As Hart writes apropos of this merging and collapsing of ascension and resuscitation into each other:

> Resurrection for Blanchot, is both beholden to death and utterly ignorant of what death truly is. It draws its force from death considered as negativity, while disregarding its obscure dimension: a dying that never begins and never ends but eternally repeats itself and therefore dissimulates "itself" ("Gospel" 2004:14).

The resuscitation alluded to in Blanchot's *récit* – itself a re-*citation* of an earlier version – invites us to think of both Lazarus's and Thomas's emergence from the tomb, but in different ways. From the Latin *resuscitare,* to "rouse again, revive",[17] the re-emergence of Thomas *qua* Lazarus is the re(sus)citing of that which did not perish completely. The character of Thomas, alone in the world, and having borrowed and then abandoned the form of *un chat supreme* (a supreme cat),[18] alludes to Lazarus only to emphasize the recurrence and repetition of death. But Thomas, emerging from the tomb resuscitated – re-*cited* – is nevertheless "still" dead. How do we account for this? If Thomas is a name – an I – searching for a body, then in entering the tomb and finding nothing so to speak, except for another name, who being dead, ensures that Thomas re-emerges empty-handed because the search, or rather its rhythm and flow, is interminable. As Blanchot tells us in "Literature and the Right to Death": "Everything physical takes precedence: rhythm, weight, mass, shape, and then the paper on which one writes, the trail of ink, the book" (327). In digging himself a tomb – a sign, an engraving of his name – Thomas completes only part of his journey.[19] All that happens when he emerges from the tomb is that he has got his name in print so to speak, re-etched so that he might go on a little further in his search. But the act of

---

[17] Which is further derived from *re* (again), *suscitare* (to raise, revive, from *sub* [up from under] and *citare* [to summon]).

[18] Indeed the motif of a cat is not chosen by Blanchot by chance: it is a reply to Sartre who, in his essay "Qu'est-ce que c'est la literature", proposes the following essentially anti-Blanchotian supposition: "The function of a writer is to call a cat a cat. If the words are ill, it is up to us to heal them. If we don't do so, much illness will come of this malady" (*Situations II* [304, my translation]). Responding to this essay in "Literature and the Right to Die", Blanchot searches instead to make lucid the separation inherent to literary and everyday language: "Let us hold onto words, then, and not revert back to things, let us not let go of words, not believe that they are sick. Then we'll be at peace [...] literary language is made of uneasiness; it is also made of contradictions [...]" (1995:325).

[19] The sense of journey evokes the eschatological concept of the seven seals is found in the Book of Revelation and references the coming of the end of the world whereupon all of the seven seals – or warnings – will have been broken. For Blanchot, or at least for the character of Thomas, we can read his journey and the events belonging to it as traversing the advent of each of the seven seals, suggesting that Thomas is thus either delivered from perishing or trapped within its eternal state, within the stone so important to Jewish religion, to Kakfa ("I am turning into stone [...] If I don't save myself in some work, I am lost"), and to Hölderlin ("I am dumb, I am made of stone") (quoted in *EL*: 62. Furthermore, the sense of a stone also gives rise to the thought of a statue viz. the aesthetic petrifaction of/within the self.

re(sus)citation – and of sepulchral inscription – does not end and so in *TO* dying *per se* cannot *come* to an end. Like the theme of revivification which haunts the work of Wordsworth, Mallarmé, Proust and most certainly Thomas Hardy, the moment of death in Blanchot is but another inscription that further ingrains some kind of truth accentuated by the authenticity of impressions.

The very impossibility of Thomas's dying *once and for all* in *TO* is, I would argue, due to the fact that Thomas begins the story as *already* dead, as already ensconced within the eternal return of death precisely because he has already, *like* Lazarus, died. Indeed in "Literature and the Right to Death", Blanchot writes:

> I say my name, and it is as though I were already chanting my own dirge: I separate myself from myself, I am no longer either my presence or my reality, but an objective, impersonal presence, the presence of my name, which goes beyond me and whose stonelike immobility performs the same function for me as a tombstone weighing on the void (324).

Instead of reading this as writing back from the margins apropos of Heidegger's possibility of being-for-death, I suggest that *TO* can be read alongside Plato's *Gorgias,* in which Sophocles evokes the angst-ridden question attributed to the lost tragedy of Euripides, *Polyidus*. "Who knoweth if to live is to be dead, And to be dead, to live?" (Lines 492e9-10).[20] This reading is closer to the anxiety that riddles Thomas, for if it were a case of not being able to engage with the possibility of death, this would assume that Thomas is yet to die, and as we know most violently in the text, Thomas is very much the embodiment of the living-dead. He cannot experience the moment of his death because, for this moment to be written, it would have to be known; neither can the author write of the *actual* moment of Thomas's death, nor can Thomas in any of his deaths find a body to replace the one he has *always already* lost. Thomas encapsulates the unquiet oscillation of a name wandering and looking for a sepulchral host (something physical), but a sepulchral host – a body, a tomb, a sema, a fall – that is an abyss and in which lives his double. And just as there is no falling, there is no transcendence. Like a crab Thomas can only move forwards in a zigzagging movement. The "Supreme Being" inherent in an onto-theology that Thomas fails to attain is, in *TO,* deferred to a cat which is "supreme" amongst its species. Nothing more.

---

[20] This reference and all subsequent ones to the *Gorgias* are from *Plato: Lysis, Symposium, Gorgias.*

## Consciousness

Thomas is riveted to consciousness *par excellence*. He perceives that "the property of my thought, [is] not to assure me of existence (as all things do, as a *stone* does), but to assure me of being in nothingness itself, and to invite me not to be, in order to make me feel my marvellous absence (*TO*: 99–100, my italics). It is for this reason that I must disagree with Kevin S. Fitzgerald who argues that Thomas is at this point experiencing the "absurd horror of existing without existence".[21] Instead, I suggest that his is an experience *for itself and in itself*, experience of an experience we can neither detach from existence nor existing.

Of the stone, Thomas curiously states this: "[...] the property of my thought, [is] not to assure me of existence (as all things do, as a stone does)". It seems that thought and stone are set in diametric opposition, with thought being the thing that assures only nothingness and the stone, knowledge of existence. We find in Plato's *Gorgias* such a reference to stones and to life. When Socrates proposes to Callicles that, "Then it is not correct to say, as people do, that those who want nothing are happy", and Callicles replies: "No, for at that rate stones and corpses would be extremely happy" (Lines 492e3-4), we understand that existence is relative to that which subsists, that is, matter. Thought as consciousness for Thomas is exactly what rivets him to *being in nothingness itself* and it is for this reason that I would argue that Thomas's textual character reads like a floating hieroglyph in search of a tablet, a head-*stone*, an inscription, a matter to be written and therefore *read*. To theorise this point further, the one hand we have the impression throughout *TO* that the character of Thomas is the leaky vessel that Socrates describes in the *Gorgias* as the undesirable state of the soul within the body, which is, according to Socrates, its tomb (493b5–8, 493c1–4). On the other hand, Thomas is the one who "flee[s] his flight" (*TO*: 119); in other words, he is a leaky name *without* a "tomb": he seeks nothing more than his material double which would bring an intimacy and a synthesis with the self — a synthesis between the perceiving *je* and the perceived *il* — and it is from this search, itself impossible, which brings the *récit* to its ultimately un-Platonic ending written in the text itself for Thomas is not imprisoned in a mortal body, but is unable to make sense of the impossibility that he is still living: "All my strength, the sense I had, in taking the hemlock, of being not Socrates dying but Socrates increas-

---

[21] Kevin S. Fitzgerald, *The Negative Eschatology of Maurice Blanchot*, no pagination.

ing himself through Plato, this certainty of being unable to disappear [...] made every instant of my life the instant in which I was going to leave life (111).

Indeed, figurative language – the double and of doubling – that Blanchot employs to render this breach between the *je* and the *il* both visible and material is powerfully captured in the use of the trope itself: differing from Terence Hawkes's assertion in *Metaphor* that "figurative language is language which doesn't mean what it says" (1), I would argue that figurative language, at least in Blanchot, means more than what it says rather than pointing to what it does not say. In other words, the figurative in Blanchot is not an empty glyph or a poetic turn of phrase, but a discernable and palpable void-like presence in which the double represents, in Coleridge's words, "the perception of similitude in dissimilitude" (quoted in Hawkes: 42). From this view, it is arguable that the trope does not render the unfamiliar more familiar, as in certain mythologies, but rather functions as a means of asserting a pause – a gauze if you will – in language so as to bring to the surface that which can only be appreciated indirectly rather than metonymically. Tropes are essential to our understanding of the everyday, as well as the literary and the textual if we apprehend their employment not as means of making the *unhemlich* more familiar, or as means of over-riding the unfamiliar with a new sense, but instead permitting a slightly different way of articulating the unfamiliar itself.[22]

Blanchot's engagement with the foreign within ourselves as a vague "synthesis of self" is expressed both grammatically and descriptively in the first chant of *TO* where it is the water that is described as giving Thomas a body with which to swim, and in the fifth chant, where it is the tomb he digs that gives him the impression of a having body. The limits of Thomas's body are defined by that which exists outside of him, as if there is more surety of what exists outside than inside. In this sense, *TO* can be understood as a search for intimacy with the self *par excellence*, an intimacy we usually seek, as Oedipus does, from a source exterior to ourselves.

This sense of duality is grammatically captured in the French of *TO* which makes abundant use of the reflexive verb, so much so that it reads like a text writing (about) itself. This is the sense of grammatical doubling, the sense of Thomas seating himself (*il s'assit*), lying himself down (*il s'etend*), raising, standing, holding himself

---

[22] We find a sense of this movement in Kafka's description of his trip to Friedland and Reichenberg in January–February, 1911: "I should write the whole night through, so many things occur to me, but all of it rough. What a power this has come to have over me, where as in the past I was able, so far as I remember, to elude it by a turn, a slight turn which was enough to make me happy" (*The Diaries of Franz Kafka 1914-1923* [237]).

up (*il essaya de se redresser*[...] *se balancer* [...] *se tenir*), merging with the storm (*il ne rencontrait aucun obstacle, il se rejoignait, il se confondait avec soi en s'installant* [...]), loving himself with revulsion (*je m'aime moi-même avec l'esprit de détestation*) multiplies the points of textual *dédoublement* infinitely into a series of "exchanged contacts with the empty" (*TO*: 20, translation adapted), so much so that we are left only with impressions belonging to the *series of seemings* that Thomas Hardy wrote of in the preface to *Jude the Obscure*. If we understand impressions to be the dissimulated inquiry into how the ontology or the being of a literary character can be expressed in fictional writing, then our appreciation of the character of Thomas, "astray in himself", is one in which character is "always flung back into being" by his relationship with words, and therefore owes his imprint, his trace, his name, sema and sign, and his ultimate materiality, to "the personal rhythm, the impersonal cadence of all things" so strikingly captured in Blanchot (1982: 258; 1995: 332; *TO*: 89).

Possibility in *TO* occurs in the resonance between the personal and the impersonal, that is, between the orbital similitude inherent to being and the moments of subjective antagonism or difference when we feel *hors de soi* (outside or besides oneself). The self perceived between the flows and breaks in character reveals a manner of being that resonates with the vertigo of tiny oscillations which return the personal self, disastrously, fortuitously, only ever back to the impersonal self. In this way, literary representations of the double can be understood as an allegorical catchment which holds, imperfectly, the self in orbit with the self. Describing this vertigo in being, Blanchot writes: "[Thomas] saw his image in the total absence of images, seized by the most violent vertigo possible, a vertigo which did not make him fall, but prevented him from falling and rendered impossible the fall it rendered inevitable" (*TO*: 74).

**Conclusion**

Attributing to Blanchot a "silence proper to him", the publisher Gallimard on the first pages of the *récit* offers us proof that Blanchot is dead, and assures us of the impenetrability of this silence: *Maurice Blanchot (1907-2003) fut romancier et critique. Sa vie fut entièrement vouée à la littérature et au silence qui lui est propre.*[23] This catachresis works perfectly within the scope of the text, and practices exactly that which Blanchot found abhorrent in Heidegger's formulation of death (that if death is our

---

[23] "Maurice Blanchot was a novelist and critic. His life was entirely dedicated to literature and to the silence which is proper to him" (*TO*: 5, my translation).

only and own possibility, then it too, like everything else within the realm of meta-physics, has been appropriated and mastered by human thought). So while the small epigraph wants to explain to the reader, in a complimentary fashion, that Blanchot, dead, is even more explicitly silent than when he was living, the reverse actually occurs, and the words produce the effect of an *epitaph* which profoundly reminds us that Blanchot is neither quietly dead nor terminally silent.

If Blanchot is the father of Thomas in the way that Shakespeare is, as Stephen Dedalus tells us, the father of Hamlet,[24] then the figure of Blanchot/Thomas, riveted to an emblem of self which confers only an inadequate apprehension of death, does not die but simply re-enacts and re-cites the "terrible discovery of his own unliving image".[25] As such, silence is *not* proper to Blanchot. As Jacques Derrida reminds us, Blanchot was never silent and it is for this reason that the last word must be left to him.[26] To further qualify: Blanchot is neither silent because he wrote (rather than spoke), nor silent because he is dead (rather than alive): he wrote because his silence, like the instance of his death, was *not* proper to him, but rather proper to others in the likeness (*semblance*) of their silence(s) and their (mis)apprehension/s of death. And while Blanchot's writings might express extreme pause and repose, solitude and absence, the silence we attribute to him is but the binary of our own silence reading his writing. It is this double movement between reader and literature mediated by the absent-presence of the author that opens a hiatus between our silence and the silence we believe to be properly Blanchot's. The work of the double in Blanchot's writing – disastrous, fortuitous – disproves all clarity and possibility that might otherwise be expected of the literary figure which serves to create the prospect, and cleavage, of difference. Blanchot's double, like the character of Thomas, is obscure in the way that similitude is constitutive: it tends to befall the self, its self, time and again, and it is for this reason that the double can only ever be understood as at least double, if by double we come to mean that which repeats itself infinitely. As a result, Blanchot's (*dés*)*astre*, his textual melody or heart-beat, like Holderlin's distant comet – "a flower

---

[24] This notion of haunting and resuscitation reminds us of Joyce's *Ulysses* where apropos of Shakespeare and Hamlet/Hamnet he writes: "in the image of the unquiet father, the unliving son lives forth" (Joyce: 249). Indeed Blanchot himself asks a somewhat similar question in his essay, "The Song of the Sirens": "What would happen if instead of being two distinct people Ulysses and Homer comfortably shared their roles, and were one and the same presence?" (447).
[25] Blanchot, *The Book To Come* (210).
[26] Derrida, "Lui laisser le dernier mot" (29–31).

of light, a star that burns but that unfurls innocently into a flower" (*EL*: 276) – does not perish but is echoed recurrently. Onward.

## Works cited

Bataille, Georges. *Inner Experience*. Trans. Leslie Anne Bolt. New York: State University of New York Press, 1988.

Benjamin, Walter. "The Image of Proust" in *Illuminations*. Trans. Harry Zorn. London: Pimlico, 1999: 192 – 210.

Blanchot, Maurice. *Thomas l'Obscur* (1941). Paris: Gallimard, 2005.

Blanchot, Maurice. *Aminadab* (1942). Trans. Jeff Fort. Lincoln: University of Nebraska Press, 2002.

Blanchot, Maurice. *Thomas the Obscure* (1950). Trans. Robert Lamberton, in *The Station Hill Blanchot Reader*. Barrytown, New York: Station Hill Press, 1999: 51–128.

Blanchot, Maurice. *The Space of Literature (L'Espace littéraire)*. Trans. Anne Smock. Lincoln: University of Nebraska Press, 1982.

Blanchot, Maurice. "Literature and the Right to Death". Trans. Charlotte Mandell. Stanford: Stanford University Press, 1995.

Blanchot, Maurice. *The One Who Was Standing Apart From Me (L'un qui me n'accompagnait pas)*. Trans. Lydia Davis in *The Station Hill Blanchot Reader*. Barrytown, New York: Station Hill Press, 1999: 263–339.

Blanchot, Maurice. "The Song of the Sirens" .Trans. Lydia Davis in *The Station Hill Blanchot Reader*. Barrytown, New York: Station Hill Press, 1999: 443–450.

Blanchot, Maurice. *The Book to Come*. Trans. Charlotte Mandell, Stanford, California: Stanford University Press, 2003.

Char, Réné. "Ma feuille vineuse" in *Chants de la Balandrane, Oeuvres completes.* Paris: Gallimard, 1983.

Coleridge, Samuel. T. *Biographia Literaria*. Princeton, NJ: Princeton University Press, 1983,

Corrigan, Robert W. "Oedipus Rex" in *Tragedy: A Critical Anthology*. New York: Houghton Mifflin Company, 1971.

Derrida, Jacques. *Margins of Philosophy (Marges de la philosophie)*. Trans. Alan Bass. Chicago: Chicago: The University of Chicago Press, 1982.

Derrida, Jacques. "Lui laisser le dernier mot". *Magazine littéraire*, 424 (2003): 29–31.

Ferrari, Enrique Lafuente. *Velasquez, Infantes and Infantas*. New York: Tudor Publishing Co, 1961.

Fitzgerald, Kevin S. *The Negative Eschatology of Maurice Blanchot*. http://www.studiocleo.com/librarie/blanchot/kf/tragic/obscure_thomas.htm

Hardy, Thomas. *Jude the Obscure*. London: Penguin Classics, 1998.

Hart, Kevin. "The Gospel of *L'Arret de* mort". *Journal of Philosophy and Scripture*, 1.2 (2004): 10–16.

Hart, Kevin *The Dark Gaze*. Chicago: University of Chicago Press, 2004.

Hawkes, Terence. *Metaphor*. London: Methuen, 1972.

Heraclitus. *Heraclitus, The Cosmic Fragments: A Critical Study*. Trans. and. ed. G. S. Kirk. Cambridge: CUP, 1954.

Goethe. *Faust*. Trans. Walter Arndt. New York: Norton, 2001.

Joyce, James. *Ulysses* (1922). London: Bodley Head, 1976.

Kafka, Franz. *The Diaries of Franz Kafka 1914-1923*. Trans. Martin Greenberg with Hannah Arendt. New York: Schocken Books, 1949.

Kafka, Franz. *Letters to Friends, Family and Editors*. Trans. Richard and Clara Winston. New York: Schocken Books, 1977.

Lévinas, Emmanuel. *De l'évasion*. Paris: Fata Morgana, 1982.

Martin, William. "The Recurrence of Rhythm: Configurations of the Voice in Homer, Plato and Joyce". Unpublished Doctoral Thesis submitted to the University of NSW, Sydney, 2006.

Miller, J Hillis. *Hawthorne & History*. Basil Blackwell: Oxford, 1991.

Nietzsche, Friedrich. *The Birth of Tragedy and the Case of Wagner*. Trans. Walter Kaufmann. New York: Random House, 1967.

Petrosino, Silvano. *La Vérité nomade*, Paris: La Découverte, 1984.

Plato. *Lysias, Symposium, Gorgias*. Trans. W.R.M Lamb. Cambridge: Harvard University Press, 2001.

Reinhardt, Karl. *Sophocles*. Trans. Hazel Harvey and David Harvey. Oxford: Basil Blackwell, 1979.

Roudaut, Jean. "Le bonheur extraordinaire" in *Magazine littéraire*, 424 (2003): 50–52.

Sarraute, Nathalie. *Tropisms and The Age of Suspicion*. Trans. Maria Jolas. London: Calder, 1963.

Sartre, Jean-Paul. *Nausea.* trans. Robert Baldick. England: Penguin Books, 1965.

Sartre, Jean-Paul. *Qu'est-ce que c'est la literature, Situations II.*. Paris: Gallimard, 1975.

Shelley, Percy B. *Prometheus Unbound.* London: Cassel,1909.

Schiller, Friedrich. *On the Aesthetic Education of Man, in a Series of Letters.* Trans. Elizabeth M. Wilkinson and L.A. Willoughby. Oxford: OUP, 1967

Stravinsky, Igor. *Poetics of Music.* Trans. Arthur Knodel and Ingolf Dahl. New York: Vintage, 1956.

Urhig, David. "Levinas et Blanchot dans les années 30: le contrepoint critique de la philosophie de Louis Lavelle" in *Levinas-Blanchot: penser la différence,* Paris: Presse Université Française, (forthcoming, 2007).

Wilde, Oscar. "The Critic as Artist" in *Collins Complete Works of Oscar Wilde.* Glasgow: HarperCollins Pub., 1999: 1108–1155.

Wordsworth, William. *The Fourteen-Book Prelude.* Ed. W.J.B. Owen. Ithaca/London: Cornell Univ. Press, 1985.

**Part Two**

# Taxonomy of the Double:
## Struggles of Cognition in the works of Vita Sackville-West and
## Walter de la Mare

Søren Landkildehus

> I was bruised and battered and I couldn't tell
> what I felt
> I was unrecognizable to myself
> Saw my reflection in a window I didn't know
> my own face
> – Bruce Springsteen, *Streets of Philadelphia*.

## Introduction

In this essay I argue that the figure of the double illustrates a fundamental change of mind. The point of my investigation is to view the double as a benign but dramatic feature of what I see as a "fundamental" transformation in one's belief system. Specifically in the context of my essay, change of mind suggests a spiritual (re)orientation in life, although this need not be religiously articulated. Vita Sackville-West provides a useful description of what I mean by a change of mind in a "fundamental sense" in her novel, *Heritage*. Here, she writes:

> Moments of revelation are intrinsically dramatic things, when a knowledge, irrevocable, undisputable, comes to dwell in the mind. All previous habitants have to readjust themselves to make room for the stranger. A great shuffling and stampeding [takes place, but], far from experiencing discomfort or difficulty in accommodating themselves to their new conditions, [...] prejudices [jump] briskly round and [present] themselves in their true shape beneath the searching glare of the revelation. (Sackville-West 1919: 48)[1]

Sackville-West's account is slightly different from the standard philosophical understanding of change of mind, since the latter often presupposes that a change in one belief entails change of all beliefs in a network.[2] The description Sackville-West offers does not necessarily include such an encompassing change. Rather, change, in her description, primarily affects the preconceptions and prejudices we harbor about what we believe. A disturbance in our network of beliefs may or may not involve a

---

I thank *The Hong Kierkegaard Library*, St. Olaf College for support, *The Kierkegaard House Foundation* for generous funding, and Mrs. Jean Britland for commenting on an earlier draft.
[1] All references to *Heritage* are from the Doran Company edition (1919).
[2] Such as in the case when "holism" is being discussed. See Jackman (1999).

complete readjustment of the beliefs we have. In any event, it should not be surprising if most of our beliefs survive the addition of new knowledge, which furthermore would serve to clarify our understanding of why we retain such beliefs in the first place. For example, we should not expect any one person to experience religious conversion without retaining most of his beliefs prior to that experience. What "changes" is the convert's ability to comprehend his beliefs as informed by the introduction of a new experience. Viewed *phenomenologically,* this would make a radical difference to the network as a whole, but it would not necessarily destabilize any individual beliefs, let alone the network of beliefs. Having said this, although the network of beliefs a person has over time may change only slightly, it would nevertheless affect the outlook of the person as a result. For example, although Adam before the fall is physically identical to Adam after the fall, his belief that he must not eat the fruit from the Tree of the Knowledge of Good and Evil is changed by the introduction of a new knowledge after he eats the fruit. Thenceforth, Adam's beliefs are significant only up to the sad knowledge that they are maintained under the new condition of having lost Eden, even though they are no less relevant. Yet, the fact that people change their beliefs over time is not in itself the reason why change of mind is interesting. Sackville-West's description of change of mind is remarkable as it pinpoints the mind's disruption and struggle to adjust to the new knowledge. What we should find interesting about Adam is not Adam-before or –after the Fall, but Adam-in-between. Being in-between reveals the struggle between the old and the new ways of thinking.

The main text I use to illustrate the phenomenon of change of mind is Walter de la Mare's *The Return* (1910). De la Mare is mainly thought of as a poet but his novels require attention as well because their style uniquely fuses exteriority and interiority, which is evident in novels such as *The Return* and *Memoirs of a Midget* (1921), and as a result, both novels display a rich vocabulary that communicates the intricacies of the mind. In my view, de la Mare's work over-all can be loosely described as "mythical" writing which, in Søren Kierkegaard's observation, "allows something that is inward to take place outwardly" (Kierkegaard 1980: 47). De la Mare's intermingling of fantasy and fact in his writings suspends the boundaries that separate the two, and thus allows the expression of the complex fusion of the outer and the inner which is a significant feature of what I have so far termed a "fundamental" change of mind. I comment on this fusion towards the end of this essay when I consider Kierkegaard's notion of reduplication.

An outline of this essay is as follows. I begin with the argument that the "double" is best seen as a term denoting individual components that comprise a whole in a variety of shapes. In the following section, I outline these shapes, and set up a theoretical framework with the purpose of providing a foundation to comprehend them, which I will then apply to the works of Charles Dickens and specifically Sackville-West. Next, I extend the theoretical framework to illustrate change of mind as depicted in de la Mare's novel. Finally, I conclude with a deliberation on the spiritual implications of my discussion.

## 1. Taxonomy of the Double

The figure of the double is complex and takes on many forms. I will offer a sketch of some varieties of the double in order to demonstrate how I arrive at *the* particular shape that exemplifies the concept of fundamental change of mind. To discuss these varieties, I will employ illustrations from various literary works. Of course, these illustrations are not *pure* examples of the various categories of the double I shall espouse, but I will delineate salient features in order to put forward my taxonomy. We should not think that we could arrive at pure *models* of the double. Consequently, I stress that this taxonomy should not be seen as exhaustive.

The double does not denote a lesser or specific "other" from the self, since there may be no criterion to distinguish an ontological priority between someone and his *so-called* double. Indeed, it is mere idealization to identify someone as the original and an "other" as his double, when in non-hierarchical language both instantiations are each other's double. An individual, in other words, *belongs* to, is part of, the double; the double, in this sense, denotes a *whole* in which the individual participates. I primarily distinguish between an outward, or manifested double, and an inward, or experiential double. In the case of the former, features of similarity are largely related to physical appearances. In the case of the latter, features are more subtly relational, usually in terms of a bifurcation of the mind. This may be difficult to identify. When we speak of the inward double, what we need to look for is a shared interiority, as for example in moral/spiritual values and belief systems. The sharing can be seen as something happening in the present, as something brought about by recollection, and as *the process of* something coming into being.[3] The last option includes the possibility of extreme disparity between the before and the after of something coming into

---

[3] Joseph Conrad's "The Secret Sharer" (1912) is an example of *sharing in the present*.

being. It is partly because of this disparity that the "in-between" is of such intrigue, because here we would have competing paradigms for our beliefs. The main categories of the double (outward and inward) have three further distinctive sub-categories: the identical, the symmetrical, and the asymmetrical. It is my view that the asymmetrical inward double is the figure that best describes change of mind.

## A. Outward Identity and Symmetry

Perhaps the most evident example of the outward double is twins.[4] In literature, twins as doubles occur, for example, in Charles Dickens's *Little Dorrit* (1857). Unknown to Mrs. Flintwinch, her husband has a brother who is his identical twin. At the beginning of the novel, upon chancing the two men together (one awake and the other asleep), she thinks she is dreaming (Dickens 2003b: 57). However, if there was any doubt "which was her own Jeremiah, it would have been resolved by his impatience" (57). The revelation of Flintwinch having a twin brother occurs very late in the novel, and this allows Dickens to use to the outward identical double to its subtlest moral extent. The brothers are literally indistinguishable. The impatience of Mr. Flintwinch, who often beats his wife, symbolizes throughout the novel the brutality of civilized men towards women, whereas the sleeping Flintwinch symbolizes the condoning indifference of individuals towards such brutality. Through the means of the identical double, Dickens conveys that there is ultimately no difference between the actual brutality against women and the passivity of bystanders.[5]

In the case of the identical twins, their similarity is indexed on their identical exteriority. On a lesser scale however, the outward double can also be detected on the level of "semblance", as in the case of family resemblance. This variety of similitude is what I term "symmetrical exteriority". While identical exteriority shared by two persons is difficult to distinguish, symmetrical exteriority is a weaker outer resemblance that provides multiple means of distinguishing one from the other. Such symmetrical exteriority is sometimes used to great effect by writers to contemplate on the intertwined destinies of different characters, as well as the choices made in life that will inevitably fuse individuals into an organic whole, or expose their divergent

---

[4] According to Otto Rank, twins may be regarded as the primordial prototype of the figure of the double. See *Beyond Psychology* (84–92)
[5] This is again repeated in the Evrémonde brothers in Dickens's *A Tale of Two Cities* (1859).

paths.[6] Vita Sackville-West's *All Passion Spent* (1932), for example, focuses on the way certain existential projects are resolved through means of the symmetrical double. Characters who exemplify this doubling share not only outward but inward similarities as well. As such, the case is *not just* of *reconciling* oneself to an originator with whom one shares only accidental exteriority (for example, a son's inheritance of his father's characteristics[7]) that an existential problem is resolved. Rather, in *All Passion Spent,* outward symmetry is located in characters' family resemblance, but augmented by an inward identity of shared existential goals which, nevertheless, can only be achieved by the double. The double is here the coming together of two family members who, united by their shared project, produce outcomes that give different practical results for each member of the double. For example, Lady Slane sees herself mirrored in her great-granddaughter, Deborah, who also shares her namesake. In the course of the novel, Lady Slane gradually fuses herself with her granddaughter:

> Fortunate Deborah! She [Lady Slane] thought, to be so firm, so trustful, and by one person at least so well understood; but to which Deborah she alluded, she scarcely knew. (Sackville-West, 1991: 282)[8]
>
> [...]
>
> "Yes", said Lady Slane, but more people are really of the same mind than you would believe. They take a great deal of trouble to conceal it, and only a crisis calls it out. For instance, if you were to die", – but what she really meant was, If I were to die – "I daresay you would find that your grandfather had understood you (me) better than you (I) think" (287).

In the first quoted text Lady Slane notices that Deborah has the same qualities of firmness, trustfulness, and empathy as she has. The empathy makes Lady Slane see herself as part of a whole (the double) that happens to be instantiated in two "Deborahs". The relative components of the double are *weakly* indistinguishable, as is evident in Lady Slane's inability to tell the difference (although her granddaughter is supposedly able to tell the difference). In the second quote, the unity of mind is asserted. The shared bewilderment of existence emphasized by "death" sets a shared goal signified by "being understood" (the icon of the grandfather symbolizes the norm-giving society), the achievement of which again produces different results for each individual. For Lady Slane, the result is reconciliation with life; for Deborah, it is the opportunity to choose her life.

---

[6] Examples include are Charles Dickens's *A Tale of Two Cities* and José Saramago's *The Gospel According to Jesus Christ* (1994).
[7] Such as the Crunchers in *A Tale of Two Cities* (esp. 55–61).
[8] All references to *All Passion Spent* are from the Caroll and Graff Pub. edition (1991).

The fusion of Lady Slane with her granddaughter happens not merely because of their outward similarity but because they entertain similar values of life. Both share an existential drive to be creative personalities. In Deborah, Lady Slane gains a new perspective of her own self: "This child, this Deborah, this self, this other self, this projection of herself, was firm and certain. Her engagement was a mistake [...]" (283). What the younger Deborah reveals to the elder is the trap of tradition in the guise of marriage. Just as the elder Deborah did not become a painter because she was married, the younger Deborah becomes a musician by refusing marriage. But through Deborah, Lady Slane can accept that what she had wanted for herself will now be fulfilled through the life of a subsequent generation:

> When she said "a musician", Lady Slane received a little shock, so confidently had she expected Deborah to say "a painter". But it came to much the same thing, and her disappointment was quickly healed. The girl was talking as she herself would have talked. (284)

In this way, the double can do what each individual could not on its own. We must not think that the younger Deborah, by herself, provides the answer to the existential problem. Rather, it is only through the unity of life experiences between the two women, and the new opportunities afforded that the older generation *through the younger* corrects its mistakes. Similarly, it is only through the united wisdom and vigor of the two women that the younger generation has a chance to progress.

Authors usually use the outward double showcased in the above examples when they wish to show that despite indistinguishable exteriority, interiority makes all the difference, consequently stressing the deceptive nature of the outward. The identity of outward features obfuscates diametrically different personalities. Often, a moral contention or situation is the tactical purpose of the outward double. The indistinguishable Flintwinch brothers invite criticism concerning dependence on outward appearances. Indeed, Mrs. Flintwinch's momentary confusion which she mistaken as "dreaming" serves to emphasize the unreliability of appearances. This theme is powerfully developed in *Little Dorrit* in which the apparent social ascent of some characters inevitably ends in failure because they rely on appearances. It is no wonder then that Amy Dorrit, Dickens's protagonist, who resists the mores of the superficial rich, repeatedly undermines outward success. In *All Passion Spent*, symmetrical exteriority highlights the social censure of women. Both "Deborahs" share the same core beliefs and values, although society has forced the older double to waste her opportunities. Benefiting from the older woman's experience, the younger double dares to resist the gendered imperatives of her social system, and successfully lives out their shared desire. Thus, it does not follow that because Lady Slane had wasted her opportunities that her life is therefore wasted, since the other individual who participates in the double can now fulfill both *their* existential project. Both individuals of the double demonstrate the unyielding permanence of the personal over the disabling externalized, societal norms that often legitimize public values and marginalize private ones.

But it is precisely due to such "permanence" that the outward double does not illustrate change of mind, as there is no shift in value paradigm. What it often does is to illustrate what it means to raise certain value claims in various contexts. In the case of the *Little Dorrit*, the identical double reveals civilization's underlying brutality and indifference which are fundamentally one and the same thing; in the case of *All Passion Spent*, the symmetrical double reveals the struggle between what society expects of a person and what that person privately desires. Nevertheless, similarity on the exterior serves in both cases as merely a "pointer" to, or signifier of, inwardness that may or may not be shared.

**B. Asymmetry, Inwardness, and Dissemblance**
The examples provided thus far suggest that the manifested double often displays a disparity between outward, perceivable features, and the interior lives of the double. The case is different with shared value and belief systems. When mirroring occurs at this level, the shape of double can be described as experiential (or inward). As demonstrated also in the preceding section, this experiential variety can be identical, symmetrical or asymmetrical. An example of the experiential double is locatable in *All Passion Spent*. The rapport between Lady Slane and Deborah is inwardly symmetrical insofar as they are passionate about art, although articulated in different forms of expression.

An example of the identical inward double can be found in Michel Montaigne's *Essays*. In "On Friendship", Montaigne speaks of his short lived but crucial relationship with Etienne de la Boétie. The sudden death of de la Boétie, however, does not sever their connection. For Montaigne, as long as he is alive, the friendship will persist.[9] True friendship is not, Montaigne writes, the manifold acquaintances we

---

[9] See Donald M. Frame, *Montaigne's Discovery of Man* (28–29).

might encourage. Rather, it is like having "one soul in two bodies" (Montaigne: 171):[10]

> Our souls pulled together in such unison, they regarded each other with such ardent affection, and with a like affection revealed themselves to each other to the very depths of our hearts, that not only did I know his soul as well as mine, but I should certainly have trusted myself to him more readily than to myself. (170–71)

The soul "mating" described here suggests that, unlike ordinary friendships – in which an individual might adore the kindness of person A, the generosity of person B, and the athletic prowess of person C, and thus divide his emotions between them – true friendship is single minded (172). Even if one could "multiply" oneself, these extra selves would still be conferred upon one's soul-mate (172). In other words, one merely happens to be two very different bodies sharing the same mind. What is sought is the identity of the interior. Importantly however, the identical particularity of the inward double does not necessarily manifest itself outwardly as symmetry. In other words, what is identical experientially need not be symmetrically manifested. The mind has been duplicated, not the outward features. This kind of soul mating portrayed by Montaigne is nevertheless rare since not even Montaigne and de la Boétie achieved it (Frame: 24).

(So far, I have merely sketched possible examples of the identical and symmetrical inward doubles. Although much more might be discussed in relation to these figures, they do not concern my discussion as they do not illustrate change of mind. Indeed, there is an almost alarming calm in the Montaigne-de la Boétie mind-merger, and were it not for the death of de la Boétie, it would not be inconceivable that such transference on the part of Montaigne may have been considered pathological. Likewise, in the symmetrical double, what characterizes it is *pro tanto* similarity which, however, does not illustrate the kind of disturbances [change of mind] identified in the passage from *Heritage*).

The shape of the asymmetrical double is characterized by dissemblance of mind: one part of the mind is subverting, hiding, or ignoring another. For our purposes, such dissemblance might reveal itself in two ways. One way is characterized by willfully ignoring evidence presented to the perceiving subject. The other way shows the subject being overwhelmed by impressions for which the perceiver has no adequate concepts. I shall explain further what I mean by this partition of mind by

---

[10] All references to *The Complete Works* of Montaigne are from the Alfred A. Knopf edition (2003).

considering the model Immanuel Kant expounds in his *Critique of Pure Reason* (A50/B74-A55/B79).[11] My use of Kant is modest, since all I am interested in appropriating is his idea of partitioning cognition into two parts: *spontaneity of understanding* and *receptivity of intuition*. The former provides us with concepts while the latter presents us with contents.

In detail, the first part, our *faculty of understanding*, makes sense of sensuous impressions. This is done *spontaneously*. Everything we experience is reticulated *immediately* by the concepts we have available. Presumably, the more we are educated the better we are at discerning the various events in our lives as well as of things around us. However, whether we have many concepts or only few, we have no experience which has not been ordered by the concepts we happen to have. This is analogous to having vocabularies of various sizes and linguistic varieties. It does not follow from having minimum vocabulary that a language user cannot be eminently eloquent. However, the risk of making cruder descriptions of things and events is higher for someone with a smaller vocabulary than for someone with a stronger command of the language. Similarly with concepts, we might get by with a small number of them, but our chance of making mistakes is increased. The spontaneity by which we conceptualize experiences indicates not only a function of mind but also its limitation. Following this line of thought, it should be clear that spontaneity of mind is limited by socio-historical structures. This does not mean that we cannot break out from such structures, but it does mean that the spontaneous understanding of experiences is constrained by whatever structures are set by a particular societal and historical era. From this, we recognize that some mistakes we make in "reading" situations and things around us often stem from the tendency of the mind to apprehend *spontaneously* what happens. We may be ignoring the fact that our limited concepts are outdated or inadequate for appropriately understanding what is going on around us. As such, one way of having a dissembled mind is to ignore that our socially inherited concepts are prone to be inadequate.

The *receptivity of intuition* is the part of mind that presents us with content. This content is made understandable to us more or less adequately by our concepts. For example, our intuition must present to us some content if we are to see an object as red, but we are also able to entertain the concepts of "red" and "object" without seeing a red object. Intuition is not reducible to any one of the senses, but is the fac-

---

[11] The scholarly standard referring to *Critique of Pure Reason* uses the A /B numbering system.

ulty of receiving input that can be *worked on* spontaneously. Whatever we feel, see, hear, taste, smell, and have a "premonition of" is delivered to us by our built-in *receptivity* to the world. The possibilities of "sensing" in our world are almost unlimited. Many of the impressions we receive have workable concepts that allow us to understand (make sense of) what is presented to us. However, it is conceivable that some impressions are misunderstood, ill-conceptualized, or even missed altogether. We might mystify this type of occurrence, and attempt to explain it as a will-o'-the-wisp kind of experience. As an example, we sense (by virtue of receptivity), and because of the immediacy of spontaneity, we conceptualize it as *something in particular*, or otherwise we would have experienced nothing. If we have no other concept, it is likely that some mythical-poetical construct will be used (Cassirer 1944: 76). This is not in itself an odious behavior. But it means an increase in becoming bewildered by experiences of which the perceiver has no proper grasp. This is the second sort of dissemblance of mind.

For Kant there can be no cognition without cooperation between the two parts of the mind. Understanding cannot *intuit* by itself, and intuition cannot *understand* anything on its own. However, by cooperating, they will dynamically produce cognition, which is the sum of the parts (spontaneity-receptivity) working together. But the parts needs not always be related cooperatively. In some cases the parts can dissemble each other. That is, although no *cognition* can arise without cooperation of the parts, this is not to say that mental activity which is on a collision course with reality cannot be possible. In the two sorts of dissembling, we see that the parts have become asymmetrically related. In the first sort, spontaneity ignores or willfully misinterprets what receptivity presents, resulting in the perceiver making choices without a proper reason to do so. This dissemblance may be understood as the tendency to *disenchant the world*. For example, we ignore deliverances of receptivity because we adhere strongly to some theory. In the second sort, receptivity floods the mind with content, but for which spontaneity has only mythical concepts, which means that the perceiver might be led into believing in something more than what is reasonable. This sort of dissemblance re-enchants or over-enchants the world, perhaps because of an adherence to a religious outlook, or is simply due to a lack of proper concepts. These formulations of dissemblance is recognizable in everyday occurrences. Spontaneity dissembles when we continue to entertain prejudicial opinions even when evidence points to a different conclusion. Receptivity dissembles when we entertain an anxiety, which, with proper reasoning should adequately disclose to us that we have really no reason to be anxious in the first place.

The dissemblance of spontaneity by receptivity is the asymmetry I identify as illustrating change of mind. The theoretical model outlined above will be used to read de la Mare's novel. But before I do so, I want to briefly discuss why the other model, that of spontaneity dissembling receptivity, does not illustrate change of mind, but instead, what I view as change of will.

## C. Dissemblance and Change of Will

In Sackville-West's *The Edwardians* (1930), the asymmetry is cleverly depicted through a pair of siblings whose desires are kept secret from (or denied by) themselves, but are revealed through the other. The novel revolves around Sebastian and Viola, who both desire Leonard Anquetil, a self-made man, who fills the role as mentor and lover. It may be helpful to note that the particular shape of the double with which we are dealing here is a whole consisting of non-communicative parts (Sackville-West 2004: 240).[12] Sebastian and Viola stand for individual parts of a dissembled mind, a *nameless beloved* (as I shall call it) in search of itself. It will be helpful also, as we progress, to note that the character of Leonard facilitates the restoration of communicative unity (348–49). In short, we should envision only two persons in our reading: the lover (Leonard) and the person beloved (Sebastian-Viola). The plot revolves around how the *nameless beloved* suffers from a dissemblance of mind due to a struggle between traditional ways of conceptualization and changes in the world, which are ignored.

Sackville-West's interest in gender roles is accentuated in the course of the novel. The gender of the *nameless beloved* is indeterminate, but both an assertion and critique of traditional ways of understanding gender is articulated through Sebastian and Viola. As a result, the asymmetry is construed in terms of gender. Sebastian, spontaneous and willful, classifies his impressions of life according to the dictates of tradition and class in society (241–48). He is initially very charmed by Leonard but refuses the self-made man's offer of an adventure abroad (94). Viola, on the other hand, receptive and willing, is more accepting of Leonard's influence (166-67, 313-314). Both siblings are busy experiencing life, within, of course, the limitations imposed by the Edwardian era. While the young and wealthy dandy Sebastian (he is a

---

[12] All references to *The Edwardians* are from the Virago edition (2004).

duke and the inheritor of a large estate, Chevron) can pretty much do as he pleases, ignoring his mentor's warnings about the snares of inheritance, his sister Viola is urgently struggling to find ways of escaping a tradition that is pernicious and stifling especially to women. As such, the setting of the novel illustrates a situation of conflict between receptive and spontaneous parts of mind, which are not allowed to exert a direct influence on another. Depicting this conflict in gender terms allows Sackville-West to demonstrate how a disenchanted worldview ignores reasons for redefining gender roles which may be in tension with society. Let us recall that spontaneity is the part of mind which supplies concepts, while receptivity delivers contents. Accordingly, the struggle is between the traditional structure of concepts that is premised on prejudice (Sebastian) and an impressionable sensibility of personal diversity (Viola) that demands less rigidity.

The struggle to recognize alternative gender roles is further complicated by the rigidity of accepted sexual ones. The novel is abundant with sexual attractions that challenge norms. After having refused the overt attentions of Leonard (92–93), Sebastian embarks on a series of affairs with women for whom he cares little. We are given hints of Viola's homosexual tendencies, such as the episode of her becoming "enrapture[d]" as she witnesses the maid dressing her mother (41). Although she is later engaged to Leonard, "He [Leonard] liked Sebastian better, and with less complication […] ardently, ardently he wished Viola away" (83–84). It is arguable that the introduction of the proposed marriage between Leonard and Viola in the last scene of the book weakens the denouement. The weakness is due to two things. Firstly, it (too) neatly reconciles Sebastian and Leonard, and Sebastian finally accepts Leonard's offer of a lengthy adventure abroad. Although Leonard and Viola are engaged to be married, this will be three years later (349), suggesting that Leonard and Viola will be separated meanwhile. Secondly, the marriage seems to have come about through a secret correspondence between Viola and Leonard. We do not know what made Leonard choose Viola over Sebastian. However, Leonard's "role" becomes evident when we view the siblings as aspects of the same person. Indeterminate sexuality becomes a strategy of dissemblance and unification. The spontaneous part of the mind of the *nameless beloved* (Sebastian) is culturally rigid. The unspoken homosexuality is at odds with social morality. But this merely signals tradition's inability to cope with the new reality to which the receptive part (Viola) is naturally open. The "content" she delivers is Leonard. In the dissembled mind, spontaneity ignores what receptivity delivers. Achieving a *collected mind* means Sebastian acknowledging Leonard. The resolution at the end of the novel marks a cooperation whereby Sebastian is finally able to will what Viola has all along accepted: the love of Leonard.

Despite Sebastian's attainment of "enlightenment" at the end of the novel, it is something *the nameless beloved* has actually intuited all along (via Viola), but to which the spontaneous part has failed to pay attention. At one point, this is noted by Viola when she remarks in frustration that:

> "Sebastian, I think, doesn't know his own mind. So far, he takes what he wants, and doesn't know why he is unhappy. He doesn't talk to me. I fancy he doesn't talk to anyone. He just lives and tries not to think. People like us must never think, for fear of thinking ourselves out of existence. If Sebastian thought at all he would go back to Chevron".(163)

This is a fragment of a lengthy discussion between Viola and a confidante in which society and tradition are criticized as instruments of human unhappiness. As long as Sebastian (the spontaneous part of mind) lives according to social rules, he will remain unhappy, and as long as he remains uncommunicative towards Viola (the receptive part of mind) he will not realize why he is unhappy. Without Viola, Sebastian cannot know his place in the complete (whole) mind. The referent "people like us" suggests the two parts of the *nameless beloved* which Viola and Sebastian embody. Only when these parts operate together in unity would the meaning of their existence in Chevron make sense. In other words, unless Sebastian starts "thinking", the self of the *nameless beloved* – which the two "parts" endeavor to become – would not emerge. (Note the irony that "thinking" will suspend the independence of the parts; this recalls the initial determination of cognition as a whole consisting of parts). In Viola's analysis of societal pressure, Sebastian's inclination to think has been blocked by social insinuations that there is no reason to exercise reflection because tradition and the class system have already provided ready-made answers to life's questions. Letting go of outmoded concepts and debilitating strategies for acknowledging reality is not, however, illustrative of change of mind. Rather, the struggle of cognition in the above example of the asymmetrical double is one of maturity. We may, perhaps, call the upshot a *change of will*. The use of our understanding is crucially tied to a continuing maturation by which we often need to repeal concepts we have merely inherited in order to *reform* them to capture our changing reality.

## 2. Asymmetry, Inwardness, and Change of Mind

As mentioned in my discussion of Kant, another form of dissemblance of mind is possible whereby spontaneous understanding is suppressed in order to privilege receptivity. In this mode, receptivity delivers more content than what spontaneity can process. The ensuing confusion would take the form of mythologizing or poetizing the content which invades the mind. Spontaneity must, under this condition, resort to imagination for ways of ordering the impressions received. With some caution, we may consider how children with very few coping strategies (concepts) are disadvantaged in ordering an overwhelming world of input, much of which they could not possibly understand. But such a disadvantage is not exclusively a childhood phenomenon. The use of mythology and archetypes allows perceivers to restructure a world that is essentially mysterious to them (Cassirer 1944: 12, 76–77). Even with the tools of mythos however, the alienated mind does not get a better grasp of the alienating reality. Spontaneity, we must imagine, is trying hard not to drown in a sea of incessant promptings. It may seem that for the dissembled mind, there is always reason to believe more than what would be warranted for a *collected* mind, precisely because the former does not have the concepts the latter has. Whereas the struggle of cognition in *The Edwardians* was characterized by willfully refusing to accept reality, the struggle in this example is the result of being overtaken by a reality that is alien because the proper concepts to order it are unavailable. Receptivity dissembling spontaneity is dramatic in the very way Sackville-West's *Heritage* (see beginning of essay) describes change of mind: the influx of impressions which overpowers spontaneity causes a "great shuffling and stampeding" (Sackville-West, 1919: 48) in the mind of the perceiver. Being overwhelmed by the deliverances of receptivity may force spontaneity to mythologize, but spontaneity may gradually acquire a more adequate, if not original, grasp on the unfamiliar reality revealed by receptivity. This can be illustrated by the following quote from Walter de la Mare's *The Return*.

> "I mean when you cease to be a puppet only and sit up in the gallery too. When you squeeze through to the other side. When you suffer a kind of conversion of mind; become aware of your senses. When you get a living inkling. When you become articulate to yourself. When you *see*. [...] then begins the weary tramp back. One by one drop off the truisms, and the Grundy-isms, and the pedantries, and all the stillborn claptrap of the market-place sloughs off. Then one can seriously begin to think about saving one's soul". (de la Mare: 138–39)[13]

---

[13] All references to *The Return* are to the Dover edition (1997).

I see here a similarity of vision shared by both Sackville-West and de la Mare. Grundy-isms (or social conventions) perniciously prevent the human being from attaining a self, or, in de la Mare's phrase, from "saving the soul". In the case of what de la Mare advocates, the process of change of mind is a profound "skinning" of the individual right down to the core of being, namely a "sense" of self. As such, *The Return* is about the loss of identity (which is socially constructed) and as a result, the increasing awareness of a lack of "self". So strongly does social identity dominate the individual that only in losing our *persona* may we realize that we have lacked *ourselves* all along.

Two separate issues are in focus. One is the experience of a radical turn of one's self-perception. That is, what happens when dissemblance of mind forces spontaneity towards mythical constructs. Another is an analysis of the mechanism that produces myth as means of coping with the dissemblance. It is my view that de la Mare's *The Return* offers illustrations of both.

### A. Possessing Lawford

*The Return* is the story of a man who slowly loses the ability to understand himself as a *persona* formed by society. In the above passage quoted from *The Return,* the character involved is Arthur Lawford, a middle-aged man who lived a more or less inconsequential existence, was indolent and lazy-minded, and with little or no imagination or curiosity. The opening scene of the novel sees Lawford wandering about an old cemetery after recuperating from influenza. He is uneasy, melancholic, and feels overtaken by an "unintelligible remorse" of something "hidden" he has "not quite reckoned with" (2). As he whiles away his time reading the inscriptions on the gravestones, he chances on one which he finds particularly haunting: the stone of one Nicholas Sabathier, a suicide. He eventually takes a nap on the stone, and upon awakening, discovers that he is in better physical shape. Upon arriving home however, he is shocked to realize that his face is no longer recognizable to himself or to his wife and servants. Throughout the novel, Lawford's feelings, projections, stray thoughts and inner promptings are carefully traced. Receptivity is persistently flooding his mind and he is unable to find any means of understanding his various experiences (109). He tries turning to medicine; but there is no help there, because he is not suffering from any physical ailment. He clutches at straws in order to find some way of conceptualizing the experiences that are radically disturbing his network of beliefs. The keen analysis de la Mare makes of the role of society, family and friends in the construction and establishment of identity (in this case, Lawford's) is what moves the plot of the novel. Through a series of encounters between Lawford and his wife, Sheila, and their mutual friends and acquaintances, Lawford's sense of alienation becomes increasingly aggravated. It is with strangers that he finds new opportunities to understand what has happened to him. A certain Mr. Herbert and his sister are two significant strangers who help Lawford reconnect his senses with his understanding of life. The gravestone, an old book of autobiography by Sabathier (supplied by Herbert), and Herbert's indulgence consequently persuade Lawford to believe, at least for a while, that the spirit of the deceased Sabathier now possesses him (83–91). This belief that he has been possessed might strike us as unreasonable but such an attempt to conceive of the change in terms of possession is indicative of a subject who is without the appropriate concepts to make sense of the content receptivity is delivering. Whereas this may help Lawford for a while (the relief of diagnosis), his wife is further alienated from him by such explanation (174).

It is helpful here to recall how de la Mare's work was characterized at the beginning of this essay: Mythical writing (or thinking) *allows something inward to take place outward.* We must understand that the allusions to outward change, namely Lawford's face, is a way of conceptualizing what is really an inward change. De la Mare mixes outward and inward events to describe the kind of all-pervasive confusion Lawford experiences. In this sense, Lawford's obsession with his changed face is in fact an attempt to deal with the incessant deliverances of receptivity. Spontaneity has no other concepts at hand than to see the impinging reality as a physical change. That this change occurs in the face is symbolic of how the stumbling spontaneity tries to conceive *outwardly* of an inward change in awareness of "self". Compare the following quotations.

[…] that other feebly struggling personality which was beginning to insinuate itself into his consciousness, which had so miraculously broken in and taken possession of his body. He could not think now. (42)

"That – that presence, that shadow. I don't mean, of course, it's a real shadow. It comes, doesn't it, from – from within?"(125)

"[…] though Sabathier had failed, though I was still my own old stodgy self, that you thought the face – the face, you know, might work in. Somehow, sometimes, I think it has. It really does haunt me".(128)

These three quotations suggest that Lawford entertains two different interpretations of what has happened to him. The first quote shows how Lawford understand his experience as an alien personality insinuating itself into his mental life. Here, the mythical conceptualization is apparent. Spontaneity is powerfully dissembled, since all spontaneity can do to understand what has happened is to conceive it as a spiritual possession. In the second quote we note a revised understanding of the experience. Now Lawford understands it not as another personality insinuating itself, but as a shadow. The mythical thinking is gradually being checked. Spontaneity, still unable to fully appropriate reality, now furnishes Lawford with concepts of an *inner* shadow. This means that the alienating force is no longer perceived as outward. Yet, the idea of having been possessed is only slightly overcome, because, from the third quote, we find Lawford still entertaining the idea that some outward force has had a role in his current situation, namely that Sabathier did try to possess him.

It is Herbert who provides helpful assistance to Lawford in understanding his change when he asks the latter:

> Isn't it possible, isn't it even probable that being ill, and overstrung, moping a little over things more or less out of the common ruck, and sitting there in a kind of trance – isn't it possible that you may have very largely *imagined* the change? Hypnotised yourself into believing it much worse […] and simply absolutely hypnotised others into thinking so, too?" (131)

This question is pivotal in three respects. Firstly, what Herbert says forces Lawford to contemplate if there has been any change to his face at all. This does not negate that there was some event which had led Lawford to believe his face has changed, but it challenges the reliability of Lawford's understanding of the event. Secondly, it underpins our interpretation of dissemblance of mind. Receptivity has overpowered spontaneity in such a way that the latter has been forced to conceive the event as a change in countenance. When Herbert suggests that Lawford has hypnotized himself, it merely means that the sheer flood of content delivered by receptivity has rendered spontaneity impotent. Accordingly, Herbert's question points to the fact that Lawford's understanding of the event is essentially mistaken. Thirdly, the quotation points to a psychological drama in which imagination plays a role of misleading Lawford and his relations. Here, the (self-)deceiver and the deceived (the self and others) mutually reinforce the deception. Lawford deceives himself into thinking he is possessed, and his relations, whom Lawford deceives too, further buttress this deception.

In fact, mythical thinking is a primordial function of our minds (Cassirer 1946: 3–49). We can trace our tendency for mythical thinking throughout recorded history (277–296). Even if there is progress of scientific thinking, there is no reason to suspect that we become less susceptible to mythical thinking when we encounter the un-known. In the context of *The Return*, this default *mechanism* is triggered precisely because Lawford is receiving more content than he can conceive within a specific conceptual paradigm. Lawford is obsessed with the idea that Sabathier has possessed him because his *understanding* fails to explain his condition adequately.

## B. The Phantasy of the Self

It will be helpful in our reading of *The Return* to see how the dissemblance outlined above can be captured using certain terms borrowed from Jonathan Lear's essay, "Restlessness, Phantasy, and the Concept of Mind".[14] Here, Lear introduces a distinc-tion between *fantasy* and *phantasy*. Whereas fantasy as a term generally covers "a family of mental states", *phantasy* is "a peculiar type of mental activity" which tends to "enact a meaning or put a meaning on display" (Lear, 1999: 92). According to Lear, phantasy will *show* a meaning rather than *say* it (92). This means that phantasy "may operate in relation to, but relatively free of, the rationalizing constraints of [...] the holistic system of an agent's beliefs and desires" (93), which could indicate the kind of dissemblance of mind whereby spontaneity has no means of dealing with what receptivity delivers.

> Phantasies are experienced as powerful because there is no obvious or easy way to bring them into the domain of thought. Thus, however active the mind may be in creating these phantasies, it often experiences them passively, as though it is suffering an experience over which it has lit-tle control. Because phantasies can remain relatively unintegrated, the mind may regularly have to suffer its own activity. (93)

Passive receptivity *shows* content but has no means of actively *conceiving it* since this is the province of spontaneity (94). Nevertheless, *something* is shown, because spontaneity *does* make a contribution of concepts, for otherwise we would have no experience at all. But the contribution might be limited to merely primitive visual and auditory concepts. This, in turn, means that we can have experiences which show meanings, but they are recalcitrant to rationalization: in other words, we do not un-derstand what is shown to us.

Lawford's obsession with Sabathier is the power of *phantasy* over his attempts at rationalization. Lawford does not understand what is happening to him, but tries to rationalize (what he thinks is) the experience of change as Sabathier's successful pos-

---

[14] Lear's essay first appeared as chapter 5 in his collection of essays *Open Minded* (1999)

session of him. When Lawford sees a changed face, it is not because his face is really changed; rather, he has no concepts available to understand what has happened other than primitive visual concepts. So, when Lawford *says* that he has been possessed, he is grasping at straws to rationalize what he cannot understand. On the other hand, phantasy *shows* meanings rather than articulates them. Phantasy reveals that what Lawford identifies as his self does not belong to him. His social "self" is groundless, a role that might just as well be played by some other persona. In the power of phantasy, Lawford *acts out* the meaning that he cannot articulate explicitly – that he is essentially a stranger to himself.

*Acting out* does not, however, ensure Lawford an intelligible means to get to grips with the loss of self. Acting out is a behavioral complex which de la Mare captures in the following way: "[Lawford] has just enriched our jaded language with a new verb – to Sabathier [...] it means 'To deal with histrionically'; or, [...] To act under the influence of subliminalisation [...] To perplex, or bemuse, or estrange with *otherness*"(de la Mare, 1997: 130). Entertaining the phantasy of having been possessed is for Lawford an indirect communication (*acting out* or *showing*) of the meaning that his preconception about himself, namely, that he has a specific self, is false. However, because Lawford is suffering from his own agency, phantasy perplexes him as well as others. What is *other*, the persona of Sabathier, is the "otherness" *with* which Lawford bemuses society and himself. Challenging this deceptive behavior may be the only way Lawford would have any chance of *collecting* his otherwise dissembled mind. Hence, the task is to question, first, whether the mythical construct of having been possessed is not mere self-hypnosis, and second, whether the experience offers Lawford the opportunity for a deeper self-understanding.

The *preconception* of what it means to have a self is described as "Grundy-isms" and "all the stillborn claptrap of the marketplace" (139). Identity is, according to de la Mare, a matter of whether our social connections will acknowledge and affirm a certain persona (90). Seeing through this masquerade practically means that change of mind starts out primarily as a dissemblance of mind. This way, receptivity presents reasons for doubting that our personality is any more substantial than a character in a play, but these reasons will only be seen as such if spontaneity can articulate them *as reasons*. In the case of dissemblance, the deliverance of such content, alien as it may be to our socially informed understanding, can only be conceived by spontaneity in mythical terms (what is inward takes place outwardly). As a result, phantasy as a peculiar mental activity *shows* the meaning of what receptivity delivers, but because of the subversion of the understanding, the individual has to *act* that meaning out.

Lawford changing his mind about self-understanding would cause a disturbance in the various prejudices and preconceptions that is owing to social inheritance. But none of his beliefs needs to be changed (166). Lawford's self-understanding is left ambiguously unarticulated at the end of the novel. On the one hand, Lawford cannot escape his social persona, his "stodgy self" (128). On the other hand, his self is nothing substantial, he is "converted", a "changeling" (163). For us, the message of de la Mare's novel consists in the notion that essential self-understanding is incommunicable. Personality is a way of *showing* who we are to others and ourselves. The meaning of the self is a phantasy: it can be *acted out* but not articulated. This suggests that we may continually be in the process of change of mind; that is to say, we are regularly experiencing a dissemblance of mind. Naturally, this would make us despair of living lives that are always *underway*. However, this despair makes the Socratic call for self-examination more urgent and less trivial.

## 3. Returning

*The Return* is a novel about an individual who awakes to a specific form of self-awareness. Lawford's experience warrants a "skinning" of the social self he has only by virtue of family and friends. So, who is Lawford then? He does not stop being that particular person with whom others are familiar. But Lawford is subjected to a change of mind which reveals to him that any persona is just a construction imbued with prejudices. With this revelation, he can now begin to concentrate on saving his soul (139).

*To return* is *to begin* to recover a spiritual life that is merely sleeping in the human being.[15] However, the human being, awakened to *see through* the social persona, is not thereby free of phantasy. We must not think that we miraculously become henceforth able to understand all there is to understand about ourselves *while* living "this urgent dream called Life"(193). Phantasy provides us, on the positive side, the ability to reveal to ourselves what we cannot codify using the inadequate concepts we have available. On the negative side however, it is a trap when we *sabathier* – as it were – ourselves into estranging, perplexing, and bemusing our loved ones. It makes

---

[15] See Pierre Hadot, *Philosophy as a Way of Life*, for connecting spiritual exercises with *returning* (109).

our account somewhat more complex. The complication can be elucidated by considering the following observation Kierkegaard makes in his *Repetition*:

> Only phantasy is awake to the dream of personality, everything else sleeps safely. In such a self-regard by phantasy the individual has no real shape, but is a shadow, or better put the real shape is invisibly present, and does not therefore make do with casting a shadow, but the individual has a multiplicity of shadows, all resembling him, and which moment by moment has an equal right to be his self. [...] Yet this shadow existence demand satisfaction, and it is never beneficial for a human being if he did not have time to live himself out, while on the other hand it is sad or laughable, when the individual was mistaken and lived himself out in this. (Kierkegaard 1963: 135-36, my translation).[16]

Kierkegaard makes a distinction between the real shape of the self and the shadows that resemble the individual in one way or another. Phantasy is a medium for the multiplicity of selves that are mere shadows. As long as they last, each shadow has a claim to be the fullest expression of who the individual is. Phantasy cannot articulate the real shape of the individual, but only shows the dream of personality. This is significant in two ways. One, personality is *a dream* which is expressed in the multiplicity of shadows. Two, the human being *dreams* of becoming the "real shape" of personality. Kierkegaard suggests that phantasy is *awake* to (or attentive to) a dream while other conceptual capacities of the mind are *asleep*. When phantasy is active, the real shape (or self) of the individual is invisibly present, hidden by the shadows that compete to express who the individual is. Phantasy shows, alongside with shadows, that there is *something more*, but can only do so by means that are misleading. Consequently, although Kierkegaard counsels that one should spend time attempting to articulate the real shape, he also cautions that whoever tries to live himself out in/as one of the shadows would render the mistaken individual a tragic-comical figure.

Change of mind, which causes the individual to become aware of the shadows, does not necessarily lead to the disappearance of the multiplicity of shadows, nor does it mean that the real shape is now somehow a substantial thing to behold. To think that the real shape of the individual is permanent over time would be to entertain an unobtainable ideal. Our clue to what the real shape is lies precisely in the nature of phantasy. Phantasy is a mere showing of meaning, and misleading at that too, and it has free reins on our existence as long as our conceptual capacities are dissembled (or asleep). The real shape would be an articulation of self which would also be a showing. That is to say, the real shape comes on display when we understand our-

---

[16] For an alternative version, see H. and E. Hong's translation of Kierkegaard's *Repetition* (esp. 154–55).

selves to be unidentical with social shadows. Expressing the real shape would require a collective effort of the mind that *returns* appropriate concepts for understanding ourselves.

To capture the kind of understanding which articulates and shows the self, Kierkegaard introduces the notion of reduplication.[17] To reduplicate means that one's existence is congruous with what one understands. In other words, the understanding one has of oneself is shown in the way one lives. Whereas in phantasy we merely reveal to ourselves what we cannot articulate, reduplication demands that we *exemplify what* we understand about ourselves. Christ is for Kierkegaard the exemplar *par excellence* of reduplication: whatever he taught, he lived (displayed) it (Kierkegaard 1991: 123). For a human being, a *benign* reduplication would be to display to oneself and others an articulated self-understanding. This might be continually underway, since over a life time the individual may undergo experiences that change how the self is understood. In this sense, the real shape is something that *takes shape of us* insofar as we are able to conceive it, which is contingent on the kind of awareness that strives to *save the soul*. Reduplication, in such a sense, could be about how we come to see through social trappings in order to concentrate on spiritual values instead. But reduplication is not a function of spiritual awakening only. Kierkegaard is aware of this when he notes the possibility of a *demonic* reduplication.[18] This particular form of reduplication involves deceiving others by precisely conforming to their expectations. Kierkegaard gives the example of the brilliant criminal who knows how to trade on the misconceptions of others by acting deceptively in confirmation of such misconceptions (Kierkegaard 1975: 3:3690).[19]

We may see these forms of reduplication as the aftermath of change of mind. An individual becomes aware that his social self is but a mere role. He may strive to improve his self-understanding and to live out this understanding in his everyday life. Another individual may experience the loss of self through a "peeling off" of social conventions in a different way. She may choose, for example, to become a confidence trickster, acting to confirm the preconceived persona others take her to be. Returning to de la Mare's novel, from this configuration, I see two options for Lawford. On the one hand, his awareness could make him strive for spiritual freedom, to save

---

[17] *Reduplication* is Kierkegaard's own term. See *Practice in Christianity* (123).

[18] Kierkegaard uses the term *demonic* to characterise an avoidance of communication. See *Concept of Anxiety* (124–25).

[19] The scholarly standard is to cite volume and entry number for this edition.

his soul as it were; on the other, his awakening could continue his *sabathiering*, viz. using his *otherness* to fool society.

Kierkegaard's answer to the dilemma of the demonically reduplicated individual is that there will always be some involuntary revelation (Kierkegaard, 1980: 124). An example of such is the character Harold Skimpole in Dickens's *Bleak House*. Although society sees Skimpole as a child-like (innocent) person, he is finally exposed as a calculatingly irresponsible individual (Dickens, 2005: 934–35). Thus, the ability to distinguish between a benign and a demonic reduplication rests on whether the demonic is caught *sabathiering*, although we may find Kierkegaard's resolution to be somewhat unpromising on these terms. As for individual *responsibility* for not becoming demonic, a Kierkegaardian position would suggest tying *change of mind* to a necessary *change of will*.

In conclusion, I want to revisit a phrase I used above: *the real shape takes shape of us insofar as we are able to conceive it*. We may strive to understand and show such an understanding of ourselves within the constraints of our conceptual capacities. This means that the shape of the individual has a multiplicity of forms, none of which, however, has supremacy. The shape is thus not a substantive personality that somewhat functions along the lines of a Platonic idea. Rather, the real shape has a conceptual function denoting a whole that is *nonetheless* fragmentarily expressed by various shadows. In this way, we may come to realize that on our own we cannot suspend the power of phantasy. Change of mind is then a way by which we become *aware* of the power and endurance of phantasy, *while* throughout our lives we are the actors and the audience of our own dramatic performance.

**Works cited**

Cassirer, Ernst. *An Essay on Man*. New Haven: Yale University Press, 1944.

Cassirer, Ernst. *The Myth of the State*. New Haven: Yale University Press, 1946.

Conrad, Joseph. "The Secret Sharer" (1912), The Secret Sharer and Other Stories. Joseph Conrad. New York: Dover Publications, 1993 (83-116).

De la Mare, Walter. *The Return* (1910). New York: Dover, 1997.

Dickens, Charles. *A Tale of Two Cities* (1859). Harmondsworth: Penguin, 2003a.

Dickens, Charles. *Bleak House* (1853). Harmondsworth: Penguin, 2005.

Dickens, Charles. *Little Dorrit* (1857). Harmondsworth: Penguin, 2003b.

Frame, Donald M. *Montaigne's Discovery of Man*. New York: Columbia University Press,
1955.

Hadot, Pierre. *Philosophy as a Way of Life*. Oxford: Blackwell Publishing, 1995.

Jackman, Henry. "Moderate Holism and the Instability Thesis" in *American Philosophical Quarterly*, Vol. 36, No. 4, October 1999

Kant, Immanuel. *Critique of Pure Reason*. Trans. P. Guyer and A.W. Wood. Cambridge: Cambridge University Press, 1998.

Kierkegaard, Søren. *Gjentagelsen* (1843), in *Samlede Værker*, 3$^{rd}$ edition, vol. 5. Copenhagen: Gyldendal, 1963. Translated as *Repetition*. Trans. H. and E. Hong. New Jersey: Princeton University Press, 1983.

Kierkegaard, Søren. *Journals and Papers*. Trans. H. and E. Hong. Bloomington: Indiana University Press, 1975.

Kierkegaard, Søren. *Practice in Christianity*. Trans. H. and E. Hong. New Jersey: Princeton University Press, 1991.

Kierkegaard, Søren. *The Concept of Anxiety*. Trans. Reidar Thomte. New Jersey: Princeton University Press, 1980.

Lear, Jonathan. "Restlessness, Phantasy, and the Concept of Mind", in *Open Minded – Working out the Logic of the Soul*. Cambridge: Harvard University Press, 1999.

Montaigne, Michel. *The Complete Works*. Trans. Douglas M. Frame. New York: Alfred A. Knopf, 2003.

Rank, Otto. *Beyond Psychology* (1941). New York: Dover,1958.

Sackville-West, Vita. *All Passion Spent* (1932). New York: Carroll & Graf Publishers, 1991.

Sackville-West, Vita. *Heritage*. New York: Doran Company, 1919.

Sackville-West, Vita. *The Edwardians* (1930). London: Virago, 2004.

Saramago, José. *The Gospel According to Jesus Christ*. New York: Harcourt, 1994.

# Dignified Chatter:
## Lessons in Redoubling from Paul Celan's *Gespräch im Gebirg*

J.D. Mininger

"Nach Auschwitz ein Gedicht zu schreiben ist barbarisch" (To write poetry after Auschwitz is barbaric).[1] We begin with this renowned and incendiary comment by Theodor Wiesengrund Adorno, only so as to epanaleptically revisit it in the end. What Adorno intended in this oft-quoted and even more frequently misunderstood provocation is not that poetry is impossible, unworthy, or completely degraded by the heinous crimes of National Socialism. Rather, with his typical dialectical rigor and with extreme rhetorical intensity, he attempts to point out the fundamental ethical dilemma in which representational art finds itself mired in the wake of the Holocaust: namely, the imperative to represent and remember the egregious crimes and the relative impossibility of faithfully and successfully doing so.

How does art – in this case poetics or simply the medium of language – answer the answerlessness of representing an atrocious crime such as the Holocaust? The fact of confrontation with unrepresentability does not enact an absolute silence in language. Rather, it unveils a paradoxical ethical imperative: to listen to that silence through further loving acts of language. Meeting this ethical imperative is one of the fundamental projects of Paul Celan's poetry.

Penned in 1960, Paul Celan's prose-poem *Gespräch im Gebirg* (*Conversation in the Mountains*) has a special relationship to Adorno. The correspondence between German literary critic Peter Szondi and Paul Celan reveals that *Gespräch im Gebirg* was written in response to a missed encounter – an aborted meeting with Adorno. Operating as intermediary, Szondi tried to arrange a get-together for the two men in the Swiss mountain town of Sils-Maria. But Celan backed out at the last second.[2] In what can only be a (perhaps perpetually) provisional manner, we will explore *Gespräch im Gebirg* as if it were a retort to Adorno's claim of the barbarity of writing poetry after Auschwitz. Celan's prose-poem operates as a kind of conversational

---

[1] Adorno, Theodor W., *Kulturkritik und Gesellschaft* Bd. 10/1, in *Gesammelte Schriften in zwanzig Bänden*, ed. Rolf Tiedemann (Frankfurt am Main: Suhrkamp Verlag, 1977), 30.
[2] See *Briefwechsel Paul Celan / Peter Szondi*, herausgegeben von Christoph König (Frankfurt am Main: Suhrkamp Verlag, 2005), especially 10–12, and 137–139.

experiment that, at least in part, answers Adorno's call for a sharper ethical awareness of the stakes of making art in the wake of the Holocaust.

The theme of a missed encounter also sponsors a point of entry into our specific reading of Celan's story, since it is on the topic of the status of the encounter between two men in the story that I wish to insert a somewhat more unusual interpretation. Though the prose-poem offers very little by way of a traditional plot, in which a reversal of fortune happens or some lesson is learned, *Gespräch im Gebirg* still manages to produce a story. A Jewish man wanders away from his home and into the mountains, where he encounters a Jewish cousin. They interact first through awkward silence, followed by a sudden, yet still discomfited loquacity. However, in his "Paul Celan: From Being to the Other", Emmanuel Levinas incisively suggests a slightly different rendition: "two Jews are there, or one Jew tragically divided against himself".[3] Proceeding from this latter premise, we will read the story as an allegory about two men who are one and the same man.

The first point of conflict for this reading arises from the fact that this is supposed to be a dialogue in the mountains, not a soliloquy. So what kind of conversation is this? If we can judge from the final line of the text, it is a conversation that leaves the man fragmented (if he was ever whole in the first place): "Ich auf dem Weg hier zu mir, oben" (I on the way to myself, up here).[4] Celan tells the story of a man who seeks himself, or rather, he seeks the materiality of what lies behind the letter (i.e. the referent) when he says "I". That "I" is a product of redoubling – retracing the trace of the Other that anchors subjectivity – explains why "I" is not precisely *myself*, but rather always "auf dem Weg hier zu mir" (on the way to myself). By itself, this is no more than a completely pedestrian observation. But the redoubling enacted by the man in the story plays a more crucial role in the text than we might at first imagine. By redoubling and retracing the path through this man's internal otherness, the text actualizes the possibility of a new, paradoxical "conversation" – a conversation of singular plurality.

Before returning to the essential question – what kind of conversation is this? – let us first embark on a significant detour through this exemplary figure of redoubling, and how Celan's text both expresses it and is expressed by it. Redoubling, *Re-*

[3] Levinas, Emmanuel, "Paul Celan: From Being to the Other", in *Proper Names*, trans. Michael B. Smith (Palo Alto: Stanford University Press, 1996), 45.
[4] Celan, Paul, *Gespräch im Gebirg*, in *Gesammelte Werke*, Dritter Band (Frankfurt am Main: Suhrkamp Verlag, 1983), 173. English: *Selected Poems and Prose of Paul Celan*, trans. John Felstiner (New York: W.W. Norton, 2001), 400.

*doublement, Verdoppelung*; it can be conceived as a rhetorical device, a linguistic trope, and a philosophical concept. By way of introducing these variations, let us examine four slightly divergent ways of defining redoubling. As the composition of the word suggests, an act of redoubling doubles its object in a somewhat dialectical manner, both negating by replacing and preserving the original. But it *re*-doubles; it doubles that which has apparently already been doubled, and suggests that a redoubling has more in common with a dynamic process of becoming than a static, wooden procedure of precisely increasing the size and measure of something times two. A redoubling also connotes an increase in intensity, such as redoubling one's speed or harnessing more power for an extra burst. The conversation that takes place in the text amplifies its intensity in this manner. In yet another version a redoubling assumes the shape of a fold, such as a piece of paper bent back on itself, or, as Celan's prose-poem teaches, a fold of earth, a mountain. Redoubling's fourth manifestation concerns a folded or bent figure, but this iteration's distinctiveness derives from the tension at the fulcrum of the fold: clenching. The radical and rather violent process of forcefully squeezing two parts together redoubles the whole of which the two parts consist. Celan's story demonstrates this in the manner in which two-men-who-are-one, like Nietzsche's Zarathustra and his shadow, seek out the common stitch that most closely sews them together.

An event of redoubling marks the entrance into the prose-poem in the form of the title, *Gespräch im Gebirg* (*Conversation in the Mountains*). The alliteration of *Ge-* [...] *Ge-*, notably capitalized in the German, underlines an essential aspect of the text's rhetorical landscape, namely, its self-production through repetition. *Ge-* helps create past participles,[5] but *Ge-* also forms aggregate, collective nouns from substantives, such as *Gebirge* (mountains). Perhaps most tellingly, *Ge-* also forms nouns that denote verbal repetition or continuation of vocal action, such as *Gespräch* (dialogue), *Geschwätz* (chatter), *Geheul* (howls), and *Gerede* (chitchat). The title foregrounds a contradictory power: the possibility to collectivize many into one and the holding-in-tension of an already-past that continues faithfully and repetitiously into the future. Thus, the space of contradiction and paradox that the mountains come to embody in the course of the story has its genesis in the title. The alliteration also sounds out an important product of its inner contradictory power in the form of an outward stuttering. While the various "inner", grammatical-syntactical valences of

---

[5] For example: *geboren* (born); *geschrieben* (written)

*Ge-* redouble in the tension of contradiction, the "outer", guttural signification stutters: *Ge-spräch im Ge-birg.* This type of pulsating, stammering vocal poetics haunts the text to its close, as it redoubles over and over at certain points.[6] However, the title's redoubling indicates still more. The title also triggers a scattering of intertextual resonances, each of which asks the text to be retuned in a different key, as if each intertext would turn back on Celan's and re-trace it anew. This invocation includes, at the very least, the names Martin Buber, Georg Büchner, Friedrich Nietzsche, and Franz Kafka.[7]

The pattern of redoubling variously introduced by the title begins to take on subtler masks in the opening lines of the text proper. The prose-poem begins as the man leaves the safety and security of his little home, and wanders up into the space of the mountains:

> Eines Abends, die Sonne, und nicht nur sie, war untergegangen, da ging, trat aus seinem Häusel und ging der Jud, der Jud und Sohn eines Juden, und mit ihm ging sein Name, der unaussprechliche, ging und kam, kam dahergezockelt, ließ sich hören, kam am Stock, kam über den Stein, hörst du mich, du hörst mich, ich bins, ich, ich und der, den du hörst, zu hören vermeinst, ich und der andere,– er ging also, das war zu hören, ging eines A-bends, da einiges untergegangen war, ging unterm Gewölk, ging im Schatten, dem eignen und dem fremden – denn der Jud, du weißts, was hat er schon, das ihm auch wirklich gehört, das nicht geborgt wär, ausgeliehen und nicht zurückgegeben –, da ging er also und kam, kam daher auf der Straße, der schönen, der unvergleichlichen, ging, wie Lenz, durchs Gebirg, er, den man hatte wohnen lassen unten, wo er hingehört, in den Niederungen, er, der Jud, kam und kam.
>
> Kam, ja, auf der Straße daher, der schönen.
>
> [One evening when the sun, and not only that, had gone down, then there went walking, stepping out of his cottage went the Jew, the Jew and son of a Jew, and with him went his name, unspeakable, went and came, came shuffling along, made himself heard, came with his stick, came over the stone, do you hear me, you hear me, I am the one, I, I and the one that you hear, that you think you hear, I and the other one – so he walked, you could hear it, went walking one evening something had gone down, went beneath the clouds, went in the shadow, his own and alien – because a Jew, you know, now what has he got that really belongs to him, that's not borrowed, on loan and still owed –, so then he went and came, came down this road that's beautiful, that's incomparable, went walking like Lenz through the mountains, he, whom they let live down below where he belongs, in the lowland, he, the Jew, came and he came.
>
> Came, yes, down this road, that's beautiful.][8]

The first sentence of the story reveals language pushed beyond its traditional boundaries: the sentence contains forty-seven commas and three dashes – an immense

---

[6] For example: "hörst du mich, du hörst mich, ich bins, ich, ich und der, den du hörst, zu hören vermeinst, ich und der andere" (do you hear me, I'm the one, I, I and the one that you hear, that you think you hear, I and the other one). German: *Gesammelte Werke*, 169. English: *Selected Poems and Prose*, 397; and "ich bin da. Ich bin da, ich bin hier, ich bin gekommen ich mit dem Gedächtnis, ich, der Gedächtnisschwache, ich, ich, ich" (I'm there. I'm there, I'm here, I've come [...] I with my memory, I feeble-memoried, I, I, I). German: *Gesammelte Werke*, 171. English: *Selected Poems and Prose*, 399.
[7] The relevant texts are Buber's *Gespräch in den Bergen* (1913) and *I and Thou* (1923), Büchner's *Lenz* (1839), Nietzsche's *Thus Spoke Zarathustra* (1892), and Kafka's *Der Ausflug ins Gebirge* (1913).
[8] German: *Gesammelte Werke*, 169. English: *Selected Poems and Prose*, 397.

amount to crowd into a single sentence, even in German. In addition, these clauses and lumps of words between commas contain frequently no more than three or four words. As the bundles of words between punctuation shrink from traditional expectations, the edges of the single sentence swell to take in the excess clusters and commas. Like Gustav Mahler composing lines that push instruments to the extreme highs and lows of their registers in order to effect a change in tone, so Celan here moves language toward its outer extremes (sentence length) and internal limits (convulsive syntagmata), drawing out a tension between the shrinking size of the word clusters, the prolific use of punctuation, and the bloated size of the sentence. This tension expresses itself outwardly in the stuttering redoubling of the clipped phrases. However, within the internal relationships of the phrases to one another, the redoubling results not in fitful immobilization but, true to redoubling, intensifies the act of coming.[9] Although their repetition layers another example of stuttering into the opening paragraph, the repetition of *ich* and *mich* slides into a smoother rhythm: "hörst du mich, du hörst mich, ich bins, ich, ich und der, den du hörst, zu hören vermeinst, ich und der andere" (do you hear me, you hear me, I'm the one, I, I and the one that you hear, that you think you hear, I and the other one).[10] "I" makes itself heard at the outset of this walk, not redoubling itself yet, but repeating "I", "you", "me", and "hear", in a kind of orienting self-assurance: I am here, on this road, continuing to move away from my secure home and heading up into the mountains.

Why does he need this self-assurance? The problem revolves around what has already sunk, set, or gone down: "die Sonne, und nicht nur sie, war untergegangen" (the sun, and not only that, had gone down).[11] It is later in the evening, after dark, when the Jew begins his journey. Among many possible interpretations, and especially given the current context of acts of orienting self-assurance, I would like to suggest that the importance of beginning at night, after the sun has gone down, recalls the Cartesian operation, which also began at night.[12] If certainty is what is at stake here, let us briefly take the example *par excellence* of the hunt for "clear and distinct"

---

[9] For example: "ging und kam, kam dahergezockelt [...] kam am Stock, kam über den Stein [...] da ging er also und kam, kam daher auf der Straße [...] er, der Jud, kam und kam" (*Gesammelte Werke,* 169).

[10] German: *Gesammelte Werke,* 169. English: *Selected Poems and Prose,* 397.

[11] German: *Gesammelte Werke,* 169. English: *Selected Poems and Prose,* 397.

[12] Descartes displaced certainty derived from a transcendent source to his own "I" that doubts all, and thus, as Thomas Pepper points out in "The Story of I/i", Descartes achieved in six nights what the God of Genesis managed in six days. Pepper, Thomas, "The Story of I/i", in *Glossalalia,* eds. Julian Wolfreys and Harun Karim Thomas (Edinburgh: Edinburgh University Press, 2003), 135.

knowledge. In contrast to Celan's wandering Jew, Descartes' "I" in *Meditations on First Philosophy* never leaves the security of his home, his fire, and his robe:

> Although the senses sometimes deceive us when it is a question of very small and distant things, still there are many other matters which one certainly cannot doubt, although they are derived from the very same senses: that I am sitting here before the fireplace wearing my dressing gown, that I feel this sheet of paper in my hands, and so on.[13]

The Cartesian project of deriving ontological certainty through doubt, represented here in the figural setting of the indubitable security of home and hearth (with the slightly voyeuristic image of Descartes alone in a dressing gown), becomes a useless myth of yesteryear in relation to *Gespräch im Gebirg*. Or, more generously conceived, it seems merely a sentimental image of the now bankrupt vision of the potential sanctuary of human autonomy. After all, it was this very kind of instrumentalized reason that made possible the terrifying precision of National Socialism. Accordingly, Celan's Jew leaves his house, perhaps precisely because more than just the sun had gone down. What else has already sunk, set, or gone under? Among many possibilities, what appears to have already gone under is the legitimacy of the Cartesian project of providing certainty and stability solely through consciousness. At least in part, this explains the man's anxious, self-reassuring, redoubled speech.

With the sun of certainty already fallen below the horizon, let us pause just a bit longer on the significance of the nighttime setting. If night takes on a vested importance for a reading of the story, then the fact of the wandering Jew's first redoubled figure, his shadow, must also be of interest, for why does he cast a shadow at night at all? A figure of plurality can be seen in the description of the shadow: "ging im Schatten, dem eignen und dem fremden" (went in the shadow, his own and alien).[14] The man walks in his own shadow—a shadow cast at night, when the light source has already secluded itself beyond the horizon. The internal otherness that the wandering Jew will eventually encounter in the form of a more concrete character already unveils itself in the immediacy of having left the security of the Cartesian home, where "I" remained the unquestioned *fundamentum inconcussum*. The shadow of plural and unstable subjectivity follows the man the moment he leaves home on his journey away from certainty. But it remains unclear whether two different shadows, his own and a strange, alien shadow follow him, or whether he simply misrecognizes

---

[13] Descartes, René, *Discourse on Method and Meditations on First Philosophy*, trans. Donald A. Cress (Indianapolis: Hackett Publishing Co., 1980).
[14] German: *Gesammelte Werke*, 169. English: *Selected Poems and Prose*, 397.

his own shadow. If even as metaphor, the multiple shadows, particularly the foreign shadow, outline a subjectivity swimming in internal plurality.

The wanderer's shadows themselves have intertextual shadows: Nietzsche's Zarathustra and his shadow. Celan's protagonist casts his shadow in the dark, one evening, after the sun, and not only that, had finished sliding down the sky. For Zarathustra, night marks the time and atmosphere for speech and for affirming the desire to intensify one's voice. Zarathustra declares, "night has come: now my craving breaks out of me like a well; to speak I crave".[15] However, the night's most stentorian voice is not Zarathustra's, but his shadow's, which haunts him with a constant redoubling presence. Nietzsche writes:

> Zarathustra was alone again, he heard a new voice behind him, shouting, "Stop Zarathustra! Wait! It is I, O Zarathustra, I, your shadow!" But Zarathustra did not wait, for a sudden annoyance came over him at the many intruders and obtruders in his mountains. "Where has my solitude gone?" he said. "Verily, it is becoming too much for me; this mountain range is teeming, my kingdom is no longer of this world, I need new mountains. My shadow calls me? What does my shadow matter? Let him run after me! I shall run away from him".[16]

Like Celan's Jew, who has just stepped out of his house, under the clouds, and walked in his own shadow, Nietzsche's Zarathustra appears to be struggling with his own alterity in the form of a shadow: that which belongs to him, takes the shape of him, remains forever tethered to him, but is not him. Zarathustra attempts to flee his own otherness, his shadow, but is unable to do so (with the exception of the great noontide, when the sun is directly overhead, at which point Zarathustra, rather tellingly, dodges consciousness by falling asleep). The same fate follows for Celan's protagonist, who does not escape, but encounters an amplification of this dynamic as his internal Other (named *Groß*) becomes an interlocutor upon entering the mountains. When Zarathustra fails to leave his shadow behind and confronts it, the shadow gives him an answer not unrelated to the descriptive lines from *Gespräch im Gebirg* that follow the image of the shadow: "ging im Schatten, dem eignen und dem fremden – denn der Jud, du weißts, was hat er schon, das ihm auch wirklich gehört, das nicht geborgt wär, ausgeliehen und nicht zurückgegeben" (went in the shadow, his own and alien – because a Jew, you know, now what has he got that really belongs to him, that's not borrowed, on loan and still owed).[17] In turn, Zarathustra's shadow answers Zarathustra with the following retort: "I am a wanderer who has already walked a great deal at your heels – always on my way, but without any goal,

---

[15] Nietzsche, Friedrich, *Thus Spoke Zarathustra*, trans. Walter Kaufmann (New York: Penguin Books, 1988), 107.
[16] Nietzsche, 272.
[17] German: *Gesammelte Werke*, 169. English: *Selected Poems and Prose*, 397.

also without any home; so that I really lack little toward being the Eternal Jew, unless it be that I am not eternal, and not a Jew".[18] In the space of overlap between Zarathustra's shadow and Celan's Jew stirs the figure of the wanderer, who moves nomadically, non-teleologically. Resonating with a concept frequently described and mobilized by Gilles Deleuze, the Jew and the shadow(s) here assume a kind of nomadic quality – a perpetual displacement of the intensities designated by property and telos. Celan's Jew does not have anything that properly belongs to him, and thus his leaving home seems more understandable, as does his wandering without a given and more recognizable aim. He simply "kam und kam" (came and came).

The second sentence, "kam, ja, auf der Straße daher, der schönen" (came, yes, down this road, that's beautiful),[19] shadows the first line the way an echo follows its source. "Kam" begins the sentence with an echo of an echo, repeating the last words of the previous sentence, which were themselves a kind of echo. In this gesture, the nomadic act of walking and wandering conjured by the frequent repetitions of "kam, kam" in the first sentence are held over into the second sentence. But this second sentence throws the trope of nomadism into relief in another sense. By comparing two possible English translations to the original German, some important nuances of this nomadism emerge. Rosmarie Waldrop translates the sentence as "Walked, yes, along this road, this beautiful road," which emphasizes the aesthetic beauty of the road.[20] John Felstiner translates it differently, suggesting: "Came, yes, down this road, that's beautiful".[21] Felstiner's translation preserves more ambiguity, which Waldrop effectively elides by choosing to repeat the word "road," a word not repeated in the original German, though still indicated in the grammar ("der schönen"). The beautiful ambiguity of Felstiner's translation choice lies in the subtlety of the appropriately wooden and direct rendering of the German: "der schönen"; "that's beautiful". The apostrophe in the English marks the relative undecidability of the phrase. It might be that the road itself is beautiful, as Waldrop would have it, invoking the possessive power of the apostrophe. It might also be that coming down the road, wandering nomadically – the experience as a whole, and not simply the aesthetic qualities of the road itself – constitutes the beauty. The apostrophe in this case displaces the suppressed letter "i", and transforms the phrase into, "came, yes, down this

---

[18] Nietzsche, 273.
[19] German: *Gesammelte Werke*, 169. English: *Selected Poems and Prose*, 397.
[20] Celan, Paul, *Collected Prose*, trans. Rosmarie Waldrop (New York: Sheep Meadow Press, 1986), 18.
[21] *Selected Poems and Prose*, 397.

road, that is beautiful". This wandering without telos, this immediate homelessness, takes up the loss of certainty which the man's journey thus far describes, and transforms it – in a word, affirms it. Though not exactly Nietzschean *Fröhlichkeit* (joy; gaiety), it is also certainly not ecstatic *jouissance*; but Celan's Jew relishes the beauty of his solitude in the mountains. Even the interjection "yes" in "came, yes, down this road, that is beautiful", redoubles the affirmative nature of the man's wandering movement along the path.

But now, at the point of a kind of displaced self-affirmation, the wandering man encounters another person, who, as it happens, is also a Jew, and his first cousin. Let us pay attention to the redoubling as it unfolds here:

> Und wer, denkst du, kam ihm entgegen? Entgegen kam ihm sein Vetter, sein Vetter und Geschwisterkind, der um ein Viertel Judenleben ältre, groß kam er daher, kam, auch er, in dem Schatten, dem geborgten – denn welcher, so frag und frag ich, kommt, da Gott ihn hat einen Juden sein lassen, daher mit Eignem? –, kam, kam, kam groß, kam dem andern entgegen, Groß kam auf Klein zu, und Klein, der Jude, hieß seinen Stock schweigen vor dem Stock des Juden Groß.
>
> So schweig auch der Stein, und es war still im Gebirg, wo sie gingen, der und jener. [And who do you think came toward him? Toward him came his cousin, his kin and first cousin, older by a quarter of a Jew's lifetime, he came along big, he too came in his shadow, the borrowed one – because I'm asking you, I'm asking, who, if God's made him be a Jew, comes along with something his very own? –, came came, came big, came toward the other one, Gross came up to Klein, and Klein, the Jew, bade his stick be silent in front of Jew Gross's stick.
>
> So the stone was silent too, and it was quiet in the mountains where they walked, himself and that one.][22]

Throughout this passage the word "kam" (came) returns, which sustains the redoubling figures of echo and nomadic movement which were initiated in the opening two sentences. It would seem that the *Geschwisterkind* (kin), *Groß*,[23] also has nomadic qualities. But if *Groß* wanders as well, what sort of encounter is this? The stakes of the passage hinge on the word "entgegen", typically translated into English as "against," "contrary to", or "towards". Waldrop translates "entgegen" with the sense of meeting and intentionality: "and who do you think came to meet him? His cousin came to meet him".[24] These lines imply that *Groß* set out to find *Klein*; that either the meeting had been previously arranged or *Groß* took it upon himself to meet up with *Klein* at some point. This intentionality would seem to belie the wandering of the opening sentences and of the refrain of "kam" from within the passage. Felstiner takes a different tack, rendering the lines: "And who do you think came toward him? Toward him came his cousin".[25] By translating "entgegen" more directly – in this case, with its directional and spatial valences in mind – Felstiner's translation pre-

---

[22] German: *Gesammelte Werke*, 169. English: *Selected Poems and Prose*, 397.
[23] *Groß* means "large" or "big" in German, but here it is also being used as a proper name, as is *Klein*, which means "small".
[24] *Collected Prose*, 18.
[25] *Selected Poems and Prose*, 397.

serves the possibility of arbitrariness in their encounter; they may have crossed each other's paths by chance. Felstiner's translation locates these two, *Groß* and *Klein*, within the wandering condition.

Precisely because of the arbitrary possibility of their encounter, this beautiful road might also be an allegorical road: a path that marks the space in which "I" grasps itself as a stranger to itself. This recalls some of Celan's meditations in his "Meridian" address, given on the occasion of receiving the Georg Büchner prize in 1961: "Finden wir jetzt vielleicht den Ort, wo das Fremde war, den Ort, wo die Person sich freizusetzen vermochte, als ein – befremdetes - Ich?" (Will we now perhaps find the place where the strangeness was, the place where a person was able to set himself free as an – estranged – I?).[26] But, as the man knows by the end of the encounter, this emergent self still remains a blur – "I on the way to myself, up here" – just as the transient space of a road is never a static station but a multi-directional place always on-the-way to somewhere else.

Owing to the opaque qualities of what little plot exists, the relationship between "I" and its otherness must receive especially close scrutiny: how does *Groß* constitute the structural Other of *Klein*, the man who walked away from his secure little home and up into the mountains? How does this particular redoubling - this one-that-is-two – operate? The man encounters *Groß* overagainst himself, "entgegen." In fact, the names they receive after comparison identify them as binary opposites of one another: *Klein* (Small) contra *Groß* (Big). But the manner of *Groß'* entry immediately complicates this binary description. *Groß* arrives in the shadow, as a figure similar to a shadow, both belonging to the body (*Klein's*) but not strictly of it: "kam, auch er, in dem Schatten, dem geborgten" (he too came in his shadow, the borrowed one).[27] These lines may also refer to *Groß* walking in his own, separate shadow. Most literally, if *Groß* really is anything within the wandering Jew, he is, quite simply, possibility. In "Michel Tournier and the World Without Others", Gilles Deleuze explains the structural Other in the following manner:

> The Other is neither an object in the field of my perception nor a subject who perceives me: the Other is initially a structure of the perceptual field, without which the entire field could not function as it does. That this structure may be actualized by real characters, by variable subjects – me for you and you for me – does not prevent its preexistence, as the condition of organization in general, to the terms which actualize it in each organized perceptual

---

[26] Celan, Paul, "Der Meridian", in *Gesammelte Werke*, Dritter Band (Frankfurt am Main: Suhrkamp Verlag, 1983), 195. English: *Selected Poems and Prose*, 407.
[27] German: *Gesammelte Werke*, 169. English: *Selected Poems and Prose*, 397.

The structural Other is thus the condition of possibility for a subject, but it is "internal", insofar as it is not a force that comes from the outside which triggers one's ability to anchor the claim "I am". The structural Other manifests itself like the silent manifestation of fear through trembling; it expresses the absent cause immanent in its own effect. In other words, the structural Other, as the condition of possibility for a subject, is always producing, but never present. This paradox of absent presence destabilizes "I" at a structural level, and constitutes, in a theoretical sense, the reason for Celan's Jew to leave home for the mountains: his home – the workplace where Descartes stands in front of the fire in his robe, with paper in hand – was never really his from the beginning.

In this context, the silence surrounding the initial encounter between *Groß* and *Klein* derives a particular significance: "der Jude, hieß seinen Stock schweigen vor dem Stock des Juden Groß. So schweig auch der Stein, und es war still im Gebirg [...]. Still wars also, still dort oben im Gebirg" (the Jew, bade his stick be silent in front of Jew Gross's stick. So the stone was silent too, and it was quiet in the mountains [...] it was quiet, quiet, up there in the mountains).[29] Like the structural Other, silence is a condition of possibility, in this case of sound, of the conversation that will finish the second half of the story. The insistent assertion of silence in the mountains redoubles the silence to emphasize that silence itself draws a path that would guide the release of words, speech, and sound. To represent this strange condition, *Conversation in the Mountains* maintains paradoxical silences: "es schweigt der Stock, es schweigt der Stein, und das Schweigen ist kein Schweigen" (the stick is silent, the stone is silent, and the silence is no silence).[30] Otherness communicates, but silently, absently.

If such a reading of *Groß* as a structural Other indeed holds, and if we can understand him as a figure through which to read an internal battle with marginality and otherness in general, and if this is really the redoubling of a single person allegorically represented as two, then the transition from silence to speech must be closely and patiently considered. The story's mode of communication alters when the absent

---

[28] Deleuze, Gilles, "Michel Tournier and the World Without Others", in *The Logic of Sense*, ed. Constantin V. Boundas, trans. Mark Lester with Charles Stivale (New York: Columbia University Press, 1990), 307.
[29] German: *Gesammelte Werke*, 169. English: *Selected Poems and Prose*, 397.
[30] German: *Gesammelte Werke*, 170. English: *Selected Poems and Prose*, 398.

narrator bows out with the words: "Gut, laß sie reden" (Alright, let them talk).[31] However, the speakers' identities remain vague. Only at one point in the exchange does an explicit indicator of speaker identity appear. Near the end of the conversation *Klein* announces that he speaks. He says, "wir, die Juden, die da kamen, wie Lenz, durchs Gebirg, du Groß und ich Klein, du, der Geschwätzige, und ich, der Geschwätzige" (173) (we, the Jews who came here, like Lenz, though the mountains, you Gross and me Klein, you, the babbler, and me, the babbler).[32] The dearth of speaker-identity markers emphasizes the relative lack of importance of that identity in the first place.

As the verbal exchange begins, two refrains emerge that redouble at various points throughout the chat: "bist gekommen von weit, bist gekommen hierher", (you've come far, you've come all the way here) and "weiß ich/weißt du" (I know/you know). Why do both speakers voice what they both already know? The text describes them as babblers or windbags ("die Geschwätzigen"). If they communicate only chatter, *Geschwätz*, then they relate nothing of importance. Rather, they simply gab, perhaps merely to be socially acceptable. However, this answers very little, especially since, prior to that label, they remain silent—truly unable to speak even a syllable: "kein Wort ist da verstummt und kein Satz, eine Pause ists bloß, eine Wortlücke ists, eine Leerstelle ists, du siehst alle Silben umherstehn" (no word's going mute and no phrase, it's merely a pause, it's a word-gap, it's a vacant space, you can see the syllables all standing around).[33] If the exchange consists only of *Geschwätz* (chatter), then what they would truly like to communicate cannot be represented in language; language fails in this instance. Not even purity of silence fills their muteness, but rather mere vacant space ("Leerstelle"), where language exists but does not move, like a mouth gaping open that cannot close.

When mute voices finally speak, an acknowledgment of prior understanding prefaces the contradictory descriptions of the landscape:

> Weißt du. Weißt du und siehst: Es hat sich die Erde gefaltet hier oben, hat sich gefaltet einmal und zweimal und dreimal, und hat sich aufgetan in der Mitte, und in der Mitte steht ein Wasser, und das Wasser ist grün, und das Grüne ist weiß, und das Weiße kommt von noch weiter oben, kommt von den Gletschern, man könnte, aber man solls nicht, sagen, das ist die Sprache, die hier gilt, das Grüne mit dem Weißen drin, eine Sprache, nicht für dich und nicht für mich – denn, frag ich, für wen ist sie denn gedacht, die Erde, nicht für dich, sag ich, ist sie gedacht, und nicht für mich –, eine Sprache, je nun, ohne Ich und ohne Du, lauter Er, lauter Es, verstehst du, lauter Sie, und nichts als das. [You know it. You know it and you see: Up here the earth has folded over, it's folded once and twice and three times, and opened up in the middle, and in the middle there's some water, and the water is green, and the green is white, and the white comes from up farther, comes from the glaciers, now you could say

---

[31] German: *Gesammelte Werke*, 170. English: *Selected Poems and Prose*, 398.
[32] German: *Gesammelte Werke*, 173. English: *Selected Poems and Prose*, 400.
[33] German: *Gesammelte Werke*, 170. English: *Selected Poems and Prose*, 398.

but you shouldn't, that that's the kind of speech that counts here, the green with the white in it, a language not for you and not for me – because I'm asking, who is it meant for then, the earth, it's not meant for you, I'm saying, and not for me –, well then, a language with no I and no Thou, pure He, pure It, d'you see, pure They, and nothing but that.][34]

The water is green, and the green is white, and the white emanates from the glaciers. Klein notes that this language of paradox – earth that folds, redoubles, thrice over, and green that is white – is not for you and not for me. This language apparently belongs to only those untouched by or divorced from an I/Thou, Self/Other binary: "eine Sprache, je nun, ohne Ich und ohne Du, lauter Er, lauter Es, verstehst du, lauter Sie, und nichts als das"(a language with no I and no Thou, pure He, pure It, d'you see, pure They, and nothing but that).[35]

    *Conversation in the Mountains* definitely appears to draw vocabulary from Buber's *I and Thou* (1923, 1937).[36] For example, the prose-poem shares with Buber an interest in the constraining aspects of language: "eine Sprache, je nun, ohne Ich und ohne Du" (well then, a language with no I and no Thou).[37] However, through the use of paradox, *Conversation in the Mountains* establishes extreme intensities of poetic language (such as the grammatical and syntactical designs of the first and last sentences), and the trope of redoubling helps amplify the contradictions and linguistic tensions. This poetic tone of the story is the veil that both helps us see and obstructs our view. The man in the mountains wants a language without I or You, but knows in spite of this that whoever speaks talks to no one – no one (*niemand*) and No-one (*Niemand*) – the particular and the universal. On the one hand, due to the opaque quality of poetic language, the protagonist finds no one (*niemand*) with whom he can connect and communicate without stuttering. If he wants certainty, he finds no one (*niemand*) in whom to anchor that certainty. On the other hand, No-one (*Niemand*), never just a single person or subject-marker, hears what is spoken, because signifiers such as "I" and "You", particularly as they redouble themselves in anxious acts of self-assurance, always simultaneously hold too little and too much: they are empty as particulars and they overflow in the universal. The man in the mountains desires a language for what hides behind the veil of self/other relations – but language is the veil itself.

---

[34] German: *Gesammelte Werke*, 170–171. English: *Selected Poems and Prose*, 398.

[35] German: *Gesammelte Werke*, 171. English: *Selected Poems and Prose*, 398.

[36] Buber, Martin. *I and Thou* (1937; *Ich un Du*, 1923), trans. Walter Kauffman and S. G. Smith (New York: Free Press, 1971)

[37] German: *Gesammelte Werke*, 171. English: *Selected Poems and Prose*, 398.

Celan's man has only the veil through which to see – only *Geschwätz* (chatter) through which to arrive at *Gespräch* (conversation). In the final two paragraphs, the dominant tropes from the story return as *Klein* recounts them to *Groß*: the candle, the beautiful road, the flowers, the talking sticks and stones, the veil, the folds of earth, their Jewish identity, and of course they themselves as figures, "du Groß und ich Klein, du, der Geschwätzige, und ich, der Geschwätzige, wir mit den Stöcken, wir mit unsern Namen, den unaussprechlichen, wir mit unserm Schatten, dem eignen und dem fremden, du hier und ich hier" (you Gross and me Klein, you, the babbler, and me, the babbler, we with our sticks, we with our names, unspeakable, we with our shadow, our own and alien, you here and I here).[38] This final act of repetition, of re-doubling, contains a vital difference: the descriptions do not come from the anonymous narrator, as earlier in the text. Rather, the character recites this litany – he speaks it. Admittedly, the characters are babblers, *Geschwätzigen*, whose gabbing amounts to mere chatter. Yet the story, as announced in the title, recounts a dialogue, a conversation, *ein Gespräch*. How does this story of redoubled *Geschwätz* transform into *Gespräch*? How does chatter become authentic dialogue?

Chatter, idle talk, chitchat, babble, blather, gibberish, prattle, drivel, bullshit – this category holds a special place in language as the space of emptiness where, as the phrase goes, language carries no weight. In the mountains, where the air is lighter, the words apparently are too.[39] However, despite lacking the weightiness of meaning, *Geschwätz* (chatter) does not constitute an absence of language, though it may be that, as Wittgenstein suggests in his *Philosophische Untersuchungen*, "die Sprache feiert" (language goes on holiday).[40] In fact, the idle talk in which *Klein* and *Groß* engage contains a number of indications that something like a more traditional *Gespräch*, or dialogue, indeed develops. They exchange some questions, which con-

---

[38] German: *Gesammelte Werke*, 173. English: *Selected Poems and Prose*, 400.

[39] Søren Kierkegaard, whose native Danish contains an especially rich and plentiful collection of descriptors for this phenomenon (e.g. snak; ævl; vås; blær; sladder; passier; vrøvl; pjadder; ordgyderi; pølsesnak; gas; tøv; munddiarré; bragesnak; barl; pip), spoke frequently of chatter. In fact, he characterized his age, the mid-nineteenth century, as an epoch distinguished from the past by its penchant for endless chatter. (Clearly, Kierkegaard's sentiments hold equally if not a great deal more true for today). On page 97 of *Two Ages*, Kierkegaard describes chatter as an "annulment of the passionate disjunction between being silent and speaking." *Geschwätz* (chatter) displaces the former emphasis on understanding (in the act of speaking) onto speech itself, producing sheer verbosity – logorrhea without content, *nihil negativum*, or in the context of Celan's story, a veil that veils nothing. For more, see Kierkegaard, Søren, *Two Ages*, ed. and trans. Howard V. Hong and Edna V. Hong (Princeton: Princeton University Press, 1978).

[40] Wittgenstein, Ludwig, *Philosophische Untersuchungen*, Zweite Auflage (Oxford: Blackwell Publishers, 1997), 19.

stitutes a defining element of Socratic dialogue. And *Klein* manages to provide a quasi-summarial conclusion to the conversation, as if something was learned or accomplished. *Gespräch* (dialogue) would seem to have as one of its guiding principles and defining goals the process of coming to an understanding of some sort.

However, the key component of *Gespräch* (dialogue) resides not in the lines, questions, and words, but in what a dialogue can produce above and beyond the sum of its internal parts and its language. Dialogue recuperates its concepts toward a "higher" telos, such that these products of the conversation matter beyond themselves. By offering *Gespräch* (dialogue) as the vital vehicle of hermeneutics, Hans-Georg Gadamer arrives at this conclusion in an emphatically banal moment of his *Truth and Method*, where he writes:

> The maieutic productivity of the whole Socratic dialogue, the art of using words as a midwife, is certainly directed toward the people who are the partners in the dialogue, but it is concerned merely with the opinions they express, the immanent logic of the subject matter that is unfolded in the dialogue. What emerges in its truth is the logos, which is neither mine nor yours and hence so far transcends the interlocutors' subjective opinions that even the person leading the conversation knows that he does not know.[41]

Certainly the emergent truth in the form of logos looks quite similar to what *Klein* says of "die Sprache, die hier gilt, das Grüne mit dem Weißen drin, eine Sprache, nicht für dich und nicht für mich" (the kind of speech that counts here, the green with the white in it, a language not for you and not for me).[42] But, unlike Gadamer's "people who are the partners in the dialogue", in this particular reading Celan's man converses with himself, or the otherness proper to him. And this produces in him and in the conversation a kind of *Du*-problem (you-problem). That a dialogue's arrival at an understanding consists of more than a simple summary answer is explained by the weakness and fragility of the position of second person within the dialectical structure, which grounds dialogue in a fundamental procedure of misrecognition (*méconnaissance*); hence the desire and need for seeking a common understanding in the first place.[43] In spite of posing questions and speaking towards *Du* (you), towards *Groß*, towards an otherness that might reflect something besides a distorted and inverted version of himself that is difficult to re-cognize, the man ends up with an "I" that is only "hier" (here), and perhaps never spoke at all: "ich hier, ich; ich, der ich dir all das sagen kann, sagen hätt können; der ich dirs nicht sag und nicht gesagt hab"

---

[41] Gadamer, Hans-Georg, *Truth and Method* (second edition), trans. Joel Weisheimer and Donald G. Marshall (London: Sheed and Wanrd, 1989), 368.
[42] German: *Gesammelte Werke*, 170. English: *Selected Poems and Prose*, 398.
[43] For a masterful reworking of this Lacanian notion of I's 'miscovery' in the mirror as it impacts dialogue, see Thomas Pepper's "The Story of I/i" (esp. 134).

(I here, I; I, who can say, could have said, all that to you; who don't say and haven't said it to you).[44] The man's *Gespräch* (dialogue) produces nothing but weightless chatter, due to this *Du*-problem. In Celan's *Conversation in the Mountains*, or in any "conversation in the mountains", *Geschwätz* (chatter) does not transform into *Gespräch* (dialogue). The title is not merely the title of the story; rather, it is also the title of a strange and unusual verbal interaction – a conversation in the mountains that is neither mere dialogue nor endless chatter. But neither does *Geschwätz* (chatter) receive its usual denigration and scorn. Through a multi-faceted program of redoubling, Celan dignifies the Jewish wanderer's chatter as a type of conversation, but not a philosophical dialogue from a Socratic, canonical tradition. This wanderer's idle talk becomes a conversation in the paradoxical space of folded earth, the mountains, where old distinctions dissolve. In Celan's *Conversation in the Mountains* the boundaries between dialogue as the midwife of logos and chatter as the absence of logos no longer hold.

What brings together redoubling with this unusual paradoxical conversation is the fact that redoubling, by virtue of its repetition and insistence, is a special mode of paying attention. All of the various forms of redoubling present in the prose-poem join forces in the attention that *Geschwätz* (chatter) receives. The wandering man asks questions to which he and his Other already know the answer. He repeats where he is, that he is, what he sees, that he is "I", and that "I knows". But by redoubling that which is already void of content (i.e. chatter), the emptiness is more clearly seen as emptiness, or as full of emptiness. The veil of language is more deeply appreciated not as that which reveals something hidden – the logos, or the real reason "warum und wozu" (why and to what end) the man leaves his home to wander into the mountains. Instead, the veil of language reveals hiddenness itself: "Ich auf dem Weg hier zu mir, oben" (I on the way to myself, up here).[45]

*Aufmerksamkeit* (Attentiveness) – allow me here to quote a saying by Malebranche from Walter Benjamin's Kafka essay that Celan recites in his "Meridian" speech – "Aufmerksamkeit ist das natürliche Gebet der Seele" (attentiveness is the natural prayer of the soul).[46] This *Aufmerksamkeit* (attentiveness) manifests itself in *Conversation in the Mountains* through a redoubling process that implicates Paul Celan, his protagonist, and the attentive reader. Is there a greater form of loving atten-

---

[44] German: *Gesammelte Werke*, 173. English: *Selected Poems and Prose*, 400.
[45] German: *Gesammelte Werke*, 173. English: *Selected Poems and Prose*, 400.
[46] German: *Gesammelte Werke*, 198. English: *Selected Poems and Prose*, 410.

tion than paying attention to the insignificant detail and banality of chatter? "I" depends on this attention paid to the magnificence of the mundane, lest we forget what Celan reminds us: "I" is only ever "on the way to myself". Chatter is typically an operation of speech that lacks everything of value. But when chatter is given the attentiveness inherent to redoubling it lacks precisely nothing, and in turn, it matters as such and for itself. *Conversation in the Mountains* dignifies chatter through its multifaceted and figural program of redoubling. Through a poetics of redoubling and chatter, Celan's prose-poem offers a textual experiment in finding a language that swerves outside of traditional forms of dialogue.

The paradoxical qualities of this text are precisely what justify its consideration as a potential answer to Adorno's wonderful provocation, with which we began, and upon which we should now redouble: "Nach Auschwitz ein Gedicht zu schreiben ist barbarisch" (To write poetry after Auschwitz is barbaric).[47] Only a poetics that manifests within itself the aporia of writing poetry after Auschwitz finds the ethical courage to trump the threat of barbarism.

---

[47] Adorno, 30.

**Part Three**

## "What you are you do not see,
## What you see is your shadow":

## The philosophical double in Mauni's fiction

Jonardon Ganeri

[1]

While the literature of the Tamil short-story writer Mauni is my subject, it is the No-
bel Prize winning Bengali poet Rabindranath Tagore who lends me my title, drawn
from the eighteenth aphorism in his prose collection *Stray Birds*. The self that I perceive, he says, is but a shadow of the self that I am. Another way to put this: I am a
shadow of my present self. What is the meaning of this bifurcation, of this claim that
there are two of me, one visible but less than fully real, the other real but hidden? It is
easy enough, perhaps, to imagine that there is a deep self and an apparent self (or, as
one might prefer to say, that there are deeper and more apparent parts or aspects of a
self), but why should one think of the apparent self as *manifesting* the deep self, as a
shadow manifests the object that casts it?

For one sort of answer, let us consider Otto Apelt's analysis of Socratic irony
(in *Platonische Aufsätze* [Berlin 1912: 96–108]), as so excellently reported by Pierre
Hadot:

> Socrates splits himself into two, so that there are two Socrates: the Socrates who knows in advance how the dis-
> cussion is going to end, and the Socrates who travels the entire dialectical path along with his interlocutor. Soc-
> rates' interlocutors do not know where he is leading them, and therein lies the irony. As he travels the path along
> with his interlocutors, Socrates constantly demands total agreement from them. He takes his partner's position as
> his starting point, and gradually makes him admit all the consequences of his position [...]. [T]he interlocutor,
> too, is cut in two: there is the interlocutor as he was before his conversation with Socrates, and there is the inter-
> locutor who, in the course of their constant mutual accord, has identified himself with Socrates, and who hence-
> forth will never be the same again. The absolutely essential point in this ironical method is the path which Socra-
> tes and his interlocutor travel together. (Hadot: 153–54)

Here are two Socratic selves, one embedded in the path, a companion and fellow
traveller, the other outside, knowing nothing other than that the path leads nowhere,
wishing that with his help his accomplice might become Socratically unknowing too.
Surely, this is not an unfamiliar trope: I have found it in the figure of Vyāsa, the author of the *Mahābhārata* according to the text's own testament, but also a character
inside the text, rubbing shoulders with Arjuna and the rest, explaining to them what it
is all about. Nor is it so different from that famous Upanisadic image, of the two birds

in a tree, one happily eating the fruit, the other looking on. We ought not say, however, that there are two Vyāsas, or two Socrates: there is one and his double, who is also he. Certainly, the Socrates who "knows in advance" is and has to be invisible, not just to the traveller but also to his embedded self as well. Or at least, the Socrates who "travels the path" must give off that he is alone if he is to convince the other that they are in the same boat.

A second answer, possibly related to the first, flows from the thought that even as we are creatures with a time, a place, a history, still we are also cosmopolitan, impartial, souls. The co-existence of these two selves was explored by George Eliot in the figure of Daniel Deronda, who only in adulthood discovers his Jewish origins:

> It was as if he had found an added soul in finding his ancestry – his judgment no longer wandering in the mazes of impartial sympathy, but choosing, with the noble partiality which is man's best strength, the closer fellowship that makes sympathy practical – exchanging that bird's eye reasonableness which soars to avoid preference and loses all sense of quality, for the generous reasonableness of drawing shoulder to shoulder with men of like inheritance. (Eliot: 745)

Two souls in one – a human, universal soul viewing the world *sub specie aeternitatis*, to which is added another, more partial, one, capable of entering into sympathic relationships with those he now counts as fellows. The problem is to see how to do justice to the call of one without silencing the other or, what amounts to the same, without splitting oneself into two. One thought is that the presence of an impartial view enables the more embedded one to preserve a certain degree of "aloofness" with respect to that newly found identity, not to be swallowed up by it. Thus undercut, it remains a somewhat shadowy expression of oneself.

[2]

The brilliant, terse, "silent" Tamil story-writer Mauni exploits the trope of the double with astonishing dexterity in several of his short stories.[1] His characters are not double-faced but genuinely double. In the background, to be sure, is a Vedāntic philosophy of self, according to which I am not really the one I take myself to be, driven by appetites and passions, thinking, talking and experiencing a multiform world. The one who is truly me stands in the wings, quiet, unmoved, and unnoticed. What Mauni explores is the relationship between these two, who are in fact one. Naturally, the

---

[1] All references to Mauni's stories are from *Fictions* (1997). "Mauni" – "the silent one" – is the pen-name of S. Mani (1907–1985), a Tamil writer who lived in Kumakonam and Chidambaram, southern India. His entire literary production consists of just twenty-four short stories, fifteen of which were published before 1938. The four stories I will discuss belong to the nine from the later period, written between 1954 and 1971.

metaphor of the shadow comes readily to hand: "Are all of us merely shadows? Of what, then, are we the moving shadows?" ("Undying Flame": 48). Here we see a first difference from the ironic Socratic split. For there is no ironic pretence but a genuine separation, an obstruction preventing me from seeing myself. What I see is my shadow. No mere game now, this is a genuine metaphysical puzzle, and one of fundamental importance. The attractiveness of the metaphor of the shadow is that it establishes a metaphysical asymmetry from the outset: the shadow depends for its existence on the more solid entity, but not vice versa. Although a shadow certainly has a life of its own (as the denizens in Plato's cave knew well), its place is always subservient and secondary. An implied master-slave relationship seems to hover in the background of the metaphor.

Mauni explores the nature of the self through the trope of the double in four brilliant stories: "From Death, Creation", "Beyond Perception", "Error", and "Wasteland". Before seeking a unifying theme, if there is one, it is best first to look hard at the particulars.

## "From Death, Creation"

In order to live, must we destroy our past self? Or is it exactly the other way round, that in each moment we destroy our own futures? In the story entitled "From Death, Creation", one threesome is placed in correspondence with another. The first involves two men and a woman, journeying together by train, the older man and his younger wife having been joined at a certain point by a young fellow traveller. The second is the Hindu trinity of Brahma, Vishnu and Siva, the legend of whom is carefully interwoven into our own narrative. Brahma and Vishnu sleep, exhausted by their labours creating the world; while they do, Siva destroys not only what has already been created but also everything that they *will* create in the future. Among our travelling threesome, it is the mature man, Subbayyar, who holds forth, recounting the Hindu myth, fetching food from the platform whenever the train pulls to stop, assured, dynamic. Gauri, his wife, dozes and daydreams, while the younger man who has happened upon this couple is startled and silenced.

The story-teller leaves us in no doubt that the two men are doubles:

"By the way, I quite forgot to ask. What is your name?" Rising to his feet, the young man said, "Subbu". "How strange! My own name! [...] It's as though we were the same person. Why, I must even have looked like you when I was younger". ("From Death, Creation": 83–4)

How uncanny that Mauni should have so nearly mirrored the Socratic triad mentioned above. A journey with two travelling companions; a third person, who is the double of one of them, somewhat removed and detached. And yet it is far from certain how the correspondences and mappings ought to work out. Who in our story would be the detached impartial Socrates? The older man, who seems more knowing, dare one say more ironic, than the other two? Or is it the younger man, a quiet presence joining the couple but not quite one of them? We come against the same enigma when we try to correlate this travelling threesome with the Hindu trinity so carefully embedded in the story. Which one is meant to be Siva, remaining awake while the other two sleep, and pre-destroying their future labours? Is it the young Subbu, watching the tense couple and knowing that he has preempted everything his later self will ever do? Is it that older self, sapping the creative energy of the younger couple in a vampirish verbosity? Or is the odd one out Gauri herself, whose presence makes the other two behave in the odd way they do, unable to reach each other in a proper communication because of their rivalry?

Reading this story, one feels the sadness of a "mistimed" couple, the man knowing that he ought to have come along earlier, that the truly happily couple is the one involving his wife and a younger him. That is emphasised by one of the many sub-narrative themes. It seems, we are informed, that Gauri was once betrothed to another man, again younger than Subbayar, whose name was Subbini; and on one of his platform visits, her husband Subbayar thinks for a minute he has seen him. The creative potential that exists between Gauri and his own young self is destroyed, the story seems to say, by the sheer fact of time. Subbayar should have been Subbini, should have been Subba. The lack of synchrony between him and his wife destroys whatever it is or was they could have been. There seems to be only one way out of such desparate tragedies that the passing of time creates, and that is if there is a final reconciliation in some point outside of time, a point represented in one tradition by the mocking Socrates and in another by the neuter *brahman*. As it is said so well in the Īśā Upanisadic, "Knowledge and ignorance – he who knows them both together passes beyond death by untruth, and by truth attains immortality". From death, creation.

## "Beyond Perception"

In "Beyond Perception" the roles are reversed. There are now two women and a man. The man, leaving his wife Sushila at home in the village, is sojourning in the town, where he happens upon another woman whom he immediately recognises and accidentally — but correctly — calls "Sushila". He tries to explain away his gaff:

> When you were little, you might have taken turns on the swing, pushing each other. The child on the swing would move at great speed past the other one pushing her. How strange that game would be if the child on the swing seemed one person at a distance, and quite another when seen close-up! In those days, the same swinging form used to appear to me in two different and alternating perspectives. But now, I seem to be using the same name for two diffferent persons swinging by. ("Beyond Perception": 103)

In this delightful metaphor, the whole paradox of personal identity is precisely described, the puzzle of finding in the very changing flux of human behaviour, experience and trait, whatever it is that lends to a person their sense of being one and the same. The Sushila who lives in the town is unsure about her own true motives, and about whether some part of her is wanting to keep Sekaran from going home to his wife. She is unsure whether any of the dispositions, habits or traits that she identifies herself with really are in any sense "her":

> Was it not a terrible thing to separate a man from his wife? And for another woman to engineer it? Who was she? And could she do such a thing? What did it mean to speak of oneself, and of one's nature and character? Is it by their transformations and opposites, even through our denials and refusals, that what we know as "I" and "mine" reveal themselves as truth? If that is so, can these characteristics that we claim for ourselves be described as firm or steadfast? What are they, really? Sushila could not work it out. It seemed that a name intervened by accident and became the target for a number of attributes,[2] roving without form or home, for these things called "I" and "my character" to pierce through and tunnel through. (106–7)

Sekaran is caught between two women, both called "Sushila", both needing him in order to reach the other aspect of themselves. Of the Sushila who is at home in the village, well "perhaps it is only when their husbands are out of sight and elsewhere, that women got some sort of pleasure in waiting for their return" (108). As for the Sushila in town, she thinks "He has a wife who has the same name as I. Is it she that I am looking for in him?" (108). He, indeed, seems to be the cause of separation, the reason for the two women's distinctness. He is what prevents either of them from realising the force of their femininity. Again, what we think of as ourselves is dissolved into something nebulous, accidental, or borrowed:

> She appeared to be womanhood itself. Do you know what fearful strength womanhood possesses? But, a woman, by the very fact of being so, must be a man's wife. And a husband tries to confine this huge notion of womanhood within the tight frame of a child's slate, and gives himself the pleasure of drawing a picture there, which he calls *Wife*. As for seeking the womanhood in her, that is a terrifying thing [...] (100)

In this story, as in the first, one couple, in the shape of a wife and her man, is unsettled by another, that of a person with themselves. The interloper, in both cases, is but that person himself or herself, in another aspect, representing a self that they might

---

[2] This "dossier" theory of names would later become familiar to analytical philosophers of language through the work of Peter Strawson and Gareth Evans.

have been or ought to have been. I find in both these stories the idea of a self in private conversation with itself, of a juxtaposition between two standpoints, one of which says to the other words to the effect, "Why are you living this way, in these relationships, fulfilling these roles and functions, when you know that that is not who you are"? At the same time, however, the story seems to acknowledge that it is only a third party who provides the conduit through which one can reach that other self. Only through Gauri can Subbaya become Subba or Subbini; only through Sekaran can Sushila become Sushila. The troubling idea that one needs another to become oneself is what prevents self-seeking from collapse into a form of solipsism. A soul cannot see itself except as reflected in the soul of another. This may remind us of Plato's idea (*Alicibiades 1* 132E–113C) that "with a soul too, if it is to know itself, it must look at a soul", just as to see one's own face one must look for its reflection in another's eye.

Here we see, I think, one dimension of the brilliance of Mauni as a philosopher. He is showing how the quest for self-fulfilment that is spoken about by the great Indian spiritual texts can be seen as a social, and not an egocentric, ambition. Finding oneself is always through another. Although it was Sakaran who abandoned the village for the city, it was his village wife Sushila who finds herself, through Sakaran, in her town-counterpart. It is through Sakaran's eyes that the two Sushilas, the one swinging far in the distance, the other nearby, are seen as one. Freedom and rootedness are brought together in the external vision of the one who sees the continuity between the two. In both these stories, it is through another that one reaches oneself.

[3]

In his later stories, Mauni's use of the double has a minimalist, pared-down, quality. Dispensed with is the need for an intermediary third person, and so is the need for a diachronic separation between a younger and an older self. It is only because he is such a technically accomplished story-writer that Mauni can achieve this degree of abstraction in the work. By the time of these stories, Mauni has extracted and separated off the puzzle of what makes a person the same in all the different states and stages of their life, a puzzle earlier explored in part by having a third person look upon the younger and older self. Now he focusses more sharply on the underlying and atemporal bifurcation, between seeing oneself as a practical subject, making decisions and commitments, inhabiting one's characteristics, and seeing oneself as an object of more impartial reflection and inspection.

## "Error"

The shifting fluidity and dream-like quality of what we call our personality or character is evident in the disconcertingly ethereal story "Error". A man sits in his room waiting for the arrival of an acquaintance he had happened to meet the previous day. Before the visitor has arrived, he decides to go out for a walk, but then finds it difficult to return:

> He wondered if he should return to his room. He thought his friend might already be sitting in his chair, in his very room, ready to upbraid him for his error, for making him wait although he had arrived at precisely the agreed time. He would not know what to say then. He gave up the thought of returning. ("Error": 142).

Instead, he finds himself at the train terminus, a place where people set off in every direction and to which they return, where they "leave behind their characters and details of their past natures", a place "where transformations happen, sometimes in error" (143). By chance he finds himself on a train, without a ticket. He gets off at a desolate station in the middle of the night. He thinks: "Even when the basis is known, can such mistakes be avoided? Perhaps, only by perceiving the whole world as a place of transformations". In the final paragraph of the story we are suddenly back at the beginning: a milk-woman arrives and knocks on the door of his room, but to no avail: "He was lost in his dream world, itself the shadow of someone else's dream" (145).

What are we to make of this strangely amorphous and surreal story, in which there is hardly any narrative or even any characterization? Perhaps without really leaving, he has left the other man sitting in his room while he goes on a journey, entirely by mistake, one which happens in a state of confusion and is also the result of a confusion. The journey that is a person's life, this story seems to say, can hardly be thought of as a progress or development in any way; rather, it is the illusion of a departure from a self left behind.[3] The decisions we make seem more accidental happenings to us than things we choose for ourselves. One of the double seems to be engaged in practical reasoning and decision making, going for a walk, getting on a train. But these "doings" are not really of his doing, and he has left behind his other self, who silently upbraids him for this neglect. The boundary between one self and its double hovers, in this story, on the brink of dissolution without ever quite disappearing. It is an artificial creation, the reflection of a neccessity, in any act of self-

---

[3] For which, see Aki Kaurismäki's film *Pidä Huivista kiina, Tatjana* "Mind Your Headscarf, Tatiana."

transformation, to imagine one's new self as distinct from one's old one. In reality, it is, as Sushila speculates in "Beyond Perception" only such imaginary separations which give one any sense of identity at all. One struggles to pull together all the rag-bag of fragments and lend them some form of dignity, and that effort to "bring to-gether the foreshadowings of the future as well as the traces of memories long gone" (140) is all there is to this insubstantial, shadow-like, sense of self.

### "Wasteland"

By the time we get to "Wasteland", Mauni's last story, all extraneous detail has been dispensed with, and the trope of the double as shadow has been reduced to its ele-mental form. A man is suddenly joined by a nameless companion whom he cannot shake off, no matter how much he roams about:

> What possible pleasure could there be in walking about the town like this? Yet they walked on and on like each other's shadows, changing places from time to time. When he looked at the man as if he were his shadow, sud-denly another notion struck him. If thought alone could effect such a conclusion, how easily he might have given the other the slip and escaped! The very thought added a spring to his steps. He heard the other call out, "What's the joke?" and calmed down a little. It had begun to dawn on him that the only way he could release himself from the shadow that was dogging him was actually by becoming the other man [...] ("Wasteland": 152).

Finding himself in a cremation ground, it comes to seem to him as if not just he but everything there is has a shadow or is the shadow of something else. The clarity for this new thought comes from the light given out by a corpse on fire:

> Everything had begun to look like a kind of joke – the cremation ground, the burning corpse, the great tree ahead; all this in the spreading wasteland. But the more he thought, and the more he gazed, each thing seemed to reveal itself as something else, this the shadow of that, that of this. Seen in the light of the burning corpse, all things seemed like a joke, nothing containing anything. (154).

Meanwhile his double, it seems, has finally become fatigued; but this too is only an appearance:

> He could see that the other was exhausted to the point of dropping off. Suddenly he seemed to vanish and then reappear at his side, only to fall to the ground beside him. In a second he realized he had been tricked. The other had swallowed his shadow. Sheer terror! His mind was swamped by sheer terror! As he saw a crazed smile on the man's face, his fear grew worse – if that were possible. With a great wearying of spirit he awoke to the reali-zation that holding on to the body is nothing but an endless addiction. (155)

To lose one's shadow is clearly a fatal mishap, but what if one's shadow is stolen from one by one's own double? To say that is to imply that the trick is one which one has played upon oneself. And have we not already been told that the way to shake off the unwelcome companion is to become the other man? In this story and the last, Mauni's use of the third person pronoun "he" is very slippery. One is left unsure which of the two men is meant to be denoted. Here, indeed, with the swapping and exchanging of identities, with each as the shadow of the other, one cannot be sure who is who and who does what. In becoming one's own shadow, and in then swallowing up that shadow who is also oneself, one is engaging in a process of self-dissolution and self-destruction, breaking down the boundaries and lines that delineate, however ethereally, one's very self. And to do that is only to acknowledge, with a laugh, that there was nothing very substantial there in the first place.

While all the four stories investigate the nature of selfhood through the trope of the double, the first two have ingredients that are dispensed with in the more minimalist later narratives, where there is no bridging third person, and no appearance of a dialogue between an earlier and a later self. In these later stories, the double enters the narrative with no name, no age, indeed, no personality or distinguishing characteristics whatsoever.

[4]

The narrative device of the double was used to brilliant effect by Jorges Luis Borges in his story "The Circular Ruins". There the struggle to invoke another's existence is taken quite literally: the main character summons up another in an act of magical creation, and since they are, after all, one and the same, he must be a magical creation too, the "shadow of someone else's dream" (see above). Personal identity is manufactured *ex nihilo* - that is what this story seems to be telling us. It so happens that friend of Mauni cut out "The Circular Ruins" and sent it to him in the post, and Borges became a favourite of his (as we hear in such echoing phrases as the one just quoted). Mauni, however, gives the trope a distinctively Indian twist: the identity that exists between the two halves of the double is made to stand for a more fundamental metaphysical identity between selves. And, as we have seen, Mauni sometimes complicates the trope in another direction, introducing a third character who witnesses the two members of the double, who constructs their identity in her gaze, and who can, in her reflections, comment on its significance.

What I have called Mauni's "distinctively Indian twist" consists in the idea that we are all the shadows of some one self. The Upanishads – the "hidden connection" or "secret teaching" – is that the self that gazes out from within my body is the same as the self that gazes out from within yours.[4] The principle (*brahman*) behind thinking is the same for each and every thinking self (*ātman*). Indeed it is this principle

---

[4] The next few paragraphs are adapted from my *The Concealed Art of the Soul: Theories of Self and Practices of Truth in Indian Ethics and Epistemology* (2007: 31–33).

that the self truly consists in, this "by knowing which a man comes to know this whole world (Mundaka: 1.3)", the "highest object of the teachings on hidden connections, an object rooted in austerity and the knowledge of the self (Śvetāśatara: 1.16)." [5] This is what Yama, the lord of death, taught Naciketas:

> As the single wind, entering living beings,
>   adapts its appearance to match that of each;
> So the single self within each being,
>   adapts its appearance to match that of each,
>   yet remains quite distinct.

> As the sun, the eye of the whole world,
>   is not stained by visual faults external to it;
> So the single self within every being,
>   is not stained by the suffering of the world,
>   being quite distinct from it. (Katha 5.10–1)

The concealed Upanisadic self is an impersonal self, the same for all. Knowing this, how could the various happenings that befall one as one threads a path through life matter so much? How could they be invested with personal significance to one who knows that one is not more *this* person than *that*? With a robust sense of self, one has to be content with one's own pleasures and pains; with only an impersonal sense of self, the pleasures (and also pains) of everyone are one's own – "You who know this self here, the one common to all men, as somehow *distinct* – you eat food. But when someone venerates this self here, the one common to all men, as measuring the size of a span and as *beyond all measure*, he eats food within all the worlds, all the beings, and all the selves." (Chāndogya 5.18.1)

That the true self is the same within each of us follows from the rule of substitution (*ādeśa*) which the sage Āruni taught to his son Śvetaketu (Chāndogya 6.1.1–7). In grammar and ritual, a rule of substitution tells us when one word or object can stand in for another, it being generally understood that the substitute resembles and behaves like the original. Here is what Āruni told his recently educated and overly proud son –

> "Śvetaketu, here you are my son, swell-headed, thinking yourself to be learned, and arrogant; so you must have surely asked about that rule of substitution (*ādeśa*) by which one hears what has not been heard before, thinks of what has not been thought of before, and perceives what has not been perceived before?" "How indeed does that rule of substitution work, sir?" "It is like this, son. By means of just one lump of clay one would perceive everything made of clay – the transformation (*vikāra*) is a verbal handle, a name – while the reality is just this: 'It's clay.' It is like this, son. By means of just one copper trinket one would perceive everything

---

[5] For abbreviations and translation, see Patrick Olivelle, *The Early Upanishads* (1998).

made of copper – the transformation is a verbal handle, a name – while the reality is just this: 'It's copper.' It is like this, son. By means of just one nail-cutter one would perceive everything made of iron – the transformation is a verbal handle, a name – while the reality is just this: 'It's iron.' That son, is how this rule of substitution works". (Chāndogya 6.1.3–6).

Thereupon Āruni teaches Śvetaketu how to look for the hidden core of things, the sap pervading the tree, the seed in a banyan fruit, the salt in salt-water, and repeatedly he says, "The finest essence here – that constitutes the self of this whole world; that is the truth; that is the self. And that['s how] you are (*tat tvam asi*), Śvetaketu" (Chāndogya 6.8.7). Knowing the "archetype" or "model", and the rule that tells us how to derive the new using the old as a pattern, puts us in a position to gain knowledge of the new. Knowing oneself is a matter of knowing the quintessence of thinking, and this is common to all. The "thin" self we discover in the phenomenology of thinking itself is not the "thick" self supported by differences between individuals with respect to the contents of their thoughts.

Indeed, and ironically, it is nevertheless a self behind which one can hide. Italo Calvino has made the point well: "Just as the author, since he has no intention of telling about himself, decided to call the character "I" as if to conceal him, not having to name him or describe him more than this stark pronoun [...]" (Calvino: 15). The Upaniṣadic self is a mask behind which individuals can hide their individuality, even as that individuality masks the self.

One of the strongest philosophical themes to emerge from Mauni's use of the double has to do with the individuation of selves: the sources of identity for a single self in projecting itself into the future or attempting to assimilate a past. In particular, what is being explored is the existence of a tension at the heart of our sense of self, which derives from the fact I must hide from myself the knowledge that my "character" or "self" is one I have made up for myself. For this invented persona does not serve as a character unless I really inhabit it and believe myself to be it; the moment I begin to look down upon it from the outside, to reflect on its ephemeral origins, it ceases to lend me an identity at all. The dual nature of our self-regard is explored by Sartre in connection with the paradox of binding oneself by one's own resolutions, for instance a resolution to give up gambling:

The resolution is still *me* to the extent that I realize constantly my identity with myself across the temporal flux, but it is no longer *me* — due to the fact that it has become an object for my consciousness [...]. It seemed to me that I had established a *real barrier* between gambling and myself, and now I suddenly perceive that my former understanding of the situation is no more than a memory of an idea, a memory of a feeling. In order for it to come to my aid once more, I must remake it *ex nihilo* and freely. (Sartre: 10)

"How," asked Sushila, "can these characteristics that we claim for ourselves be described as firm or steadfast?" ("Beyond Perception": 107). given that it is always possible for us to see them as external elements and artifacts? How do I retain an internal relationship with my past resolutions and decisions? In the end, the sum of all these "characteristics" constitutes only a shadow that follows us around and is hard to shake off. The double is a mocking presence, reminding us that all the attributes we ascribe to ourselves and which give our sense of self its necessary robustness are really quite hollow. No wonder it is a joke, no wonder the double is so often described by Mauni as smiling a little sarcastically. After all, isn't there sarcasm too in the "embedded" Socrates, ironically pretending to be one of us? For all our efforts to identify ourselves with our future plans, or to see what has happened to us in the past as shaping us, there is no escape from the ever-present and unsettlingly ironic smile. The dissonance between Subbayyar and Subbu, or between the town Sushila and her married namesake in the village, is a reminder of how uncomfortable one is with one's past or future self. But, as the final two stories show, no escape from this is to be found by seeking to remain wholly in the present. The dissonance is not, at bottom, a temporal one. It is rooted in the conflict between the irrepressible need to believe that one is the person one seems to be and the certain knowledge that one is not. Diogenes, the first "world-citizen" and the founder of Cynicism, thought himself to be a true follower in the footsteps of Socrates. And perhaps one can admit that both swallow up their shadows.


**Works cited**

Borges, Jorges Louis. "The Circular Ruins", in *Collected Fictions*. Trans. Andrew Hurley London: Penguin, 1998. 96–100.
Calvino, Italo. *If on a Winters Night a Traveller*. Trans. London: Vintage, 1998.
Eliot, George. *Daniel Deronda*. London: Penguin, 1995.
Ganeri, Jonardon. *The Concealed Art of the Soul: Theories of Self and Practices of Truth in Indian Ethics and Epistemology*. Oxford: Clarendon Press, 2007.
Hadot, Pierre. *Philosophy as a Way of Life*. Oxford: Blackwell, 1995.
Olivelle, Patrick. *The Early Upanishads*. Oxford/New York: Oxford Univ. Press, 1998.
Mauni. *Fictions*. Trans. Lakshmi Holmström. New Delhi: Katha, 1997.

Sartre, Jean-Paul. *Being and Nothingness*. Trans. Hazel Barnes. New York: Washington Square Press, 1956.

# The Problem of Miniaturist Art as Reflection of Reality in Orhan Pamuk's *My Name is Red*

Mustafa Kirca and Firat Karadas

Orhan Pamuk's *My Name is Red* opens with an epigraph from the Koran – "To God belongs the East and the West" – which, for us, suggests that a vital theme is the relationship between the East and the West, and especially their conceptions of "reality" (see also Kirchner: 12) which, despite radically divergent, should not be construed as opposed but complementary.[1] In the novel, the best expression of their co-presence is the Sultan's book, around which the entire novel revolves. The Sultan commissions an illustrated book to demonstrate his power to the Venetian Doge and the whole novel centers on the preparation of this book by the various important miniaturists of sixteenth century Turkey. Although the novel provides a detailed elaboration of the tradition of the art of miniature in Ottoman Istanbul, because the Sultan's book is aimed at marrying Frankish art and miniature art, both styles are equally represented and through this, the novel elucidates several important concerns such as the tension and interaction between the Western and Eastern modes of artistic representation, the threat Western art poses for the art of miniature, and the applicability of the Western concept of perspective in art to miniature art. Orhan Pamuk thus transforms the novel into a playground where he can discuss art form and style; the relationship between art and morality, society and religion; the effects of Western ideas on the Islamic art of miniature; and the future of Ottoman art and its naqqashes, a term used for the illustrators and painters of miniature. Through the hybrid characteristics of the illustrations in the Sultan's book, the novel contrasts the two artistic styles and questions their efficacy to depict reality, especially in relation to religion and the position of the artist in his work. Through the multivocal points-of-view of the novel, which *formally* alludes to the hybrid nature of the Sultan's book, a panorama of the social and private lives, ideas and conflicts of this historical moment is carefully and vividly drawn.

---

[1] The novel was originally published in Turkish as *Benim Adım Kırmızı* in 1998 by İletişim. In 2001 Faber and Faber published its English translation. All the references to the text are from the English edition.

This essay considers art as a kind of "double" to both artists and historical contexts, whose representation mirrors not only the artist's religious and social positions, but also the historico-cultural context of the time. The Sultan's book, we argue, not only depict the tension and interaction between East and West, but how these circumstances directly impact on artists, who then translate them into their work. In other words, we are interested in discussing not only the different manner in which Eastern and Western conceive reality but arts' relation to this reality is as well. There is also another mirroring at work on a metafictional level; here Pamuk's *My Name is Red,* a work that deals with the tension between two artistic styles, is the double of the book Enishte Effendi illustrates for the Sultan. To what extent each "text" corroborates with, or cancels out, the other will be a point of interpretation which this essay will offer in the conclusion.

**The Great Divide: Art, Reality, and Meaning**
In the book commissioned from a renowned naqqash, Enishte Effendi, the Sultan wants the Western technique of perspective to be applied to the art of miniature, a technique which the Sultan has observed and admired in paintings by important Frankish and Venetian artists. At the center of this painting will be the figure of the Sultan himself – a proposition that is in violation of Islamic principles, which forbid human portraits because they imply idolatry. Although troubled, Enishte orders his team of talented illustrators to begin painting but in parts, disallowing them from seeing the whole picture. However, the Sultan's intent is eventually discovered, which results in turmoil and Elegant's and Enishte Effendi's murders by one of the painters. Part detective fiction, the novel attempts to identify the killer, and whilst doing so, delve into art theory. One of the main contentions which the narrative raises is the differences between Eastern and Western views on reality and art; the Frankish style is arguably closer to reality than Islamic illustration because it employs perspective. But the Islamic miniaturists claim that their work is truer to a representation of reality because it is reality as Allah would see it, whereas Venetian art depicts what can only be seen by the artist's naked eyes, and hence is limited and illusory.

Moreover, in Islam, drawing human figures is seen as blasphemous because according to the Koran, "to produce the image of an object" is similar to "creating" – an act which only Allah is capable of (İpşiroğlu: 9). As the murderer in *My Name is Red* declares to Enishte: "in the Glorious Koran, 'creator' is one of the attributes of Allah. It is Allah who is creative, who brings that which is not into existence, who gives life to the lifeless. No one ought to compete with Him. The greatest of sins is committed by painters who presume to do what He does, who claim to be as creative as He" (193). Muslims believe that representing equivalents of objective reality in painting bar them, as the murderer informs, "from [entering] the gates of Heaven" because the Prophet Mohammad has warned that "on Judgment Day, Allah will punish painters most severely [...] the idol makers will be asked to bring the images they've created to life. [...]. Since they'll be unable to do so their lot will be to suffer the torments of Hell." (193). In order to avoid such a punishment, Muslim painters draw what they perceive as the "meaning" behind the objects instead of exact equivalents; this art form is generally known as "conceptional illustration" (İpşiroğlu: 10).

As such, miniaturists do not replicate objects in the material world in their work but the meanings or "shadows" of these objects. As the tree in the chapter "I am a Tree" declares: "I don't want to be a tree, I want to be its meaning" (61), or to put in another way, the "story" behind the painted tree. The Sultan, despite his blasphemous order, seems to also appreciate this subtle point while commissioning the book from Enishte when he says that: "It is the story that's essential [...]. A beautiful illustration elegantly completes the story. An illustration that does not compliment a story, in the end, will become but a false idol" (132). Hence, when meaning in art is sacrificed for perspective and objective accuracy, what becomes lost in the process is "reality". This observation is made clearly by Master Osman, the head of the Ottoman naqqashes, who says to Black, one of Enishte's artists: "Meaning precedes form in the world of our art. As we begin to paint in imitation of the Frankish and Venetian masters, as in the book that Our Sultan had commissioned from your Enishte, the domain of meaning ends and the domain of form begins" (387). In order to distort the illusion of objective reality in Islamic art, only shapes and appearances without shade and light are depicted. This is to achieve a kind of distance from the object portrayed so that art inevitably points to Allah as the unchanging power behind it and to remind its viewer of the objective world's illusory nature. Only by drawing meaning and dealing with concepts, instead of "imitating", can art harmonize with Islamic teaching. In a thoughtful essay about Islam and painting, Zeynep U. Elkatip argues that the art of miniature in the sixteenth century prepared the ground for the legitimization of Islamic painting by destroying the illusion of reality and rejecting the imitative function of art; instead, as she states, "Islamic illustrators, who depict Allah's world in the way Allah would see it and in accordance with the order of importance in Allah's mind, would not in this way produce an imitation and not draw exactly what they see" (371: our translation).

Depicting the world as Allah would see it and considering Allah as supreme lead the miniaturists in *My Name is Red* to employ "the Persian way of depicting the world from above" (303), as if observed "from the balcony of a minaret" (205). In contrast, as the prejudiced miniaturists view it, Frankish and Venetian art deals with what is ordinary and represents it "from the perspective of a mangy street dog" (191). To use perspective in drawing entails the presence of a center, from which the outer world is reflected; this creates a hierarchy between objects and the beliefs they represent. Such a way of reflecting the world is not without problems in Islam because it encourages "an unforgivable sin by daring to draw, from the perspective of a mangy street dog, a horsefly and a mosque as if they were the same size –with the excuse that the mosque was in the background– thereby mocking the faithful who attend prayers" (191).

In the narrative, discussion on art mainly revolves around the depictions of three images – a dog, a tree and a horse, all of which are part of the illustration in the Sultan's book; as such, a comparative study between Eastern and Western art arises precisely from the situatedness of these objects in this book. Interestingly however, the arguments of these three images are not presented as conflicting with each other but in the form of a Bakhtinian dialogue, each expressing its view as a response to the other. In the chapter "I am a Tree", the illustrated tree expresses its desire to be imbued with a story in a miniature, to either provide "shade for Mejnun disguised as a shepherd as he visited Leyla in her tent", "to fade into the night, representing the darkness in the soul of a wretched and hopeless man," or "to shade Alexander during the final moments of his life on his campaign to conquer Hindustan" (59). Defending miniature against Frankish perspective, the tree argues that to look at a *drawing* of a tree is more pleasant than to look at a tree, implying that Western art is not really drawing because it is too exact a copy. Consequently, miniature is, for the tree, better because it represents meaning rather than the material object. In this regard also is an idealized view of objective reality depicted in Islamic illustration. The tree criticizes Frankish painters for depicting "the faces of kings, priests, noblemen, and even women in such a manner that after gazing upon the portrait, you'd be able to identify that person on the street" (61). "I thank Allah," the tree says, "I, the humble tree before you haven't been drawn with such intent. And not because I fear that if I'd been thus depicted all the dogs in Istanbul would assume I was a real tree and piss on me: I don't want to be a tree, I want to be its meaning" (61).

The arguments of the illustrated horse-narrator in the chapter "I am a Horse" can be read as a response to the tree from a Frankish-style point of view. Here, the horse complains that the grace of its midsection, the length of its legs and the pride of its bearing as represented in miniature art do not foreground the uniqueness of a real horse but of the miniaturist who illustrated it. It says: "everyone knows that there is no horse exactly like me. I'm simply the rendering of a horse that exists in a miniaturist's imagination" (264). The special emphasis placed on memory and remembering as the predominant source of artistry in miniature should be seen as another juncture where Eastern and Western art differentiates. We learn from Master Osman that a dexterous miniaturist draws not what he sees but what he remembers (92). The fact that the miniaturist "holds" the horse *image* in his mind and then transcribes it onto his art, rather than copying directly and accurately a *real* object, is a fundamental feature in Islamic illustration. Master Osman explains the virtue of such a depiction: "the horse that a master miniaturist has drawn tens of thousands of times eventually comes close to God's vision of a horse, and the artist knows this through experience and deep in his soul. The horse that his hand draws quickly from memory is rendered with talent, great effort, and insight, and it is a horse that approaches Allah's horse" (306). Here again, what the miniaturist depicts is not a replica of a real, material horse but its meaning, or appearance as it exists in Allah's mind. But the problem with this, as the horse laments, is that "All miniaturists [would] illustrate all horses from memory in the same way even though we've each been uniquely created by Allah, Greatest of all Creators [...]. Because they're attempting to depict the world that God perceives, not the world that they see" (264). As a counterpoint to Master Osman's argument, the horse declares:

> I am sick of being incorrectly depicted by miniaturists who sit around the house like ladies and never go off to war. They'll depict me at a gallop with both my forelegs extended at the same time. There isn't a horse in this world that runs like a rabbit. If one of my forelegs is forward, the other is aft. Contrary to what is depicted in battle illustrations, there isn't a horse in this world that extends one foreleg like a curious dog, leaving the other firmly planted on the ground (265).

The horse makes a sophisticated point when it theorizes that miniaturists who draw from memory (in fact, the best miniaturists are blind, because then they can only ever draw *from memory*) are possibly committing a sin. It wonders if the discontentment with the object they physically see, which then translates into thousands of drawings of the same object that eventually achieves comparative status as Allah's imagination

127

of a horse, do not eventually result in a kind of competition with Allah. In contrast to this, the horse sees in the Frankish style the sole purpose of which is to create a realistic *illusion*. To illustrate its point, it provides an example; there is a story of a Frankish king who once examined the portrait of a woman whom he is contemplating on marrying. In the painting, she is seated on a mare. Suddenly, the king's stallion became aroused and "attempted to mount the attractive mare in the painting, and the horse grooms were hard pressed to bring the ferocious animal under control before he destroyed the picture and the frame with his huge member" (263). The horse-narrator surmises that it is not the beauty of the Venetian mare that has aroused the Frankish stallion but "the act of taking a particular horse and painting a picture in her exact likeness" (263). In this regard, the horse argues, "the new styles of the Frankish masters aren't blasphemous, quite the opposite, they're the most in keeping with [horses'] faith" (265). The logic of the horse can be understood this way: the Frankish painters depict in their art a replica of the real object, which creates in the viewer the *illusion* that what is depicted is not an artistic image but the real object itself. This way of painting, for the horse, is not contradictory to religious belief because Frankish artists *depict* the beauty of God's creation in his art, not attempting to *create* it out of nothing.

From the horse's argument, it is obvious that the Frankish/Venetian style of perspective brings art closer to reality than its Islamic miniaturist counterpart. (With this, the gold coin in the chapter "I am a Gold Coin" certainly agrees: "When these Venetian infidels paint, it's as if they aren't making a painting but actually creating the object they are painting" [126]). A Venetian painting makes one feel that he is "no longer looking at a page from a book but at the world seen through a window" (485). Venetian artists do not depict the world as seen from the balcony of a minaret as miniaturists do; they depict, as Enishte claims, "what's seen at street level, or from the inside of a prince's room, taking in his bed, quilt, desk, mirror, hid tiger, his daughter and his coins. They include it all" (206). Discussing the play of shade and light in Frankish painting, Enishte notes:

Eyes can no longer simply be holes in a face, always the same, but must be just like our own eyes, which reflect light like a mirror and absorb it like a well. Lips can no longer be a crack in the middle of faces as flat as paper, but must be nodes of expression – each a different shade of red – fully expressing our joys, sorrows and spirits with their slightest contraction or relaxation. Our noses can no longer be a kind of wall that divides our faces, but rather, living and curious instruments with a form unique to each of us (166).

Yet, whether one supports Islamic illustrations or favors Western methods, art's problematic and relative relationship with objective reality is evident in all styles. Whether Frankish or Islamic, no representation of an object can achieve the status of the object itself. Constructed by the iconic imagination of the artist, art is both similar to and different from the object depicted; the stillness and placidity of the depiction announce its contrast to the liveliness of its origin in the material world. Indeed, this difference-in-similarity is expressed by both the tree and horse illustrations, although with opposite conclusions. While the horse takes comfort in that what is illustrated will never truly represent the way things "really are", however accurate the copy ("We horses scrounge for and eat the green grass at our feet when nobody is looking. We never assume a statuesque stance and wait around elegantly, the way we're shown in paintings. Why is everybody so embarrassed about our eating, drinking, shitting and sleeping?" [265]), the tree laments that its depiction, although exact, does not meaningfully capture its interrelatedness with the rest of the natural world around it ("there are no slender trees beside [it], no seven-leaf steppe plants, no dark billowing rock formations [...] Just the ground, the sky, [itself] and the horizon." It says: "my story is much more complicated" [56]).

An even more profound consideration of the nature of art's "reality" is made by the illustrated dog in the chapter "I am a Dog." Drawing attention to art's construction as an artifact, the dog avers: "I have no problem with the fact that my portrait was drawn on such cheap paper or that I'm a four-legged beast, but I do regret that I can't sit down like a man and have a cup of coffee with you. We'd die for our coffee and our coffeehouses – what's this? See, my master is pouring coffee for me from a small coffeepot. A picture can't drink coffee, you say? Please! See for yourselves, this dog is happily lapping away" (16). For the dog, it does not matter whether perspective or miniaturist style is deployed because art, however much it represents aliveness, movement and meaning, is ultimately artificial and static. In fact, Black, while contemplating an illustration of a naval fleet heading off to battle in a miniature in Master Osman's workshop (71), comes to realize that artificiality and deadness is much more palpable in miniature art because of its lack of perspective, and with its distortion of the proportions of physical objects. Both these techniques widen the gap between the object and its representation in miniature art even further.

But it is precisely the point that art is always artificial, we argue, that the narrative wishes to make – a point which ultimately derives from the epigraph that heads the narrative. In the final analysis, all art is unreal; miniaturist art cannot be seen as being closer to God's reality, nor Frankish art as blasphemous, because the static nature of painting already announces its artist's *humanity*. An artist can never create, however wonderful or accurate the artifact, but merely *depict*. Sadly, this point is completely missed by the murderer, resulting in the loss of a great naqqash and the ruination of a wondrous artwork.

## The Problems of the Center

Enishte's discomfit stems not only from the fact that the Sultan wants his portrait in the illustration for the book. Another issue with which a Muslim artist has to grapple if he or she were to adopt Western technique is centrality (which is related to perspective) – a crucial feature in Western art, but one prohibited by Islamic illustrations because it implies idolizing whatever occupies this position. One of the main criticisms against Enishte's illustration for the Sultan's book arises from emplacing the Sultan at the center. Not only is this idolatrous, it also results in "depicting Our Sultan, the Caliph of Islam, the same size as a dog [and] rendering Satan the same size, and in endearing light" (477). In fact, such a leveling paradoxically decenters the Sultan; instead, Satan, in being painted "as large as life and his face in all its detail"(477) seems more important and grander. Arguably then, for the miniaturists, the straight-forward rendition in Frankish painting that "centers" the object of representation is perhaps the greatest of sins in the Muslim faith not only for its idolatry but for its re-duction (aggrandizement) of illustrious (dangerous) elements. Instead, the lack of a center in miniature art is in accordance with Islam. As Enishte's murderer states:

> because the illustrations of the Persian masters and even the masterpieces of the greatest masters of Heart are ul-timately seen as an extension of border ornamentation, no one would take issue with them, reasoning that they enhanced the beauty of writing and the magnificence of calligraphy [...]. However, as we make use of the methods of the Franks, our painting is becoming less focused on ornamentation and intricate design and more on straightforward representation. This is what the Glorious Koran forbids and what displeased Our Prophet. (478)

The fact that Islamic art is decorative and always already "an extension of border or-namentation" suggests that centrality is altogether and deliberately eschewed. In fact, it is arguable that the lack of center *is* the characterizing feature of Islamic illustra-tion: it helps distance the illustrated world in miniature art from objective reality and in the process, transforms the artwork into a depiction solely of meaning. The func-tion of the center in glorifying and exalting the object of representation is viewed with grave trepidation by the miniaturist – and this point is strikingly rendered to-wards the end of the novel when the murderer replaces the Sultan's portrait with his own in order to make a critical point:

> In the center of this world, where our Sultan should've been, was my own portrait, which I briefly observed with pride. I was somewhat unsatisfied with it because after laboring in vain for days, looking into a mirror and erasing and reworking, I was unable to achieve a good resemblance; still, I felt unbridled elation because the picture not only situated me at the center of a vast world, but for some unaccountable and diabolic reason, it

made me appear more profound, complicated and mysterious than I actually was... I was both the center of everything, like a sultan or a king, and, at the same time, myself. (485)

In a sense, we can read this as a sliding from art to evil, which demonstrates the extent to which art plays a serious role in religious life, and that the contravening of its conventions can lead to tragic consequences. Alternatively, the above passage can be read as a sliding in the reversed order; by centering himself in the artwork, the murderer is merely confirming his diabolism. In any case, these two contrasting possibilities of reading the killer's intent of course mirror the argument in this essay that centrality in art both exalts and diminishes/displaces the object of that center. In the end, is the murderer acting on his own volition or is he an instrument of fate/faith? That the artwork in question is a hybrid merely attenuates this ideological conundrum that the narrative is driving: in a painting where Eastern and Western styles are represented, centrality is revealed as both locative and displacing.

## Conclusion: Metafictional Double

As already said in the introduction, the novel opens with the word "To God belongs the East and the West." Enishte Effendi claims that the Eastern style of miniature and the Western style of perspective can be employed simultaneously in the art of painting. He argues that this is what he endeavors to realize in the illustration of the book he prepares for the Sultan. He explains:

Two styles heretofore never brought together have come together [in the book] to create something new and wondrous. We owe Bihzad and the splendour of Persian painting to the meeting of an Arabic illustrating sensibility and Mongol-Chinese painting. Shah Tahmasp's best paintings marry Persian style with Turkmen subtleties. Today, if men cannot adequately praise the book-arts workshops of Akbar Khan in Hindustan, it's because he urged his miniaturists to adopt the styles of the Frankish masters. To God belongs the East and the West (194).

According to Enishte, "It was Satan who separated East from West". He reiterates this point even beyond death when, approached by the angel Azrael in a dreamlike sequence, he penetrates the mystery of the *Book of the Apocalypse* which is revealed to be an angel "with one thousand wings spanning East and West", holding "the whole world in his hands" (213). Painting, for him then, is an instrument through which he can bridge the East-West divide, and he attempts this principally through the application of perspective to miniature art; at the least, this hybrid practice will help promote better understanding between the two cultures which often view each other with suspicion. This theme is, as several critics have noted, reflected on a metafictional level as well. Özlem Uzundemir, for instance, regards the novel's metafictional form as "construct[ing] a [...] dialogue between the East and the West"

(112). Another critic, Eric J. Iannelli, claims that *My Name Is Red* is meant to achieve the same kind of bridging objective as Enishte's painting. Pamuk himself seems to confirm this when he says that "I wrote all my books by blending styles, methodologies, conventions and histories of both the East and the West. To this intersections, I am indebted for the richness of my novels" (1999: 155, our translation).

*My Name is Red* is hailed by its readers as a form of miniature art itself (Kuyaş: 353) in which Orhan Pamuk is able to reflect a world without a center and without a hierarchical order. It is "drawn" like a piece of miniature art in which hierarchy is subverted by the lack of a single unifying perspective customary of the novel. Here, there is no main character, no single narrator, and omnipresent authorial voice. Each chapter has its own narrator with its distinctive perspective(s), and, each narrator, like individual figures on a miniature, is simultaneously isolated from, and harmonizes with, the others in order to enact the entire painting. Thus, the plurality of perspectives is achieved, not just those of animate or important beings (the Sultan, the naqqashes), but of inanimate and trivial ones (gold ring, tree, dog) as well. Each voice, to borrow Mikhail Bakhtin's notion, enters into a dialogic relationship with another to form a *carnivalesque* (or, to put it more properly, *miniaturesque*) structure within the novel. To a point, this argument may suggest that Pamuk is privileging Islamic art after all, for his novel is unconcerned with hierarchy and having to represent objects from a certain point of view; but when we consider that this *miniaturesque* aspect of the novel is conveyed in the Western stylistic convention known as the postmodern novel (Uzundemir 2001), it is then clear that the writer's intent for *My Name is Red* is precisely to collapse Eastern and Western art into each other to produce a hybrid work.

According to Black, both Eastern and Western arts have their strengths, and their differences should be allowed to overshadow their uniqueness, in the way Enishte's murderer and the miniaturist Black do. For unlike Enishte who believes that "To God belongs the East and the West", Black believes that "East is east and West is west" (488). In response, Butterfly, another master miniaturist in Master Osman's workhouse, quips: "An artist should never succumb to hubris of any kind [...] he should simply paint the way he sees fit rather than troubling over East or West" (488). But Black's point, on a more affirmative level, can be read not so much as the twain never meeting, but that the meeting should never be premised on one tradition attempting to reduce the other into the category of the self (same). There is almost a Derridean venture here in embracing the other as totally Other. A dialogue between the East and the West is achievable not by interpreting one in terms of the other but by accepting the fact that both are fundamentally different. The hybrid miniature art depicted in Pamuk's novel can proffer the hope of bridging East and West that Enishte Effendi entertains as long as their differences are carefully encouraged and maintained.

## Works Cited

Elkatip, Zeynep U. "Geleneğin Kırılışından Türk Modernleşmesine, *Benim Adım Kırmızı*'da Resmin Algılanışı" (From the Breaking Up of the Tradition to Turkish Modernism, the Conception of Painting in *My Name is Red*) in Kılıç, 1999. 361 – 80.

Iannelli, Eric J. 2001. http://www.raintaxi.com/online/2001winter/pamuk.shtml. (accessed on 3 February 2007)

İpşiroğlu, Mazhar Ş. *İslamda Resim Yasağı ve Sonuçları* (*The Prohibition of Painting in Islam and its Consequences*). Istanbul: Yapı Kredi, 2005.

Kılıç, Engin. (Ed). *Orhan Pamuk'u Anlamak* [*Understanding Orhan Pamuk*]. Istanbul: İletişim, 1999.

Kirchner, Mark. "Muhasar-i Kal'e-i Doppio – Orhan Pamuk Üzerine Notlar"(The Seige of Doppio Castle — Notes on Orhan Pamuk), in Kılıç, 1999. 9–14.

Kuyaş, Nilüfer. "Seks, Yalanlar ve Minyatür" (Sex, Lies and Miniature)] in Kılıç, 1999. 351–60.

Pamuk, Orhan. *My Name is Red*. London: Faber and Faber, 2001.

Pamuk, Orhan. *Öteki Renkler* (*Other Colours*). Istanbul: İletişim, 1999.

Uzundemir, Özlem. 2001. "*Benim Adım Kırmızı*'da Doğu ile Batı, Geçmiş ile Günümüz Arasında Diyalog Arayışları" (The Search for Dialogue Between East and West, Past and Present in *My Name is Red*). *Doğuş University Journal*, 2. 1 (2001). [112-119]

# Part Four

# Confessing the Post-Romantic Subject: *Fight Club* as "Rematch" of Rousseau and Hobbes

Brian Burns

*I'm not a nihilist. I'm a romantic.*

– Chuck Palahniuk

Despite the hyperbolic and often disturbing nature of Chuck Palahniuk's 1996 novel *Fight Club*, much of the novel is familiar territory. Palahniuk's story of the struggles of a young man trying to find a place for himself in the world conforms to much of the conventional plot of the confessional and *bildungsroman*. Make the young man schizophrenic, as happens in Palahniuk's novel, and these familiar genres become marked by the "schizo" sensibility that Baudrillard, Jameson, and Deleuze and Guattari locate in the postmodern subject.[1] The uncanny in *Fight Club*, beginning with the unnamed narrator's *doppelgänger* Tyler Durden, is part of a wider return in the narrative to Romanticism's critique of the Enlightenment's sense of what it means to be human. Oscillating between the emotional sensibilities and pugilistic tendencies of the narrator and his double, Tyler Durden – and therefore between the philosophies of Rousseau and Hobbes, *Fight Club* enacts a schizophrenic postmodernity that is also highly "post-romantic", in that the narrative's overdetermined sense of Rousseau as a signifier of the postmodern subject works to collapse almost the entire history of criticism of the Enlightenment back to the age of Romanticism. This essay will not only consider *Fight Club's* neo-Gothic *doppelgänger* as exemplifying Freud's notion of the uncanny as the "familiar made unfamiliar", but it will also argue for *Fight Club* as a strangely familiar narrative which returns to the confessional, gothic, and philosophical interests of Jean-Jacques Rousseau and the Romantics.

If we define the postmodern, as many do, by beginning with Lyotard's observation regarding postmodernity's drive to dispense with the meta-narratives of the Enlightenment, then *Fight Club* is made particularly uncanny due to its *doppelgänger* forcing a "rematch" or uncanny return to one of the original and most enduring cri-

---

[1] For these discussions of the "schizophrenia" of postmodernity, see: Baudrillard, "The Ecstasy of Communication", Jameson, "Postmodernism and Consumer Society", and Deleuze and Guattari, *Anti-Oedipus: Capitalism and Schizophrenia*.

tiques of the Enlightenment located in Rousseau's very familiar "fight" with Hobbes in the *Discourse on the Origins of Inequality*. My sense of a "post-romantic" subject is meant both to mark the place of Rousseau and the Romantics in illuminating the problems of modernity and postmodernity, and to help illustrate the centrality of Rousseau's confessional discourse in defining the postmodern subject in literature and popular culture.

With the notable exceptions of Jean Starobinski, Christopher Kelly, and a handful of others, critics in a number of fields have tended to separate out Rousseau's *Confessions* (1781 and 1789) as being too literary and personal to be included in any in depth discussions of Rousseau's political and philosophical *oeuvre*. Recently, Christopher Kelly has gone the farthest in championing the *Confessions* by insisting that "[i]n addition to being a behind-the-scenes look at the private life of a public man, the *Confessions* is at the center of Rousseau's philosophical enterprise" (Kelly, "Introduction": xxxii).[2] In his recent book *The Romantic Subject in Autobiography*, Eugene Stelzig observes that Rousseau's description of his own development is part of his wider philosophy "concerned with the refractory issue of what is original in human nature" (Stelzig: 47). The stubbornness of this issue is one reason that Rousseau decides to approach it autobiographically at the end of his career in his *Confessions, Dialogues*, and *Reveries of a Solitary Walker*. Michael Davis addresses this in *The Autobiography of Philosophy*, when he describes how the professionalization of philosophy has removed the field from earlier, more intuitive connections made between autobiography and the study of philosophy. Davis argues ambitiously that "the ground for all philosophy" is found first in how "for Heidegger and Aristotle, Plato, and Nietzsche philosophy is essentially autobiographical and second [...] in what amounts to a philosophical psychology, Rousseau makes the autobiographical character of philosophy thematic" (Davis: 1, 8). Although my hopes for philosophy in this essay are not so ambitious, the ethos of Davis's reading of philosophy as autobiography and his recognition of the importance of Rousseau in this remain central to my thinking. Where Davis and I diverge is mainly in emphasis, in that he chooses to read Rousseau's philosophy through his *Reveries of a Solitary Walker*, while I choose to consider Rousseau's *oeuvre* using his *Confessions*. I give the *Confessions* priority because of the manner in which Rousseau's rhetoric continues to wash over us in sup-

---

[2]For Christopher Kelly's work on Rousseau's *Confessions* see, *Rousseau as Author: Consecrating One's Life to the Truth*, and *Rousseau's Exemplary Life: The Confessions as Political Philosophy*.

port of Foucault's observation regarding the explosion of modern confessional discourse in *The History of Sexuality*:

> The confession has spread its effects far and wide. It plays a part in justice, medicine, education, family relationships, and love relations, in the most ordinary affairs of everyday life, and in the most solemn rites [...]. One confesses [...] things that would be impossible to tell anyone else, the things people write books about. One confesses – or is forced to confess [...]. Western man has become a confessing animal. (Foucault: 59)

Foucault's image of the "confessing animal" suggests that this modern type is a major change in emphasis or perhaps even a replacement for Aristotle's "political animal", which the Enlightenment philosophers, including Hobbes and Rousseau, sought to either update or replace. "Confessing" can replace "political" in its pairing with "animal" because since Rousseau, the confessional has in many ways become political. For both Rousseau and Palahniuk's narrator, confessional discourse is, as Foucault describes it, "a ritual of discourse in which the speaking subject is also the subject of the statement [... and] a ritual that unfolds within a power relationship" (61). Sexual disclosures are, of course, one of the confessional's master tropes, so in our time when for example, the pop singer Madonna produces significant personal power and celebrity through her public sexual confessions, we should take notice. Very early in her career, Madonna took a page right from Rousseau's playbook in confessing to finding sexual pleasure in being spanked.[3] If the confessee can dispense with the authority of the "father confessor", which in Foucault's thesis for the secularized confession is "one's doctors, one's educators, one' parents, one's educators" *ad infinitum*, the confessing subject can then control, direct, and often predict the power of his or her own confessions, rather than having them filtered and claimed as a right of power by an authority figure (Foucault: 59). Despite this, the implications of Foucault's statements regarding the centrality of confessional discourse in defining the modern subject have gone largely unexplored.[4] This reading of the *Confessions* alongside *Fight Club* will work to explore the implications of this dynamic. Rousseau and Palahniuk's narrator seek power, both personal and political, through the control

---

[3] It also cannot be ignored that *Fight Club* evolves its own more violent version of this same confessional commonplace, driving Slavoj Žižek to describe the "knot of love and violence" in Palahniuk's novel as one of its most salient features (112).

[4] Two recent exceptions are Jeremy Tambling, *Confession: Sexuality, Sin, and the Subject*, and Peter Brooks, *Troubling Confessions: Speaking Guilt in Law and Literature*.

of their own confessional discourse, and issues of sexuality play a defining role in both of their confessional narratives.

While it is a commonplace to fix Rousseau at or near the beginnings of the trajectory to modernity, as is the case for Richard Velkley, Marshall Berman, and Charles Taylor,[5] it is less common to consider Rousseau firmly within the context of postmodernity as I insist here. Graeme Garrard's recent *Rousseau's Counter-Enlightenment* ends with the cogent observation that:

> Even though there are clear echoes of Rousseau's earlier denunciation of the Enlightenment of his age in recent intellectual movements such as critical theory, hermeneutics, pragmatism, feminism, postmodernism, and communitarianism – all of which contain some version of the charge that the pathologies of our civilization have their origins in the eighteenth-century Enlightenment – his name is rarely invoked in this context. Yet he was the first enemy of the Enlightenment, a status that both Rousseau and the *philosophes* would have thought self-evident. (Garrard: 120)

*Fight Club* is such a convincing condensation of Rousseau's voice and thought that it is clearly much more than just an echo of the earliest days of modernity in the mid- to late-eighteenth-century counter-Enlightenment, and, I would add, much more than just a mirror of a confessional culture "that people write books about". It is substantially more because it goes as far as allegorizing Rousseau in a manner which suggests that the postmodern subject has internalized Rousseau's ideas and rhetoric so that Jean-Jacques's original views regarding modernity have become a defining characteristic of the voice of postmodernity.

Rousseau is not purely postmodern by a long shot, but neither are most postmodern autobiographers. There is a predeliction in postmodernity to want to cling to portions of a unified self, the littered remains of Descartes's *cogito*, in order to make the decentered postmodern subject make sense. The result is rarely completely satisfying. Timothy O'Hagan sees this predilection – and its result – emerge quite clearly in Rousseau's work:

> For Rousseau, the self is still the starting point, and perhaps the end point too, of all our reflections. But the self has become an unstable, shifting unity. It is both encountered and constructed; it is contested and fought for in a battle of amour-propre. With Rousseau, Cartesian doubt is transformed [...]. "We see neither the soul of the other, because it hides itself, nor our own, because we have no mirror of the mind," wrote Rousseau in 1757, and in the *Reveries of a Solitary Walker*, composed at the very end of his life, he confessed: "the real and basic motives of most of my actions are not as clear to me as I had long supposed". (O'Hagan: vii)

Confessional discourse is the rhetoric of this balancing act between the Enlightenment and the present, allowing for a dusting of reason to stick – sometimes lightly

---

[5] See Richard Velkley, *Being After Rousseau*, Marshall Berman, *All That is Solid Melts into Air: The Experience of Modernity,* and Charles Taylor, *Sources of the Self: The Making of Modern Identity.*

and at other moments more heavily – to efforts to construct a working notion of a contested and increasingly fractured subjectivity. Modern confessional discourse is "schizophrenic" from the start because of what it attempts (there are few commentators who do not see Rousseau as a paranoid psychological case first and foremost, beginning with his most recent biographers Cranston and Damrosch), reflecting that the transition from Rousseau's torn and paranoid subject in the *Confessions* to Palahniuk's schizophrenic subject in *Fight Club* is not as dramatic as it may appear at first glance.

Confessional discourse is a prescient tool for measuring the history of affect. If Rousseau were alive today, he would likely recognize *Fight Club* as a confessional artifact in the history of human culture and affect that he envisioned at the beginning of his *Confessions*. Palahniuk's culture of the future would be recognizable as one where *amour-propre* is now "on steroids", dominated by messages delivered electronically, whether the subject wants to see and hear them or not, and where, as John Berger describes as early as 1972 in *Ways of Seeing*, the ultimate cost is the "self being split in two" because "the publicity image steals her love of herself as she is, and offers it back to her for the price of the product" (Berger: 134). This future merely confirms Rousseau's canny theories in the *Discourse on the Origin of Inequality* regarding the centrality of "love of one's self" and the move from simple *amour de soi* to increasingly complex layers of *amour propre* throughout the development of human societies.

As the schizophrenic projection of the confessional first-person narrator in *Fight Club*, Tyler Durden is the natural inheritor of Rousseau's confessional discourse, which tracks the effects of postmodernity's ever-present forms of *amour propre* on the individual subject. Confessional discourse was modified by Rousseau to direct attention away from original sin and place it on the defects or "sins" of the wider culture. The *Discourse of Origin of Inequality* sees the "fall of man" as emerging out of the intensification and urbanization of human culture, while the *Confessions* shows the ill effects of this cultural formation on the lifespan of an individual. This focus on environment and the cultural criticism that goes with it are among the most central characteristics of confessional discourse since Rousseau, and it is these qualities that *Fight Club* utilizes in its own explosive critique of the postmodern condition.

Before going any further, a brief review of the major points of the plot of Chuck Palahniuk's *Fight Club* is necessary; otherwise, the odd and wildly allegorical plot may distract later from my argument. The novel opens with Tyler Durden holding a gun in the mouth of the unnamed narrator, and threatening to shoot. If this is not dire enough, Tyler has also set a bomb to detonate in several minutes in the highrise they occupy. The rest of the novel provides the enlarged context by which the narrator and Tyler Durden arrived here, seemingly prepared to die as part of an anarchist plot. Tellingly, the narrator admits: "I know all of this: the gun, the anarchy, the explosion is really about Marla Singer" (Palahniuk: 14), and as the narrative unfolds the narrator's relationship with Marla Singer moves from being a secondary detail to becoming the primary motivation for the narrator's schizophrenic delusions. The narrator begins retracing his life as he describes meeting Marla Singer while attending numerous self-help groups for sufferers of maladies such as testicular cancer and brain parasites. Neither the narrator nor Marla is sick, but mixing with terminally ill patients not only allows them both to feel, something they struggle with in their daily lives, but the groups have the added benefit of relieving the narrator's sleeplessness. The narrator's frequent business travel for an unfulfilling job, as well as his lack of a personal life, leave him both marginalized and an insomniac. It is only the emotional release provided by the self-help groups that allows the narrator any sleep.

After a chance meeting with Tyler Durden on a nude beach following one of his routine business trips, the narrator returns home to find his condominium destroyed by an explosive device (Tyler Durden will later admit to this). With nowhere else to turn, he moves into Tyler Durden's place, which is really a squat in a dilapidated house. Soon after arriving there, the narrator works to fight back his jealousy when Tyler begins having a sexual relationship with Marla Singer. It is about this same time that the narrator and Tyler begin the practice of punching each other and find that not only is feeling pain better than feeling nothing, but punching and being punched are oddly exhilarating. Soon, they are forming a network of "fight clubs", groups where men beat each other severely as a way to self-actualize. The clubs grow in popularity, until the narrator begins to notice that his partner Tyler is using the fight clubs to organize cells of an anarchist paramilitary group called "project mayhem". The narrator begins to track Tyler's movements, only to find that Tyler Durden is a schizophrenic projection of himself, who organizes Fight Clubs and Project Mayhem, all while the narrator believes he is asleep. Tyler is a variety of neo-gothic *doppelgänger*, acting on the desires of the narrator to be powerful and desirable. The narrator finally confronts Tyler when the story returns to the narrative frame, where Tyler's effort to kill the narrator culminates instead with the narrator successfully "kill-ing" Tyler with a gunshot that passes only through the narrator's cheek. The novel ends with the narrator being kept as a patient on a mental ward where the verisimilitude of the entire confessional diatribe is left up in the air. As the narrator always feared, Marla "likes" him, but does not love him the way she did Tyler Durden.

*Fight Club*'s strange constellation of symbols pushes for an allegorical reading that is critical of postmodern culture, fueled by the fact that the unnamed narrator and Tyler Durden together embody and rail against the problems of the postmodern subject.[6] But, even before the arrival of the narrator's *doppelgänger*, the novel develops an uncanny network of ideas and symbols that act as the embodiment of both Rousseau and the Romantics. Much of the interweaving of Rousseau with *Fight Club* is locatable in the confessional plot that Rousseau gave to his life in his autobiography. The marginalized and potentially unstable young man fighting against his society's expectations regarding his career and future, goes a long way toward encapsulating the plots of both Rousseau's *Confessions* and Palahniuk's *Fight Club*. At the end of Book One of the *Confessions*, Rousseau, the "wretched apprentice", describes fleeing Geneva and the injustices of a petty master in an effort to take control over deciding his future occupation (*Confessions*: 41). Using the story of his life in a manner which predicts psychoanalysis and Sigmund Freud, Rousseau goes on to describe the effect that the death of his mother and his absent father have had on his own drive to love and feel loved. *Fight Club* develops a similar basic plotline and psychology in which the unnamed narrator retreats into the system of fight clubs as a way to move away from a job with a "nagging, ineffectual, petty, whining [...] boss," which offers little in terms of independence or excitement (Palahniuk: 98). Although the narrator in *Fight Club* is much older than the 16-year-old Rousseau leaving the gates of Geneva in 1728, the narrator's statement early in *Fight Club* that he is "a thirty-year-old boy" (50) who is alienated from both of his parents and the world, places him on par with the childish and still searching thirty-year-old Rousseau who finally leaves Madame de Warens, his lover, protector, and "Mamman," and makes his way toward Paris in 1742.

---

[6] For readings of *Fight Club* that consider a prominent role for postmodernity and the logic of late capitalism in the novel and/or film see: Krister Friday, *"A Generation of Men Without History"*: Fight Club, Masculinity, and the Historical Symptom", Henry A. Giroux and Imre Szeman, "IKEA Body and the Politics of Male Bonding: Fight Club, Consumerism, and Violence", Peter Mathews, "Diagnosing Chuck Palahniuk's *Fight Club*", and Kevin Boon, "Men and Nostalgia for Violence: Culture and Culpability in Chuck Palahniuk's *Fight Club*."

These parallels between Rousseau's life and the narrator's life would be little more than the shared symptoms of modern life (the dissolution of the family, alienation, and so forth), if Palahniuk's narrator did not make a series of moves that speak directly to Rousseau's interest in regaining humankind's emotional center. Early in the *Discourse on the Origin of Inequality*, Rousseau announces that "[p]erceiving and feeling" are humankind's original sensibilities and "human understanding owes much to the passions [...] [f]or one can desire or fear things only by virtue of the ideas one can have of them, or from the simple impulse of nature; and savage man [...] feels only the passion of this latter sort" (*Discourse*: 26). Despite Rousseau's undeserved reputation for wanting to return to the cave with his version of "natural man", the *Discourse on the Origin of Inequality* assigns the highest priority to what Tzvetan Todorov described recently as Rousseau's "middle way", the place between natural man and present day social man where the power of the culture of modernity could be mitigated. Although Rousseau knew that it was impossible to move back in time, he did see something attractive in what he called the "period of first revolution" in the *Discourse on the Origin of Inequality*, where property and the effects of *amour propre* were new, and family and family life still ruled supreme:

> The first developments of the heart were the effect of a new situation that united the husbands and wives, fathers and children in one common habitation. The habit of living together gave rise to the sweetest sentiment known to men: conjugal love and paternal love [...]. Women became more sedentary and grew accustomed to watch over the hut and the children, while the men went to seek their common subsistence. With their slightly softer life the two sexes also began to lose something of their ferocity and vigor. But while each one separately became less suited to combat savage beasts, on the other hand it was easier to assemble in order jointly to resist them. (*Discourse on the Origin of Inequality*: 47–48)

In *Confessions* and *Fight Club*, both conjugal and paternal love experience the decay or "denaturing" that is more than implied in the above quotation, but is not necessarily negative in its milder forms. For Rousseau and the Romantics, a retreat into nature at Les Charmettes, Les Hermitage, or the Lake District allowed for a simpler life away from some of the withering effects of *amour propre*. For Palahniuk's narrator, locating a balance between strong interpersonal relationships and a simpler life proves to be far more problematic.

At the beginning of *Fight Club*, the narrator describes seeking out self-help groups for terminally ill patients in an effort to find an emotionally authentic place in an increasingly fraught world. Like Rousseau, whose father leaves him with an uncle at age ten and remarries, the narrator's family life in *Fight Club* is characterized by an absentee father who "sets up franchises" as he moves on to other relationships, leaving his child to fend for himself. The self-help group for men with testicular cancer allows the narrator to locate his own version of "Mamman" in a former body-builder named "Bob" whose earlier steroid use led to testicular cancer. Taken as part of a wider allegory of the trials and vicissitudes of the postmodern subject, the narrator's meetings with Bob becomes a stand-in for the romantic search for the more emotional and feminized self present in the family at the time of Rousseau's "first revolution":

> Bob's big arms were closed around to hold me inside, and I was squeezed in the dark between Bob's new sweating tits that hang enormous [...]. Going around the church basement full of men, each night we met: this is Art, this is Paul, this is Bob [...]. His arms wrapped around me [...].
> "It will be alright," Bob says. "You can cry now" [...].
> Bob's shoulders inhale themselves up in a long draw, then drop, drop in jerking sobs [...] I've been coming here every week for two years, and every week Bob wraps his arms around me and I cry [...] Bob cries because six months ago, his testicles were removed. Then hormone support therapy. Bob has tits because his testosterone is too high. Raise the testosterone level too much, the body ups the estrogen to seek a balance. (16–17)

In this postmodern version of Romantic *sensibilité*, the male subject cannot ignore the necessity for emotional release, despite the feminizing context of emotions and tears. Using too much effort simply to appear more masculine forces the mind and the body to compensate. Bob and the narrator will later overreact to the regendering of themselves in the self-help groups by forming and joining the fight clubs. The fight clubs fail in the end, in part, because, "testosterone" and "estrogen", denoting the physical and the emotional, as well as the male and female aspects of both the self and the wider society, are still out of balance. If postmodern society has a castrating influence, then, as Palahniuk appears to be saying, it is difficult to compensate for this outside of strong familial and conjugal relationships.

The combination of three of the most important signifiers connected to Rousseau and the Romantic cult of *sensibilité* – tears, breasts, and the maternal – are difficult to ignore in the scenes at the self-help groups with Bob. Rousseau's place in the push for increased sensibilité began with his earliest *Discourses* and reached its height in *La Nouvelle Héloïse*. Timothy O'Hagan is correct in noting that Rousseau balances "romanticism and rationalism" when you consider his entire *oeuvre*, but given the opportunity, Rousseau would often contradict himself, as he does frequently in *La Nouvelle Heloïse* in order to merely "increase the erotic temperature of the novel" (O'Hagan: 32; Cranston: 209). In order to make his point about emotion and natural man and to excite his public, Rousseau was often willing to overdo it, a quality that he clearly shares with Pahlaniuk. In *La Nouvelle Heloïse*, love is rapturous and virtuous no matter what its circumstances and consequences, because the emotions are both intense and honest. Within this emotional landscape, tears are pushed frequently to the foreground. In the famous scene in the *Confessions* where Rousseau attends the opening of his opera dressed casually and unshaven in order to become a version of natural man, Rousseau describes being "moved to the point of tears which [...he] could no longer contain after observing, after the first duet, that [... he] was not the only person who was weeping" (*Confessions*: 369). In his history of the French Revolution, Simon Schama describes Rousseau as leading the "first hot eruption of Romantic sensibility" leading to "the creation of a spoken and written manner that would become the standard voice of the Revolution" (153). Tears are part of this performance, and are "especially prized as evidence not of weakness but sublimity [...]. So Rousseau's heroes and heroines, beginning with himself, sob, weep, and blubber at the slightest provocation" (Schama: 150–1). The narrator of *Fight Club* momentarily understands the sublimity of his tears in his twice-a-month visits to Bob and the testicular cancer group. Like Rousseau at the opera, the narrator needs the people around him to cry before he is able to drop his self-conscious *amour propre* and weep himself. In Rousseau's case in the *Confessions*, this urge to take emotional cues from others is a sign of the continued effect of *amour propre* in leaving him in a location between the emotional necessity and spontaneity of natural man, and the restrained sensibilities of social man.

Throughout his *Confessions*, Rousseau enscribes the female, especially the mother, as the signifier of the confused potential for a return to childhood, nature, and by extension human prehistory, that is ultimately impossible. In taking Augustine's title of "Confessions" for his autobiography, Rousseau was alerting his readers to an ongoing conversation with Augustine in his life narrative. Whereas Augustine's desire to be loved leads him first away from his mother, Monica, and into the arms of his mistress, he is able, later in life, to return to the Christian thinking that Monica had been espousing for him all along. Rousseau leaves Geneva at a similar moment in his life and attaches himself to several mistresses, but in his version of the confessional, an Augustinian-style return "home" is not possible without either a mother or a father available (Rousseau's mother died within days of his birth and legal problems forced Rousseau's father to leave Geneva). Rousseau's "unnatural" environment will not allow a replay of Augustine's conversion and return home, and as a result, when he meets women, he needs them to be both mother and lover. Madame de Warens, Mademoiselle de Lambercier, Madame de Larnage, and Thérèse Lavasseur are each a different version of Rousseau's drive to capture both a "Mamman" and a lover in the same woman.

*Fight Club*'s narrator is located in this same confused place. Marla, the narrator's love interest in the text, is standing across the room at the testicular cancer self-help group meetings, but the narrator reaches out for "Bob", his version of "Mamman". Like Rousseau, a return to a fuller emotional and sexual life is blocked by the need to relocate the maternal in order to make sense of the world. The marginalized confessional subject needs a mommy, or as Rousseau notes in *Emile*, it is the "tender and foresighted mother" who will allow her child to grow to adulthood in a healthy mental and physical state (*Emile*: 37). Bob's new breasts themselves speak to maternity through a symbol that Rousseau worked to reinvent throughout his career.[7] For Rousseau, the breasts are for lactation and not seduction and it is our denatured state that has taken us away from considering breasts as maternal. In *Emile*, Rousseau goes as far as to see the return of the breast to its original occupation as the first step back to nature: "[…] let mothers deign to nurse their children, morals will reform themselves, nature's sentiments will be awakened in every heart, and the state will be repeopled" (46).[8] The importance given to the maternal and "working" breast over the highly-sexed breast on display in the fashionable décolletage of Rousseau's age is recognizable in Eugène Delacroix's canvas "Liberty Leading the People" (1830).[9] The exposed breasts of Liberty coming over the barricades are not primarily sexual, but they speak rather to an allegory of both liberty and maternity in the Romantic French construction of revolutionary fraternity that is recognizeable in the person of Bob in *Fight Club*. Of course, even at the most superficial level, Bob's breasts are merely the narrator's supplement for the mother and the lover in the text, and like the breasts of Liberty on Delacroix's famous canvas, it is difficult to remove breasts entirely from the cultural codes of desire.

In *Of Grammatology*, Derrida explores the question of absence and presence in Rousseau's *Confessions* by noting that the text is governed by a system of textual supplementarity, with a "chain of supplements" placing the maternal alongside a number of signifiers including Madame de Warens, Thérèse Lavasseur, and ultimately nature herself (Derrida: 152–57). Derrida consciously chooses Rousseau's *Confessions* for his close reading of the supplement because Rousseau's philosophical framework in the *Confessions* is designed to probe and problematize the issues –

---

[7] For discussion that highlights Bob and the problem of the maternal in *Fight Club* see Jesse Kavadlo, "The Fiction of Self-Destruction: Chuck Palahniuk, Closet Moralist", (esp. 9– 0).

[8] For Rousseau's extended argument regarding breastfeeding and nature, see *Emile* (esp. 43–46).

[9] For a related discussion of breasts and breastfeeding in the cult of *sensibilité,* see Simon Schama, *Citizens: A Chronicle of the French Revolution* (esp. 145 – 49).

beginning with presence, writing, nature, and truth – that Derrida feels are ill-served by the structuralists' sense of definitions based on binary opposition. But the supplementarity of confessional discourse itself runs far deeper than this. In its focus on the permutations of selfhood and writing, confessional discourse forces the subject to become not only subject and object in its own discourse, but the confessing subject's marginal status in the confessional since Rousseau has made the confessing subject almost always *other* in his or her own discourse. Confessional discourse has a predilection for the production of supplementary *doppelgängers* or "split selves".

Rousseau frequently renames the self-conscious versions of himself, who are both him and not him, "Jean-Jacques" or "Rousseau" in his discourse, but his alterity is also exemplified throughout the *Confessions* by his status as a frustrated natural man living in a denaturing society. This self is forever two or more selves torn by culture and *amour propre*. As Rousseau announces in Book One of the *Confessions*:

> Such were the affections that marked my entry into life; thus there began to take shape or to manifest themselves in me this heart, at once proud and tender, and this character, effeminate and yet indomitable, which, continually fluctuating between weakness and courage, between laxity and virtue, has to the end divided me against myself [...]. (*Confessions*: 11)

The qualities described here come out of Rousseau's disagreement with Hobbes in the *Discourse on the Origin of Inequality*. Rousseau notes that his major problem with Hobbes and the Enlightenment philosophers was that while many spoke of "returning to the state of nature, none of them has reached it", so that when "they spoke about natural man [...] it was social man that they depicted" (*Discourse*: 17). Whereas Hobbes sees mankind, in *Leviathan*, as slipping into a hostile state of nature "where every man is enemy to every man [...and] in such condition, there is [...] consequently [...] no arts; no letters; no society; and which is worst of all, continual fear, and danger of violent death; and the life of man, solitary, poor, nasty, brutish, and short" (Hobbes: 84), Rousseau sees a very different state of nature and vision of humanity in that while man is "intrepid" as Hobbes argues, he is not seeking "only to attack and fight" (*Discourse*: 20). Natural man lives a solitary life in Rousseau's conception in which his bravery is born of understanding his skill and power when faced with the danger of wild animals and enemies wherein "he learns not to fear them anymore" (20). Rousseau's natural man only fights for reasons of self-preservation, preferring in most cases to withdraw from both human contact and conflict, while in the *Leviathan* and elsewhere, Hobbes's alleged mistake is having "wrongly injected into the savage man's concern for self-preservation the need to satisfy the multitude of passions which are the product of society and which have made laws necessary"

(35). Bouncing between weakness and courage and so on, Rousseau circulates be-
tween natural man and social man as a litmus test of his denaturing throughout the
*Confessions*. What is perhaps most striking in the quotation from Book One of the
*Confessions* above is that the process of denaturing is already quite advanced in
Rousseau's childhood, which suggests an othered or divided identity in modern con-
fessional discourse from the earliest years.

Just as Rousseau's confessional discourse bounces its subject between the attributes of natural and social man, the violent *doppelgänger* in *Fight Club* emerges
out of this same web of notions. As a schizophrenic's vision of a more primitive or
natural self, it is telling that Tyler Durden first appears to the narrator naked and involved in producing a primitive sundial. Everything about this sequence adds to the
feeling of being transported back in time to produce an odd version of natural man:

> How I met Tyler was I went to the nude beach. This was the very end of summer and I was asleep. Tyler
> was naked and sweating, gritty with sand, his hair wet and stringy, hanging in his face.
> Tyler had been around a long time before we met.
> Tyler was pulling driftwood logs out of the surf and dragging them up the beach. In the wet sand, he'd al-
> ready planted a half circle of logs up the beach [...]. If I could wake up in a different place, at a different time,
> could I wake up a different person?
> I asked if Tyler was an artist.
> Tyler shrugged and showed me [...] the line he'd drawn in the sand, and how he'd use the line to gauge the
> shadows from each log. (Palahniuk: 32 – 33)

For Rousseau, nakedness and exposure are two of natural man's overriding and formative characteristics: "Accustomed from childhood to inclement weather and the
rigors of the seasons [...] and forced, naked and without arms, to defend their lives
and their prey against other ferocious beasts [...] men develop a robust and nearly
unalterable temperament" (*Discourse*: 19). In the *Confessions*, Rousseau ironizes his
own denatured sexuality and location somewhere between "primitive" man and social
man when he describes exposing himself to the servant girls at a well in Savoy in "a
spectacle more risible than seductive". Unlike the intrepid man in the state of nature
as described in the *Discourse on the Origin of Inequality*, Rousseau is fearful of being
caught and flees only to be cornered by "a big man, with a big moustache, a big hat,
and a big sword, escorted by four or five old women armed with broomsticks" (87).
Here for Rousseau, the combination of fear and nakedness marks the unhealthy and
unnatural doubleness in his personality as he is moved farther from the state of nature. This scene predicts how the naked and more natural Tyler Durden on the beach
signals both the narrator's doubleness and "denatured" status within the logic of late
capitalism in *Fight Club*. Just as nakedness invents the "primitive" in Rousseau's
rhetoric of selfhood, *Fight Club*'s narrator is himself naked and sleeping on a nude

beach when the naked and "primitive" Tyler Durden first appears. Tyler "has been around a long time" because he not only a part of the narrator's identity, but he is also a version of the Enlightenment and Romantic takes on the primitive as well as a conduit back into the depths of human prehistory.

In Rousseau's estimation, allow "a civilized man to gather all his machines around him [...and he will defeat] savage man. But if you want to see even more unequal fight, pit them against each other naked and disarmed, and you will soon realize the advantage of constantly having all of one's forces at one's disposal [...] and of always carrying one's entire self with one" (*Discourse*: 20). This point is particularly timely in this context. The invention of Tyler Durden by the narrator creates a persona who can operate outside of the "machines around him", while this scene also is a unique take on the ability of the narrator to "carry one's entire self with one" by becoming more than one. Tyler Durden fits directly into Derrida's theory of the supplement as a recognizable take on the collision of absence and presence, nature and culture, time and timelessness. His "writing" on the beach suggests a supplemental narrative and point of view, and using Derrida's own terms, Tyler Durden becomes the perfect embodiment of the self's own supplementarity in confessional discourse:

> It is the strange essence of the supplement not to have essentiality: it may not always have taken place. Moreover, literally, it has never taken place: it is never present, here and now. If it were, it would not be what it is, a supplement, taking and keeping the place of the other. (Derrida: 314)

Focusing on, among other things, the complex interplay of subjectivity and the environment, the subject's movement through time in a life narrative, and the desire to control a variety of what is often called the "inner voice", the confessional's own native supplementarity multiplies into the region of identity itself. The postmodern subject's own decentered status expands in a discourse that is a glutton for its own fractured and supplementary form.

The epigraph to Rousseau's *Confessions*, "Underneath and in the skin" (*"Intus, et in Cute"*), points directly to the revolutionary "inner" voice at the heart of Rousseau's project. In melding his ideas regarding the denaturing effects of the wider culture with the story of himself, Rousseau, who was widely seen as the greatest rhetorician of his age, announces that the *Confessions* will need to invent "a whole new language" for penetrating human feelings and describing the personal and social realities of everyday life (*Confessions*: 648). David Fincher's 1999 movie version of *Fight Club* signals the beginnings of both the novel's and the film's acceptance of this now familiar rhetoric of romantic interiority by performing a striking filmic version of

Rousseau's epigraph. As the opening credits roll, a dark and strange terrain appears on-screen, illuminated by frequent electrical flashes and a strange glow. The "eye" of the movie camera appears to fly like an airplane inside a cave or dark enclosed space, while giving the audience only a "rear window" view of the terrain as it vanishes in the near distance. As a visible network of fibrous material thickens and the camera then emerges onto the sweaty and magnified surface of what is unmistakably human skin, it becomes clear that the movie camera has itself been under, inside, and now has arrived outside the skin. Given this context, the viewer can now regard the earlier web of fibrous material as the narrator's brain and neural network, and the flashes of light as electrical impulses along his neurons. The film version then arrives where the novel begins, with Tyler Durden holding a gun in the narrator's mouth. This is the frame narrative and the eventual location of the denouement of both novel and film. Not only does the film's opening sequence unintentionally but rather cannily revisit Rousseau's epigraph, but when the camera emerges from the narrator's brain and the surface of his skin it assumes the point of view of Tyler Durden. The double consciousness represented by the novel's narrator and what is ultimately a schizophrenic projection of himself, as well as the movie camera's insistence on using a "rear view" when emerging from the narrator's brain, also reinvents Rousseau's confessional intentions visually. The Rousseauian confessional narrative is an attempt by the self to look both at and inside the self in this manner.

In *Fight Club*, Tyler Durden looks at the narrator from within the narrator in what turns out to be a disembodied way. From the start of his *Confessions*, Rousseau is extremely self-conscious of two or more "selves" invented by the process of looking back on and narrating a life. In the Neuchâtel preface he notes that the *Confessions* "will be painting a double portrait of [his] state of mind, at the moment when the event happened and the moment when [he] described it" (648). Rousseau continues, noting that his choppy confessional approach is itself "part of the story", because his uneven personality and radical effort to describe himself and his feelings demand that he invent new rules of style, and "in whatever style this work is written, it will always, because of its very object, be a book that is precious to philosophers; it offers [...] a point of comparison for the study of the human heart, and it the only such document in existence" (*Confessions*: 648). In the end, *Fight Club*'s confessional discourse is even more uneven and choppy than that of the *Confessions* in its effort to bring a schizophrenic point of view to what has long been identified as a schizophrenic culture. Pahlaniuk's narrator's confessions turn inward to expose his raw emotional core, personified in the projection of Tyler Durden, which illustrates a "doubled portrait" of the narrator's state of mind.

In *Fight Club*, the discourse of alterity and interiority takes a page from another popular and strikingly uncanny confessional form that echoes the desire to construct a discourse that goes "in and under the skin". In the abandoned house he occupies with Tyler Durden, the narrator "found stacks and stacks of *Readers Digest* in the basement and now there's a pile of *Reader's Digest* in every room". These magazines are present throughout the narrative and the narrator soon finds that "in the oldest magazines, there's a series of articles where organs in the human body talk about themselves in the first person: I am Jane's Uterus. I am Joe's Prostate" (Palahniuk: 58). From this point on in the narrative, the narrator alerts the reader to his inward turn and ultimately his schizophrenia by way of the formula "I am Joe's $x$", where "x" reflects on the affective rather than physical anatomy of the narrator. For example, "I'm Joe's Raging Bile Duct" and "I'm Joe's Grinding Teeth" describe the narrator's frustration and jealousy at hearing Tyler Durden describe his sexual relationship with Marla Singer (59). These are fitting additions to confessional discourse in a number of ways beyond their pointing to the confessional's effort to describe the emotions and therefore the "inside" of the narrator. Not only is the first-person narrator a necessary ingredient of most confessional discourse, but the confessional since Augustine is itself a discourse focused on the body, especially the sexual body. Rousseau expanded on the confessional's traditional interest in sexuality when his *Confessions* became a tracking of the problems associated with his own body's unnatural medical history.

Rousseau was a notorious hypochondriac, who attempted to be in touch with his body as well as his feelings. In Book Six of the *Confessions*, Rousseau remarks that "what set the seal of [...his] disquiet" was reading physiology and anatomy texts so that "constantly revising the multitude and functioning of the parts of which [...his] body was composed [...he] expected to feel it go wrong twenty times a day" (*Confessions*: 242). The formulaic voice of the "I am Joe's/Jane's" series is nothing if not disquieting in how it both makes the reader feel, and in how it predicts the plot of *Fight Club*. As in "I am Joe's Heart", which I will use as an example, the uncanny talking body part announces that Joe is not taking good care of himself and admits such things as "Joe had a heart attack five years ago and didn't even know it" and that he frequently skips a beat while Joe is sleeping (Ratcliffe: 60). Joe's and Jane's body parts work and talk while Joe and Jane sleep, while admitting things about Joe and

Jane that they themselves do not know. The total effect is uncanny, to say the least, and *Fight Club*'s narrator internalizes this and projects another disquieting version of this "inner voice" in the persona of Tyler Durden, who himself acts while the narrator sleeps.

Rousseau's confessional discourse warns specifically about the power of reading to shape the imagination in dangerous and unforeseen ways. In Book One of the *Confessions*, Rousseau describes the negative effects of imaginative literature on his life in some detail. After reading the Greek and Roman classics, such as Plutarch's *Lives*, as well as his mother's romances, Rousseau begins to imagine himself a Greek or Roman or romantic hero rather than himself. The effect lasts well into adulthood and left him "with some bizarre and romantic notions about human life, of which experience and reflection never quite manage to cure [him]" (*Confessions*: 8). Within the broader context of the modern subject, Rousseau is offering himself as an exemplum of the power of the culture of information to insinuate itself into the identity of the individual and help to produce numerous versions of the self. This same problem, increased by the machinery of what we now call "the information age", can turn seemingly benign texts into overwhelming metaphors of selfhood, as happens with the "I am Joe's" articles in *Fight Club*.

In his 1925 essay "*Das Unheimliche*", Freud defines the uncanny as "the familiar made unfamiliar" and uses this idea to consider the uncanny effects of the double in examples ranging from the *doppelgänger* in E.T.A. Hoffmann's "The Sand-Man" to Freud's own personal experience of seeing, but not instantly recognizing his own image in a mirror upon boarding a darkened train. Often latent in Freud's categories of the uncanny is some aspect of repressed sexuality. Late in his essay, Freud recalls the uncanny repetition that went with a trip to Italy. What is important here is the combination of sexual repression and repetition in the formation of the uncanny:

> Strolling one hot summer afternoon through the empty and to me unfamiliar streets of a small Italian town, I found myself in a district about whose character I could not long remain in doubt. Only heavily made-up women were to be seen at the windows of little houses, and I hastily left the narrow street at the next turning. However, after wandering about for some time without asking the way, I suddenly found myself back in the same street, where my presence began to attract attention. Once more I hurried away, only to return again by a different route. I was now seized by a feeling that I can only describe as uncanny [...]. (Freud: 145)

Here, sexual desire and repression, combined with the repeated return to the red light district, produce a distinctly uncanny experience. The "heavily made-up women" of the quarter recognize immediately what Freud can only know later upon reflection, that it is sexual desire that is motivating this "compulsion to repeat" which is so often characteristic of the uncanny more generally (145). In *Fight Club*, the double plays the familiar gothic role of ameliorating the necessity to face a meaningful relationship, in this case with Marla Singer. In his essay, Freud uses E.T.A. Hoffmann's gothic tale, *The Sand-Man*, as the paradigmatic example of the uncanny *doppelgänger*. In this story, the *doppelgänger* only appears to interrupt Nathaniel's healthy personal and sexual relationship with Clara, which leaves Freud to ask "why does the Sand-Man always appear as the disruptor of love" (140)? In many ways this question answers itself, in that the *doppelgänger* is the sign of the repression of, or flight from sexual desire and sexual relationships in both *Fight Club* and *The Sand-Man*. In *Fight Club*, the *doppelgänger* performs this by being the supplementary lover himself:

> One morning, there's the dead jellyfish of a used condom floating in the toilet.
> This is how Tyler meets Marla.
> I get up to take a leak, and there against the sort of cave paintings of dirt in the toilet bowl is this. You have to wonder, what do sperm think.
> *This?*
> *This is the vaginal wall?* (Palahniuk: 56, Palahniuk's emphasis)

The narrator then announces that despite his dreams of having sex with Marla Singer, which appear to be confusing him here, it is Tyler Durden's condom in the toilet that is his first clue that Marla and Tyler are sleeping together. Before his description of his experience in Italy, Freud remarks that an uncanny feeling " recalls the helplessness we experience in certain dream-states" (Freud: 144). The narrator's "dream" is just such a moment when the confident and attractive Tyler Durden becomes the narrator's preferred version of himself. Freud describes this as the uncanny *doppelgänger*'s *modus operandi*: "a person may identify himself with another and so become unsure of his true self; or he may substitute the other's self for his own. The self may thus be duplicated, divided, and interchanged" (142). Confused by his desire for a relationship with Marla Singer and his desire for a mother (signaled by the strange sexual/natal description of the "vaginal wall"), the narrator projects a version of "primitive" sexuality in Tyler Durden that has a direct antecedent in Rousseau's confessional discourse.

Even in his description of the toilet, *Fight Club*'s narrator has evoked a primitive setting somewhere in human prehistory by describing the bowl as marked by some "sort of cave paintings of dirt". As a matter of course, Rousseau transports himself back into human history figuratively in the *Confessions* in a manner that suggests aspects of this highly sexualized "return to the cave" in *Fight Club*. Late in Book Six, and just after Rousseau announces the disquieting effects of medical literature considered above, Rousseau describes traveling down the Rhône River to take a cure for vapours and meeting enroute Madame de Larnage, a forty-four year old mother of ten children who very much fits into Rousseau's vision of the mother/lover. As a sign of his denaturing, Rousseau notes that he is unable to act on Madame de Larnage's advances, and in order to increase his confidence he automatically "invents" his own version of the *doppelgänger*:

> For some bizarre reason that escapes me, I decided to pass myself off as English: I presented myself as a Jacobite, which seemed to satisfy them, called myself Dudding, and was known to the company as M. Dudding [...]. I managed to get away with it, relieved that no one had thought to question me about the English language, of which I did not know one single word. (*Confessions*: 244)

The more Madame de Larnage presses for his attentions, the more he is "in a torment" until "she broke the silence" by kissing Rousseau in a way that "spoke too clearly to leave me in any doubt" (246). Rousseau goes on to describe himself at this point as "a changed man" who for four days experienced "the most voluptuous pleasures. Their taste was pure and strong, unmixed with any pain. They were the first and only ones [... he had] tasted that way" (247). The lovers separate without remorse, and Rousseau chooses not to renew the relationship with a visit he had promised. This construction of a pure, uncomplicated sexuality appears to be right out of human prehistory in the *Discourse on the Origin of Inequality*, where Rousseau describes "primitive" human sexuality as "limited merely to the physical aspect of love [...] each man peacefully awaits the impetus of nature, gives himself over to it without choice, and with more pleasure than frenzy; and once the need is satisfied, all desire is snuffed out" (40). Like the narrator in *Fight Club* who places his double Tyler Durden in a cave and other "primitive" settings rather than face a relationship with Marla Singer, Rousseau projects Dudding in his place as a flawed and confused version of prehistoric man and prehistoric sexuality. The status of Dudding as a Jacobite fits the anti-despotic political message underlying Rousseau's interest in human prehistory and gives Rousseau's *doppelgänger* a mild variety of the revolutionary persona that will occupy the foreground in *Fight Club*.

*Fight Club*'s interest in human prehistory finally completely joins with Rousseau's conversation with Hobbes in the *Discourse on the Origin of Inequality* late in the narrative as the narrator begins to question Tyler Durden and other individuals in the fight clubs about the organization's activities, aspirations, and ideology. When he questions a fight club member, with the menacing name of "the mechanic", about the organization, his responses are "pure Tyler Durden" as he wanders through a number of revolutionary slogans until he states, "imagine hunting elk through the damp canyon forests around the ruins of Rockefeller Center" (Palahniuk: 149–150). Later, as the narrator searches for ways to destroy Tyler Durden, the same sentence reemerges in the narrator's own discourse: "Imagine stalking elk through the deep canyon forests around Rockefeller Center" (199). The ultimate goal of Tyler Durden's anarchist movement is the erasure of history and a return to human prehistory based on a pugilistic and Hobbesian view of the state of nature.[10] In a manner that suggests the intrusion of the qualities of postmodernity, for Tyler Durden, the state of nature becomes an utopia, an aesthetic, and a preferred reactionary life style. The anti-aesthetic postmodern artist who originally appeared building a primitive and shadow-casting sundial while naked, now wishes to act again in his own much larger piece of primitivist performance art in the shadows of Rockefeller Center.

The violent tensions between the narrator and Tyler Durden regarding "project mayhem" can be read as an echo of the ongoing debate over whether the French Revolution can be blamed on Rousseau and his confessional discourse. People began to understand the power of the confessional voice beginning in Rousseau's day, where Edmund Burke and numerous others saw a Rousseau-style search for an "inner voice" as a symptom of a dangerous and revolutionary turn, one that was parroted on the streets of Paris during the French Revolution. François Furet notes that "the urge

---

[10] Krister Friday reads *Fight Club* as taking on the larger problem of postmodern historicity. He notes that the text offers an alternative to Jameson's well-known idea that the "omnipresence of a totalizing spatial logic of global capitalism [has] preempted all attempts to "think the totality"." Friday continues:

> With the absence of a viable conceptuality to "think the totality" of the present in ontological , historical, or material/cultural terms, we are still left with the exigencies of constructing identities – a process that nonetheless still invokes History and periodization as the necessary, transcendent horizons for framing identity, even if these are large empty, formal categories without content or closure. For this reason, perhaps Jameson was right to suggest that fictive narrative articulates "our collective *fantasies* about history and reality" (emphasis added) (*Political Unconscious*: 34), but only if an emphasis on fantasy obliges further exploration of how psychoanalysis can frame the historiographic impulse, especially as it underwrites identity. In other words, "thinking historically" is a process that can never locate its object qua period/identity, but according to *Fight Club*, what may be more important is the way that the process of failure becomes itself a more fundamental dynamic of identity formation in postmodern historicity. (para.: 32)

I would only add that by imitating Rousseau's use of a "primitive" type as one of their "transcendent horizons for framing identity" and revisiting the Rousseauian confessional's own emphasis on "the process of failure [...] as a fundamental dynamic of identity formation", *Fight Club*'s author and narrator connect themselves to a long struggle to "think the totality" within constructions of identity that points to Rousseau and the Romantic attacks on the Enlightenment as a formative moment in the postmodernity that Friday describes here.

to cast Jean-Jacques Rousseau as the author of the French Revolution is as old as the event itself". Rousseau's place in framing the French Revolution is clearest when Robespierre "wielded his power by means of an ideological authority in which the cult of Rousseau figures not only centrally but almost exclusively" (Furet: 168). *Fight Club*, then, can be seen as returning to and reinventing the revolutionary and reactionary history of Rousseau's confessional and anti-aristocratic voice through Tyler Durden's efforts to turn the fight clubs into Project Mayhem's "great revolution against culture" that will not only "redistribute the wealth of the world", but ultimately rewrite history by destroying "the national museum, which is Tyler's real target" (149 and 14). Although Rousseau may have never intended his work as revolutionary, in the "barricades" sense of the term, there is something of Tyler Durden in the Rousseau at the end of the Geneva manuscript of the *Confessions* who added this note for a public reading of the work before an aristocratic audience in 1770:

> I have told the truth. If anyone knows things that are contrary to what I have just set out […] he knows lies and deceits […]. As for me, I hereby declare publicly and without fear: that anyone who, without even having read my writings, examines with his own eyes my nature, my character, my morals, my inclinations, my pleasures, my habits, and can think me a dishonourable man, is himself a man who ought to be choked. (*Confessions*: 642)

And perhaps this is a consciously crafted "palatable" version of the potentially violent, if only in his rhetoric, denatured "social man" that Rousseau felt had been the major error of Hobbes in his effort to locate a fighting man in the state of nature. Tyler Durden will ultimately make a version of the same Hobbesian mistake in *Fight Club*, feeling that embracing and controlling our brutish natures in the rules and laws of fight clubs would allow a more natural and authentic self to emerge. Charles Taylor notes that "what is often mistaken for primitivism in Rousseau is his undoubted espousal of austerity against a civilization of increasing needs and consumption" (Taylor: 359). Rousseau would certainly see Tyler Durden and the narrator as reacting rightly against the warped logic of the consumer culture, but he would also see their primitivism as something that ignores the realities of postmodern life. The so-called "noble savage", as the name implies, was meant only as a barometer of human goodness and possibilities, and not as a license to destroy.

Within the parameters of confessional discourse, the production of the uncanny, and the neo-gothic interests of postmodernity that I have been considering here, it is likely that there are numerous other places in current popular culture where allegories of a kind of fear and fascination with our own alterity, return once again to the original critics of the Enlightenment. In my mind, this is the uncanny Freudian "compulsion to repeat" that is most central in *Fight Club*: the postmodern subject desires a return to the maternal and uncanny moment of its own birth in the Romantics' most powerful critiques of the Enlightenment, and when we arrive there, we often see an uncanny version of ourselves. Not surprisingly, this double is often a version of the confessional, troubled, and marginalized modern subjectivity first described by Jean-Jacques Rousseau.

The uncanny may be a priviledged mechanism for calibrating a return to the Romantics' original critiques of the Enlightenment because, like Rousseau's secular version of confessional discourse, the uncanny was "invented" by the Romantics as a reaction to the Enlightenment. Terry Castle has noted an important and highly suggestive historical trajectory which unpacks the uncanny as a reaction to the Enlightenment:

> the Freudian uncanny is a function of *enlightenment*: it is that which confronts us, paradoxically after a certain light has been cast, and it is then connected to this that the eighteenth century in a sense "invented the uncanny": that the very psychic and cultural transformations that led to the subsequent glorification of the period as an age of reason or enlightenment – the aggressively rationalist imperatives of the epoch – also produced, like a kind of toxic side effect, a new human experience of strangeness, anxiety, bafflement, and intellectual impasse." (Castle: 7–8)

Castle proposes quite rightly that the uncanny develops out of a reaction to Enlightenment reason and is exemplified perhaps at its purest in E.T.A. Hoffmann's romantic *Tales* beginning in the 1790's. Freud's uncanny can be read as both "a historical allegory" and a "diachronistic structuring" that is "a version of the familiar psychoanalytic distinction between archaic and the contemporary, the "primitive" and the "civilized". Castle points out that for Freud:

> what makes the *doppelgänger* now seem uncanny (a "ghastlyharbinger of death") is precisely the fact that we have grown out of that "very early mental stage" when the double functioned as a figure of existential reassurance – just as human culture as a whole has moved beyond the animistic beliefs characteristic of "primitive" or magic-based societies". (9)

Of course, this is the same trajectory – from the state of nature to the modern – that is at the center of Rousseau's philosophy and is still center-stage in the confessional constructions of the narrator in Pahlanhiuk's *Fight Club*. As a discourse focused on describing modernity's effects in a manner frequently parallel to the uncanny's "encompassing sense of strangeness and unease [which] Freud finds so characteristic of modern life", (Castle: 10) the often confessional voice of the postmodern subject is very much rooted in ongoing concern with a "primitive" or "natural" way of seeing or living.

In *Fight Club*, placing Rousseauian confessional discourse and the Gothic within a postmodern context exposes the proximity between Romantic and Postmodern constructions of the subject, in part because the Romantic position regarding selfhood was never simply an across the board belief in a whole and unified self. *Fight Club*'s status as both Romantic and Postmodern illustrates that the perceived differences between the Romantic and Postmodern are part of the evolution and intensification of modernity within postmodernity, and are, therefore, often merely differences in degree rather than in substance. Romantic discourses frequent postmodernity, because, as the original critics of the Enlightenment, Rousseau and the Romantics helped to develop the metaphors of selfhood and other critical equipment that have become part of the standard toolbox for describing, diagnosing, and deconstructing the postmodern condition.

## Works cited

Baudrillard, Jean. "The Ecstasy of Communication". Trans. John Johnston, in *The Anti-Aesthetic: Essays on Postmodern Culture*. Ed. Hal Foster. Seattle: Bay Press, 1983. 126–34.

Berger, John. *Ways of Seeing*. London: BBC and Penguin, 1972.

Berman, Marshall. *All That Is Solid Melts Into Air: The Experience of Modernity* (1982). New York: Penguin Books, 1988.

Boon, Kevin. "Men and Nostalgia for Violence: Culture and Culpability in Chuck Palahniuk's Fight Club." *Journal of Men's Studies: A Scholarly Journal about Men and Masculinities*. 11.3 (2003): 267–76.

Brooks, Peter. *Troubling Confessions: Speaking Guilt in Law and Literature*. University of Chicago Press, 2000.

Castle, Terry. "Introduction." *The Female Thermometer. Eighteenth-Century Culture and the Invention of the Uncanny*. Oxford: Oxford University Press, 1995. 3–20.

Cranston, Maurice. *The Noble Savage : Jean-Jacques Rousseau, 1754-1762*. New York: Penguin, 1991.

Damrosch, Leo. *Jean-Jacques Rousseau*. New York: Houghton Mifflin, 2005.

Davis, Michael. *The Autobiography of Philosophy: Rousseau's The Reveries of the Solitary Walker*. Lanham: Rowman and Littlefield, 1999.

Deleuze, Gilles and Felix Guattari. *Anti-Oedipus: Capitalism and Schizophrenia*. Trans. Robert Hurley, Mark Seem, and Helen R. Lane Minneapolis : University of Minnesota Press, 1983.

Derrida, Jacques. *Of Grammatology*. Trans. G.C. Spivak. Baltimore: Johns Hopkins University Press, 1997.

Elsaesser, Thomas. *Metropolis*. London: British Film Institute, 2000.

*Fight Club*. Screenplay by Jim Uhls. Dir. David Fincher. 20th Century Fox, 1999.

Foucault, Michel. *The History of Sexuality, Vol. 1: An Introduction*. Trans. Robert Hurley. New York: Vintage Books, 1978.

Freud, Sigmund. *The Uncanny*. Trans. David McLintock. New York: Penguin, 2003.

Friday, Krister. "'A Generation of Men Without History': *Fight Club*, Masculinity, and the Historical Symptom". *Postmodern Culture*, 31.3 (2003). Available at http://muse.jhu.edu/journals/postmodern culture.

Furet, François. "Rousseau and the French Revolution", in *The Legacy of Rousseau*. Ed. Clifford Orwin and Nathan Tarcov. Chicago: University of Chicago Press: 168–82.

Garrard, Graeme. *Rousseau's Counter-Enlightenment: A Republican Critique of the Philosophes.* Albany: State University of New York Press, 2003.

Giroux, Henry A., and Imre Szeman, "IKEA Body and the Politics of Male Bonding: Fight Club, Consumerism, and Violence." *New Art Examiner* 28 (2000/2001): 32–37 and 60–61.

Hobbes, Thomas. *Leviathan*. Oxford University Press, 1996.

Jameson, Frederick. "Postmodernism and Consumer Society", in *The Anti-Aesthetic: Essays on Postmodern Culture*. Ed. Hal Foster. Seattle: Bay Press, 1983: 111–25.

Kavadlo, Jesse. "The Fiction of Self-Destruction: Chuck Palahniuk, Closet Moralist." *Stirrings Still: The International Journal of Existential Literature.* 2.2 (2005): 3–24.

Kelly, Christopher. *Rousseau as Author: Consecrating One's Life to the Truth*. University of Chicago Press, 2003.

Kelly, Christopher. "Introduction". *Confessions*. Trans. Christopher Kelly. Hanover: University Press of New England, 1995: xvii–xxxvi.

Kelly, Christopher. *Rousseau's Exemplary Life: The Confessions as Political Philosophy*. Ithaca: Cornell University Press, 1987.

Mathews, Peter. "Diagnosing Chuck Palahniuk's Fight Club." *Stirrings Still: The International Journal of Existential Literature.* 2.2 (2005): 81–104.

O'Hagan, Timothy. *Rousseau*. New York: London, 1999.

O'Hagan, Timothy. "Preface". *John-Jacques Rousseau and the Sources of the Self.* Ed. Timothy O'Hagan. Brookfield VT: Ashgate, 1997: vii–viii.

Ratcliffe, J.D. "I am Joe's Heart." *Reader's Digest.* April 1967: 59–62.

Rousseau, Jean-Jacques. *Confessions.* Trans. Angela Scholar. Oxford UP, 2000.

Rousseau, Jean-Jacques. "Preface to Neuchâtel Manuscript of Confessions", in *Confessions.* Trans. Angela Scholar. Oxford UP, 2000. 643–49.

Rousseau, Jean-Jacques. *Emile or On Education.* Trans. Allan Bloom. New York: Basic Books, 1979.

Rousseau, Jean-Jacques. *Discourse on the Origin of Inequality.* Trans. James Miller. Indianapolis: Hackett Publishing, 1992.

Rousseau, Jean-Jacques. *Julie, or, The new Heloise: Letters of Two Lovers who Live in a Small Town at the Foot of the Alps.* Trans. Philip Stewart and Jean Vaché. Hanover: University Press of New England, 1997.

Rousseau, Jean-Jacques. *Rousseau, Judge of Jean-Jacques, Dialogues.* Ed. Roger D. Masters and Christopher Kelly. Trans. Judith R. Bush, Christopher Kelly, and Roger D. Masters. Hanover : University Press of New England, 1990.

Schama, Simon. *Citizens: A Chronicle of the French Revolution.* New York: Knopf, 1989.

Stelzig, Eugene L. *The Romantic Subject in Autobiography: Rousseau and Goethe.* Charlotteville: University Press of Virginia, 2000.

Tambling, Jeremy. *Confession: Sexuality, Sin, and the Subject.* New York: St. Martin's Press, 1990.

Taylor, Charles. *Sources of the Self: The Making of Modern Identity.* Cambridge: Harvard University Press, 1989.

Todorov, Tzvetan. *Frail Happiness: An Essay of Rousseau.* Trans. John T. Scott and Robert D. Zaretsky. University Park: Pennsylvania State University Press, 2001.

Velkley, Richard. *Being After Rousseau.* Chicago: University of Chicago Press, 2002.

Žižek, Slavoj. "The Ambiguity of the Masochistic Social Link." *Perversion and the Social Relation.* Eds. Molly Anne Rothenberg, Dennis Foster, and Slavoj Žižek. Durham: Duke University Press, 2003: 112–25.

# A Body of Information: Posthumanism, the Digital Doppelgänger and Don DeLillo's *White Noise*

Natalia Lizama

This essay interrogates the theme of the double in relation to the philosophy of posthumanism, focusing on Don DeLillo's novel, *White Noise*.[11] Within the narrative of *White Noise*, the double is manifested as a form of digital doppelgänger, a technologised other that doubles the original subject, Jack Gladney, and portends his death. Where the doppelgänger has historically been imagined as an incorporeal entity (comprised perhaps of ectoplasm or completely insubstantial) or one that takes monstrous corporeal form, the doppelgänger in *White Noise* takes the form of digital information derived from medical diagnostic technologies. The complex representation of the digital doppelgänger in *White Noise*, when considered in relation to posthuman theory, elucidates the potential for both a new reading of the novel and an understanding of the posthuman subject that, following N. Katherine Hayles, accounts for embodied subjectivity.[12] The posthuman in such a context need not be constrained by technological determinism wherein the "authentic", non-technologised "human" is posited in opposition to the technologised "posthuman" as "other" or doppelgänger, but rather, posthuman ontology exists as a circular and reciprocal mode of embodiment, situated in the unstable and shifting interaction between individual and doppelgänger.

Since its publication in 1984, *White Noise* has been the subject of repeated analysis and critique, particularly in relation to postmodern theory, with critics suggesting that the recurring images of simulacra throughout the novel exemplify the trope of postmodernity.[13] Indeed, as Matthew J. Packer points out, analysis of White Noise in terms of postmodern simulation is so exhaustive that the novel is by now "is own 'most photographed barn in America'" (Packer: 648). In light of this, it might seem that yet another critique of *White Noise* is superfluous. However, whereas previous analyses of *White Noise* have interrogated the novel from postmodern and ecocritical perspectives, this essay sheds new light on *White Noise* by contextualising the novel in relation to posthuman theory and the trope of the doppelgänger. In turn, the

---

[11] All references to *White Noise* are to the Picador (1984) edition, hereafter cited in parenthesis.
[12] See Hayles, *How We Became Posthuman: Virtual Bodies in Cybernetics, Literature, and Informatics* (1999).
[13] See for example, Laura Barrett (2001–2002), Leonard Wilcox (1991), and Dana Phillips (1998).

representation of the doppelgänger within *White Noise* provides insight into a model of the posthuman that focuses on shifting subjectivity rather than human-posthuman binary categorisation.

*White Noise* revolves around a series of remarkable events in the life of its protagonist, Jack Gladney, an academic at a fictional Midwestern university in the United States. Early in the novel, Jack is exposed to a toxic chemical agent during an industrial accident termed the "Airborne Toxic Event", during which a train laden with poisonous chemicals is derailed, resulting in the formation of an enormous black chemical cloud in the air. The airborne cloud travels across the land and Jack and his family are forced to evacuate their homes and seek sanctuary in an abandoned Boy Scout campground as the cloud approaches their home town. Whilst travelling to the campground, Jack leaves the safety of his car to refuel and in doing so is exposed to the cloud's toxic chemical, Nyodene D., for several minutes. Upon arrival at the campground, he then undergoes a medical assessment to determine the implications of his exposure to the chemical. This assessment accounts for both the duration of his exposure to Nyodene D. and his entire life history, incorporating "[his] medicals, [his] psychologicals [and his] police-and-hospitals" (DeLillo: 141). The prognosis for Jack is both disturbing and ambiguous: the test results that form his "whole data profile" appear as "bracketed numbers with pulsing stars" on a computer screen that the medical technician is unable to decipher (141–42). Throughout the course of the novel, Jack undergoes repeated medical tests using a variety of diagnostic technologies, all of which result in the same pulsing stars and bracketed numbers that comprise his "whole data profile".

This essay contends that Jack's whole data profile comprised of this cryptic information functions as a form of informatic double or "digital doppelgänger". Like the doppelgänger of fiction and myth, the digital doppelgänger similarly evokes the trope of the supernatural and portends death. Yet, unlike the traditional doppelgänger, the digital doppelgänger is comprised of digital information, and in this way the informatic double is an ulterior self embodied within technology. Additionally, whereas the traditional doppelgänger narrative typically involves an original subject who is threatened by the double in the form of a sinister impostor of the self, Jack and his digital doppelgänger are involved in a complex exchange of selfhood wherein neither his embodied or informatic selves are privileged as authentic. In this way, the relationship between Jack and his digital doppelgänger can be understood to reveal a posthuman ontology that is based upon reciprocity between multiple technologised subjects. This essay will firstly outline the ways in which the informatic double in *White Noise* functions, in many ways, similarly to the spectral doppelgänger of Gothic and science fiction through its seemingly supernatural capacity to portend death, before discussing the reconfiguration of the doppelgänger in terms of digital information and its incorporation of posthuman ontology.

## Digital Doppelgängers

The term "doppelgänger", meaning literally "double-goer", was coined in the late eighteenth-century by Jean Paul Richter in his novel *Siebenkäs*. Richter uses the term in relation to the novel's protagonist who encounters his own double, and describes the term in a footnote as denoting "people who see themselves" (Živković: 122).[14] During the nineteenth century the doppelgänger motif became popularised in Gothic literature, such as that of E.T.A. Hoffman, Edgar Allen Poe, Mary Shelley and Robert Louis Stevenson.[15] In the fictions of these authors, the figure of the doppelgänger was portrayed as a shadowy and often supernatural entity that mirrored and threatened the self, frequently serving a harbinger of death or evil, and appearing as a grotesque and frightful figure. In the early twentieth century, the figure of the doppelgänger was re-visited and reinterpreted in light of psychoanalytic theory, with Otto Rank conducting a study of *Der Doppelgänger* and Sigmund Freud extrapolating on the trope of the double in relation to the uncanny.[16] In such analyses, the doppelgänger was seen to present a radical threat to ontological stability; by replicating the self, and in doing so challenging an individual's uniqueness, it presented, as Dimitris Vardoulakis notes, "a notion of the subject/subjectivity that [was] defective, disjunct, split, threatening, spectral" (Vardoulakis: 100). Following this historical trajectory, the doppelgänger in western culture is seen to threaten the self through its presage of death and its embodiment of dual subjectivity, wherein the authenticity of selfhood is problematised.

---

[14] In a footnote to *Siebenkäs*, Richter describes the term doppelgänger thus: "So heissen Leute, die sich selbst sehen." (So people who see themselves are called").
[15] As Hillel Schwartz notes, western culture is permeated with narratives of "cloning gone wrong", in which the creation of the human-like life is seen to result in disaster for its creator. Novels such as Mary Shelley's *Frankenstein* or Robert Louis Stevenson's *The Strange Case of Dr Jekyll and Mr Hyde*, in which a monstrous being brings destruction and despair to its creator, exemplify this cultural myth and are indicative of a profound cultural anxiety about the ethics of replicating human life (Schwartz: 351). For a further discussion of the doppelgänger in relation to speculative fiction, see Frank Dietz (1998).
[16] Otto Rank (1971), Sigmund Freud (1955).

The term "digital doppelgänger" has been used recently within the popular press to describe a number of phenomena. In her article, "Digital Doppelgängers", Lisa Bode notes that the term has been used to denote an actor's digital duplicate in the form of a computer-generated image (Bode: 4). As Bode explains, within the context of digital cinema, a "digital likeness" of an actor is "birthed in a computer and made to gesture in the performer's stead"; in such an instance, "digital doppelgänger" denotes a duplicate body existing within the imagined world of digital cinema (8).[17] In addition to Bode's theorization of the term, "digital doppelgänger" has also been used in popular media to denote, variously an online presence or identity; a digital image such as an avatar used to represent an online persona; or the digital footprints left by an individual's travels through cyberspace.[18] Yet, with the exception of Bode's article, in which she briefly mentions the capacity of the double to elicit a fear of "decorporealised detachment from one's own likeness", the use of the term doppelgänger in such examples, for the most part, tends to disregard its potential for eliciting anxiety and fear through functioning as a presage of death. Rather, "doppelgänger" is used almost synonymously with duplicate, indicating a likeness or representation, albeit in digital format. This essay contends that the term "digital doppelgänger", when considered in relation to the informatic double of *White Noise*, elucidates a model of posthumanism in which the ambiguous ontology of the double is reconfigured in accordance with technology.

The digital doppelgänger in *White Noise,* in the form of Jack's whole data profile, contains not only information about the ramifications of his exposure to Nyodene D., but also incorporates his entire life's history; as the technician at the campground informs Jack, because of the "massive data-base tally, [...] you are the sum total of your data" (DeLillo: 141). Thus Jack's whole data profile denotes, within the discourse of medical informatics, the sum total of his self, the entirety of his being. It simultaneously mirrors his entire self and exists separately from him as a discrete entity, a body of information comprising indecipherable computerised symbols. By replicating Jack in this way, the whole data profile functions within the narrative of *White Noise* as a digitised doppelgänger, a double that reproduces and destabilises the original subject in a way similar to that of the traditional doppelgänger.

---

[17] Angela Ndalianis (2002) refers to such entities as "synthespians".
[18] See for example Ron Magid (1998), Ben Fritz (2003), and Dawn Chimielewski (2005). Schwartz also suggests that "musicians have made a pact with their Doppelgängers" in reference to digitally edited music production in which "Doppelgängers do the definitive, replayable work" of musicians (Schwartz: 377).

Indeed, the digital doppelgänger of *White Noise* has a number of similarities with the traditional doppelgänger, first evident in the representation of Jack's data profile as imbued with "supernatural" qualities. This is foreshadowed during the Airborne Toxic Event, in the black cloud of Nyodene D. drifting through the air that will eventually be incorporated into Jack's informatic data profile. The cloud of Nyodene D., described by the media variously as a "feathery plume", a "black billowing cloud", and finally the "airborne toxic event" (113–17) is, like the figure of the doppelgänger, an ethereal and shadowy form, an ominous and supernatural portent that incites fear and anxiety in the characters within the novel. As Peter Boxall describes the Airborne Toxic Event, the characters in the novel regard the black cloud of Nyodene with an "awed approach" that recalls "sublime biblical revelation" (Boxall: 113). Indeed, as Jack describes in the novel, the black cloud is conceived by those who see it "in a simple and primitive way, as [...] something not subject to control" (DeLillo: 127). This notion of the black cloud as "a death made in the laboratory" (127) that nonetheless defies scientific rationality resonates with nineteenth-century representations of doppelgängers, such as Stevenson's Mr Hyde or Shelley's monster created by Frankenstein.[19] In such examples the double is manifested as a grotesquely primitive and bestial entity, one that exists beyond the realm of the rational despite its being a by-product of science. Nyodene D. is similarly imbued with this sense of the supernatural and primitive through its immunity to quantitative or rational scientific categorisation, remaining as mysteriously incomprehensible as the billowing black cloud that loomed ominously during the Airborne Toxic Event.

Throughout the novel, Jack undergoes repeated medical tests to determine the ramifications of his exposure to Nyodene D., yet is unable to obtain a clear diagnosis of his condition. The most informative prognosis that that can be obtained from his whole data profile is one of an imminent "nebulous mass" resulting from Nyodene D. exposure that will eventually grow within his body and ultimately lead to his death. When Jack attempts to obtain further information about the specificities of this "nebulous mass", he is informed that it is a "possible growth in the body" and that "[i]t's called a nebulous mass because it has no definite shape, form or limits" (280). The mystery that surrounds Nyodene D. is again reinstated when Jack seeks information about its side-effects; he learns that it causes rats to grow "urgent lumps" (111) and sends them "into a permanent state" (139) yet what exactly a "permanent state"

---

[19]Shelley and Stevenson's narratives depict the doppelgänger as an artificially created monstrous double. However, within Gothic fiction, the doppelgänger also often appears in the form of an apparition or spectre.

or an "urgent lump" is never clarified. The nebulous mass that lurks embodied within Jack's informatic double, portending death, is, like the doppelgänger, shrouded in ambiguity and resists conceptualisation by scientific or medical discourse.[20]

Just as the characters within the novel conceive of the black cloud of Nyodene D in a "primitive" and pre-scientific way, as if with a sense of apocalyptic doom, so too does Jack reflect upon the magnetic scanner that can detect Nyodene within his body with an almost religious awe and trepidation:[21]

> Dr Chakravarty wants to insert me once more in the imaging block, where charged magnetic particles collide, high winds blow. But I am afraid of the imaging block. Afraid of its magnetic fields, its computerized nuclear pulse. Afraid of what it knows about me. (325)

In the same way that the doppelgänger has the potential to prophesise an imminent and frightening future that would otherwise remain unknown to the original subject, so too is the medical imaging block capable of supernatural premonition through its capacity to predict Jack's future medical condition by rendering visible his digital doppelgänger. Here, the digital doppelgänger of *White Noise* can be understood in relation to Joseph Francavilla's assertion that the double is "uncanny in its remarkable shrewdness, acuteness, and its almost magical wisdom, intuition, and power" (Francavilla: 5). This same sense of omnipresent foresight is projected onto Jack's whole data profile as it is deciphered by the medical scanner. The imminent nebulous mass concealed within Jack's informatic body can be revealed by a scanner that can predict future events in a way that human beings cannot; the cryptic stars and brackets that comprise the digital doppelgänger resist comprehension by medical practitioners, yet can somehow be understood by the magnetic scanner.[22] In this way, the power of the traditional literary doppelgänger to incite fear and anxiety in the individual whom it doubles is transposed in *White Noise* from the supernatural to the

---

[20] This notion of the doppelgänger as radically at odds with scientific reason can be viewed in light of Margrit Shildrick's discussion of the monstrous posthuman, in which she notes that monsters are "opposed to the epistemological, ontological and ethical paradigms of reason" (Shildrick: 2). For Shildrick, monsters signify "the otherness of possible worlds, or possible versions of our selves, not yet realized"(8). In this sense, the doppelgänger can be seen as a monstrous other, one that signifies "the other of the humanist subject" through its defiance of epistemological reason (2).

[21] Packer discusses the representation of the sacred in *White Noise*, noting "the religious awe looming in the airborne toxic event" (Packer: 649).

[22] This capacity of the doppelgänger to portend death through the use of medical technologies can be seen as indicative of the role of computerized diagnosis in the contemporary medicine. As Deborah Lupton explains this,

> [b]efore the advent of medicine, the most potent symbol of death was the grim reaper, a skeletal figure dressed in black and carrying a scythe. In the late twentieth century, death is represented by a biological lesion or a test result: for example, a positive result for the presence of cancer in a [...] biopsy. (Lupton: 44)

Technologies such as MRI and CT are intertwined with death because of their potential for medical prognoses of terminal illness or disease. In this regard, death is represented in the form of images of pathological abnormalities and is perceived to lurk within the body, able to be rendered visible by medical imaging technologies. From this, death shifts from being a sensory or physical reality, indicated by the experience of illness or pain, but is transformed into visual information.

technological. Rather than the doppelgänger existing within the realm of the ghostly and being devoid of corporeality, the digital doppelgänger instead exists within the realm of technology, comprised of information and visible only through technologised eyes. The ominousness of the supernatural body is thus transposed onto the body technologised by medicine, and in this way there is an implicit connection between mortality and digital imaging technologies, wherein the reconfiguration of the body into data raises the spectre of death.

Indeed, in the closing paragraph of the novel, this same sense of the supernatural that characterises the doppelgänger is again projected onto technology when Jack reflects upon the rearrangement of the supermarket shelves:

> There is agitation and panic in the aisles, dismay in the faces of older shoppers. They walk in a fragmented trance [...] trying to figure out the pattern, discern the underlying logic. [...] Smeared print, ghost images. [...] The terminals are equipped with holographic scanners, which decode the binary secret of every item, infallibly. This is the language of waves and radiation, or how the dead speak to the living. (325–26)

The supernatural world of ghosts and shadows is thus reconfigured in accordance with digital information as a new language that can incorporate the ambiguity of death and dissolution. The spectre of death is transposed onto the realm of the digital, and can be imagined and imaged only by the scanning machine that can cross the boundaries between the dead and the living.

This notion of the digital doppelgänger as imbued with death relates to the way that the figure of the doppelgänger has historically been seen to presage death. For Otto Rank, the doppelgänger serves as "a reminder of the individual's mortality, indeed, the announcer of death itself" (in Živković:.123 – 24), where this capacity of the double to portend death is founded on an inherent fear of death in which the double performs the role of immortal soul. Death in *White Noise* is similarly prophesised by the double in its data form. The "passage of computerized dots" that comprises Jack's whole data profile indicates his mortality: as he laments, this cryptic information "register[s] my life and death"(DeLillo: 140). Death exists within Jack's computerised body of information as an unavoidable fate that "no man escapes" (141). In this sense, the body of information that comprises Jack's digital double is the administrator of his mortality in the same way that the doppelgänger is for Rank. As Jack reflects:

> "Death has entered. It is inside you. You are said to be dying and yet are separate from the dying, can ponder it at your leisure, literally see on the X-ray photograph or computer screen the horrible alien logic of it all. It is

when death is rendered graphically, that it is televised so to speak, that you sense an eerie separation between your condition and yourself." (141–42)[23]

Jack's yet-to-be-revealed "nebulous mass" functions as the symbol of death in the same way that the digital doppelgänger functions as a memento mori, signifying mortality and serving as a reminder of the transience of life.[24] Indeed, as Dr Chakravarty reminds Jack, he is, simply by virtue of being alive, effectively engaged in the process of his own dying; even when he is not situated within the boundaries of the hospital or clinic, Jack is nonetheless a "permanent patient" whose inevitable death shadows him constantly. In this way, the presence of Jack's digital doppelgänger highlights an already existing reality: his own pathological status as patient, one whose "death is progressing" (325). Death is thus no longer a tangible or corporeal event but, rather, dying instead transformed into an informatic process, a pathological condition to be monitored rather than an inevitable cessation of life. Indeed, for Jack, "[t]hat little breath of Nyodene has planted a death in my body. It is now official, according to the computer. I've got death inside me."(150). The presence of Nyodene D. within Jack's body is a visible manifestation of his mortality; once death is deemed to be inescapable and has been legitimised by the language of the computer, it becomes imbued with a visual reality and thanatopsis is unavoidable. Through its capacity to portend death in this way, the informatic body that comprises Jack's whole data profile parallels the doppelgänger of literature and psychoanalysis. Like the doppelgänger, the informatic double of *White Noise* similarly elicits anxieties about death and the dissolution of self, reincorporating into digital code the elements of supernaturalism and ominousness that typify the traditional doppelgänger. In doing so, the digital doppelgänger functions as an informatic ulterior self derived from imaging technologies and can be viewed in light of models of posthumanism that revolve around the reconfiguration of the human in accordance with the technological.

---

[23] This description of the alien logic of seeing one's death represented visually can be understood in relation to the self-alienation that results from viewing images of one's body-interior. Francisco Varela explains this phenomenon in his essay "Intimate Distances", in which he discusses his experience of undergoing a liver transplant. Varela describes the experience of watching an ultrasound image of his body displayed upon a computer screen, whilst his doctors simultaneously view the same image. During this experience he has a profound sense of estrangement and alienation from himself, where he experiences his embodied self at the same time as being radically divorced from it; his body "redoubled in a scanner's image" elicits a "mixture of intimacy and foreignness" (Varela: 2). This sense of alienation derived from viewing the body-interior resonates with the "horrible alien logic" Jack experiences upon seeing his dying body rendered graphically, and can be viewed as a consequence of the disjunction between self and body that occurs when the body is represented in an unfamiliar way.

[24] Although Jack's death is imminent, its exact time cannot be specified, and in this way, his overall prognosis is, ironically, no different to what it would have been prior to his exposure to Nyodene D.; even without having been exposed to the chemical Jack would invariably die at some future, and probably unknown, point in time. In this sense, Nyodene has not necessarily caused Jack's demise, but has rather imbued him with a heightened awareness and fear of mortality and in this way, the lingering presence of Nyodene D. as computerised information functions similarly to a memento mori.

## Posthuman Doubles

Like the doppelgänger, the posthuman has been the subject of repeated debate and discussion. Theorisations of posthumanism offer disparate and often contradictory explanations of the term, ranging from those that are sufficiently vague so as to effectively categorise virtually any human being (technologised or otherwise) as "posthuman", to others that are so specific as to be relevant in only a limited number of circumstances. In discussing the doppelgänger in relation to posthumanism, this essay examines the way in which the representation of the digital doppelgänger in *White Noise* might elucidate theorisations of the posthuman, specifically those of N. Katherine Hayles, that allow for the fluctuation and ambiguity of human-technological exchange.

One of the key difficulties surrounding theorisations of the posthuman is the chronological determinism that almost invariably results from "post-isms". To speak of the posthuman is, implicitly, to assume the previous existence of the "human", wherein the characteristics of the posthuman are presumably absent in the "human". From this, a difficulty arises in that a binary system of objects is virtually unavoidable, and the philosophy of posthumanism is thus fraught with both a desire for and simultaneous anxiety about binary classification. In addition, many theorisations of the posthuman adhere, often problematically, to a Cartesian dichotomy, wherein a "body" is deemed to be a machinic prosthesis enhanced by technological apparatuses, or a "mind" can be completely synthesised with technology, whereupon the body is abandoned and disregarded.[25] A number of theorists avoid this problem by approaching posthumanism from a perspective not limited to the technological. Judith Halberstam and Ira Livingston, for example, posit that posthuman bodies "emerge at nodes where bodies, bodies of discourse, and discourses of bodies intersect to foreclose any easy distinction between actor and stage, between sender/receiver, channel, code, message, context" (Halberstam and Livingston: 2). While such a definition is useful for reconfiguring bodies that resist linear categorisation, the lack of specificity of this conceptualisation of the posthuman means that virtually any body could be considered posthuman: within social and cultural discourse, human beings rarely conform to

---

[25] Hayles cites robotics researcher Hans Moravec's "transmigration scenario" as exemplary of this particular mode of posthuman thought. Moravec envisions a "post-biological" future in which it will one day be possible to "transmigrate"; to download a human being's complete consciousness into a computer, whilst, presumably, their remaining body is discarded (Moravec: 108 – 9).

clear distinctions, such as those between actor and stage or sender and receiver. Indeed, as Halberstam and Livingston go on to note, the posthuman body:

is a technology, a screen, a projected image; it is a body under the sign of AIDS, a contaminated body, a deadly body, a techno-body [...], a queer body. The human body itself is no longer part of "the family of man" but of a zoo of posthumanities. (3)

The posthuman in this instance functions as an umbrella term, under which a wide range of bodies and embodied experiences can be classified. Concomitant with such generalised definition of posthumanism is an underlying and problematic assumption that the "human" is in fact devoid of the ontological instability and ambiguity that supposedly characterises the posthuman.

To this end, N. Katherine Hayles offers a far more specific and useful definition of the posthuman in *How We Became Posthuman: Virtual Bodies in Cybernetics, Literature and Informatics*. Drawing from the fields of cybernetics and information theory, Hayles focuses on the representation of technologised bodies in science fiction, suggesting that posthuman philosophy is centred on a belief that human being "can be seamlessly articulated with intelligent machines" (Hayles: 3). For Hayles, the posthuman is not limited to the reinstatement of a liberal humanist model of selfhood wherein subjectivity is radically decorporealised whilst flesh is technologised. Rather, Hayles's model of posthumanism forms the basis for reconceptualising human-technological interaction and engagement in a way that accounts for actual and embodied human subjectivity (287). The posthuman is thus characterised by the fact that the distinctions between corporeal and machinic existence are problematised, wherein "there are no essential differences or absolute demarcations between bodily existence and computer simulation" (3). Thus, Hayles's model of posthumanism focuses on technologically-based reconfigurations of the human rather than on any number of contexts in which bodily ontologies are problematised.

Hayles's model of posthumanism is congruent with the digital doppelgänger in *White Noise*, in which Jack as a human being comprises multiple and technologised selves, all of which make up the entirety of his embodied subjectivity. In this case, Jack and his double are both posthuman subjects whose digital and corporeal bodies construct and reconstruct one another. The digital doppelgänger is not a technological phenomenon that exists externally from Jack, decorporealised within the machine, but is rather an integrated part of him, one that informs his being: it is the "sum total" (DeLillo: 141) of himself just as he is rendered "transparent" (276) by the scanner that deciphers his corporeality. Indeed the figure of the doppelgänger has, historically, often been represented as a fundamental part of the individual whom it doubles, even whilst it simultaneously jeopardises that individual's ontological integrity. To return to Stevenson's narrative, this dualism of the doppelgänger is illustrated in the relationship between Dr Jekyll and Mr Hyde; the doppelgänger in the form of Mr Hyde does not masquerade as Dr Jekyll, but forms an essential part of Dr Jekyll himself, embodying his inner desires, such that the two individuals are inseparably intertwined and must eventually meet the same fate. In the same way, Jack's digital doppelgänger can be seen as an entity that, while existing as visible information on a computer screen or a printed readout, has tangible ramifications on Jack and informs his being; it not only indicates his death, but imbues Jack with an awareness of his own mortality, his perpetual "status as a patient" (260). Because of the ambiguity surrounding the effects of Nyodene D., Jack's data profile does not necessarily have any concrete implications for his physical health, but nonetheless entirely dictates his experience of embodiment throughout the novel. It is essentially the combination of Jack and his digital doppelgänger that form the "sum total" of himself.

This form of doubled embodiment can be understood in the context of Hillel Schwartz's notion that, referring to conjoined twins, doppelgängers exhibit "the horror and terror of a Siamesed bond" (Schwartz: 64). Schwartz suggests that the figure of the doppelgänger evokes the notion of an incomplete subjectivity, one that yearns for wholeness through reintegration with its vanished twin other yet is fraught with fear of being doubled (49). In this regard, Jack's embodied subjectivity, with the concomitant sense of fear it elicits, is borne from the conjunction between himself and the informatic technologies that construct and frame his being (89). As Hayles describes this situation, Jack's whole data profile is "a striking image of how his corporeality has been penetrated by informational patterns that construct as well as predict his mortality.[26] Jack's digital doppelgänger is thus not an foreign body or a simulation, but a twin self through which his individual ontology is constructed and reiterated; in this context, the pulsing stars that comprise the digital doppelgänger are not simply manifestations of abstract information but are shadows of Jack's own heartbeat.

The way in which the digital doppelgänger in conjunction with its corporeal counterpart combine in *White Noise* to form a single subject that embodies both human subjectivity and machinic existence can thus be viewed as evoking a form of

---

[26] Hayles briefly refers to *White Noise* in *How We Became Posthuman*, suggesting that *White Noise* "offers a vision of subjectivity constituted through the interplay of pattern and randomness rather than presence and absence" (Hayles: 40).

posthuman embodiment. In this context the posthuman subject, in the form of Jack, functions as an individual being whose subjectivity and ontology is formed through the integration of various technological and non-technological facets. There is no clear distinction here between the biological and the technological self, no dichotomy in which organic and artificial are posed in opposition to one another. Rather, Jack, by being constructed through the doppelgänger's presence, is rendered informatic in the same way that his digital counterpart is profoundly corporealised. Ultimately, the binaries between self and double are rendered indistinguishable and Jack and his digital doppelgänger meld into one posthuman being: the computerized scanners that "decode the binary secret of every item" (DeLillo: 326) including human bodies, eradicate any differentiation between information and corporeality, such that the resulting technologised embodiment elicits a posthuman ontology.

**Works cited**

Barrett, Laura. "How the Dead Speak to the Living". *Journal of Modern Literature* 25 (2001 – 2002): 97–113.

Bode, Lisa. "Digital Doppelgängers". *M/C Journal*, 8. 3 (2007).

Boxall, Peter. *Don DeLillo: The Possibility of Fiction*. London/New York: Routledge, 2006.

Buell, Lawrence. "Toxic Discourse". *Critical Inquiry*, 24. 3 (1998): 639–65.

Chimielewski, Dawn. "Meet Sunny's Digital Doppelganger". *The Age*, 5 January 2005.

Cooke, Brett, George E. Slusser, and Jaume Marti-Olivella (eds.). *The Fantastic Other: An Interface of Perspectives*. Amsterdam: Rodopi, 1998.

Danow, David K. "The Enigmatic Faces of the *Doppelgänger*". *Canadian Review of Comparative Literature*, 23. 2 (1996): 115–28.

DeLillo, Don. *White Noise*. Basingstoke: Macmillan, 1984.

Dietz, Frank. "Secret Sharers: The Doppelgänger Motif in Speculative Fiction", in *The Fantastic Other: An Interface of Perspectives*. Eds. Brett Cooke, George E. Slusser and Jaume Marti-Olivella. Amsterdam: Rodopi, 1998. 209–20.

Francavilla, Joseph. "The Android as Doppelgänger", in *Retrofitting Blade Runner: Issues in Ridley Scott's Blade Runner and Phillip K. Dick's Do Androids Dream of Electric Sheep?* Ed. Judith Kerman. Bowling Green: Bowling Green State University Popular Press, 1991. 4–15.

Freud, Sigmund. *The Standard Edition of the Complete Psychological Works of Sigmund Freud, Vol.XVII.* Trans. James Strachey. London: The Hogarth Press, 1955.

Fritz, Ben. "Garner Finds Viewing Her Digital Doppelganger Surreal". *Variety*, 27 August 2003.

Graham, Elaine L. (ed.). *Representations of the Post/Human: Monsters, Aliens and Others in Popular Culture.* New Brunswick: Rutgers University Press, 2002.

Halberstam, Judith, and Ira Livingston (Eds.). *Posthuman Bodies.* Bloomington: Indiana University Press, 1995.

Hayles, N. Katherine. *How We Became Posthuman: Virtual Bodies in Cybernetics, Literature, and Informatics.* Chicago: University of Chicago Press, 1999.

Kerman, Judith (ed.). *Retrofitting Blade Runner: Issues in Ridley Scott's Blade Runner and Phillip K. Dick's Do Androids Dream of Electric Sheep?* Bowling Green: Bowling Green State University Popular Press, 1991.

Lupton, Deborah. *Medicine as Culture: Illness, Disease and the Body in Western Societies.* London: Sage, 1994.

Magid, Ron. "New Media: Invasion of the Body Snatchers". *Wired* 3 March (1998).

Moravec, Hans. *Mind Children: The Future of Robot and Human Intelligence.* Cambridge: Harvard University Press, 1988.

Ndalianis, Angela. "Digital Stars in Our Eyes", in *Digital Stars in Our Eyes: The Star Phenomenon in the Contemporary Era.* Eds. Angela Ndalianis and Charlotte Henry. Connecticut: Praeger, 2002. 165–78.

Packer, Matthew J. "'at the Dead Center of Things' in Don DeLillo's *White Noise*: Mimesis, Violence and Religious Awe". *Modern Fiction Studies*, 51. 3 (2005): 648–66.

Phillips, Dana. "Don DeLillo's Postmodern Pastoral", in *Reading the Earth: New Directions in the Study of Literature and Environment.* Eds. Michael P. Branch, Rochelle Johnson, Daniel Patterson and Scott Slovic. Moscow, ID: University of Idaho Press, 1998. 235–46.

Rank, Otto. *The Double: A Psychoanalytic Study.* Trans. Harry Tucker Jr. Chapel Hill: University of North Carolina Press, 1971.

Rank, Otto. *Beyond Psychology.* New York: Dover, 1958.

Schwartz, Hillel. *The Culture of the Copy: Striking Likenesses, Unreasonable Facsimiles.* New York: Zone Books, 1998.

Shelley, Mary. *Frankenstein, or, the Modern Prometheus.* London: Wordsworth Editions, 1993.

Shildrick, Margrit. "Posthumanism and the Monstrous Body". *Body & Society*, 2.1 (1996): 1–15.

Stevenson, Robert Louis. *The Strange Case of Dr Jekyll and Mr Hyde and Other Tales of Terror*. London: Penguin, 2002.

Vardoulakis, Dimitris. "The Return of Negation: The Doppelgänger in Freud's "The 'Uncanny'"". *SubStance*, 35. 2 (2006): 100–16.

Varela, Francisco J. "Intimate Distances: Fragments for a Phenomenology of Organ Transplantation". *Journal of Consciousness Studies*, 8. 5–7 (2001): 259–71.

Wilcox, Leonard. "Baudrillard, DeLillo's *White Noise* and the End of Heroic Narrative". *Contemporary Literature*, 32. 3 (1991): 346–65.

Živković, Milica. "The Double as the 'Unseen' of Culture: Toward a Definition of Doppelganger". *Linguistics and Literature*, 2.7 (2000): 121–28.

**Contributors:**

**Brian Burns** is a Visiting Assistant Professor of English and Humanities at Michigan State University. He is currently rewriting his dissertation "Confessional Discourse as Autoethnography" into a manuscript for publication. The book will read Rousseau and DeQuincey as early practitioners of field anthropology/sociology by considering their confessions alongside the works of Bronislaw Malinowski and Margaret Mead.

**Jonardon Ganeri** is Professor of Philosophy at the University of Sussex. His major research interest is in the philosophical literature of classical India, and has published many books, the most recent of which is *The Concealed Art of the Soul: Theories of Self and Practices of Truth in Indian Ethics and Epistemology* (OUP, 2007). In this, and in future work currently being planned, he investigates the relationship between philosophical theory and literary form, as that relationship bears upon the search for selfhood and identity.

**Firat Karadas** and **Mustafa Kirca** are research assistants and doctoral students of English Literature at the Middle East Technical University, Turkey. Their fields of study include postmodernist poetics, literary theory and philosophy.

**Søren Landkildehus**, a Danish national, received his doctorate in philosophy from The University of Reading, 2005. His main interests are moral and epistemological questions concerning spirituality and religious belief. Dr. Landkildehus is currently research fellow at the Hong Kierkegaard Library, St. Olaf College. Currently, he writes on Kierkegaard and Dickens.

**Natalia Lizama** is a PhD candidate in the School of Social and Cultural Studies at the University of Western Australia. Her doctoral thesis, entitled "Post-biological Subjects: Medicine, Technology and the Body Resurrected" examines ways in which the body is resurrected in a number of contexts, including the Visible Human Project, Gunther von Hagens' *Body Worlds,* and immortal cell lines. Her research interests include the intersections between corporeality, subjectivity, medicine and technology.

**J.D. Mininger** earned his Ph.D. in Comparative Literature from the University of Minnesota in 2006. He has published (inter alia) on Paul Celan, Søren Kierkegaard, and Immanuel Kant, and is currently finishing a study on the poetics of anxiety.

**Andrew Hock Soon Ng** is lecturer in contemporary fiction and postcolonial and diasporic literature at Monash University, Malaysia. His primary research interest is in postmodern horror and Gothic narratives. He is the author of *Dimensions of Monstrosity in Contemporary Narratives* (Palgrave, 2004) and *Interrogating Interstices* (Peter Lang, 2007), and has contributed articles to journals such as *Women Studies, Mosaic, Concentric* and *Journal for the Studies of the Old Testament*.

**Claire Potter** is the author of two chapbooks of poetry, *In Front of a Comma* (2006) and *N'ombre* (2007). She holds a B.A. from the University of Western Australia, a B.A.Hons from the University of NSW and a Masters II from Université Paris VII. She is currently doctoral candidate in English at Université Paris VII and the University of Western Australia.

**Daniel P. Watt** is Lecturer in Drama at Loughborough University. His research interests include philosophical and literary influences on theatre and performance in the twentieth century, particularly the work of Samuel Beckett and Tadeusz Kantor. Publications include *A Performance Cosmology: Testimony from the Future. Evidence of the Past*, (with Judie Christie and Richard Gough, Routledge, 2006), and articles in *Performance Research, Oxford Literary Review, Journal of Cultural Research* and *Wormwood*. He is also series editor for InkerMen Press' Axis Series.

# Index of First Names

*ibidem*-Verlag

Melchiorstr. 15

D-70439 Stuttgart

info@ibidem-verlag.de

www.ibidem-verlag.de
www.edition-noema.de
www.autorenbetreuung.de

1142971R0

Printed in Great Britain by
Amazon.co.uk, Ltd.,
Marston Gate.